❖ Engendering Transitions

Women's Mobilization, Institutions, and Gender Outcomes

Georgina Waylen

OXFORD

UNIVERSITY PRESS

OXFORD
UNIVERSITY PRESS

Great Clarendon Street, Oxford OX2 6DP

Oxford University Press is a department of the University of Oxford.
It furthers the University's objective of excellence in research, scholarship,
and education by publishing worldwide in

Oxford New York

Auckland Cape Town Dar es Salaam Hong Kong Karachi
Kuala Lumpur Madrid Melbourne Mexico City Nairobi
New Delhi Shanghai Taipei Toronto

With offices in

Argentina Austria Brazil Chile Czech Republic France Greece
Guatemala Hungary Italy Japan Poland Portugal Singapore
South Korea Switzerland Thailand Turkey Ukraine Vietnam

Oxford is a registered trade mark of Oxford University Press
in the UK and in certain other countries

Published in the United States
by Oxford University Press Inc., New York

British Library Cataloguing in Publication Data

Data available

Library of Congress Cataloging in Publication Data

Data available

Typeset by SPI Publisher Services, Pondicherry, India
Printed in Great Britain
on acid-free paper by
Biddles Ltd., King's Lynn

ISBN   978–0–19–924803–2
ISBN   978–0–19–924804–9 (Pbk.)

1 3 5 7 9 10 8 6 4 2

❖ Preface

The purpose of this book is to engender the study of one of the most important political phenomena of the late twentieth century—namely democratization. It examines transitions from a range of non-democratic regimes that have different transition paths and outcomes that differ in the quality of their subsequent democracy. An understanding of the role of women in these different transitions and the impact of those transitions on gender relations has been missing from much of the democratization literature to date. Just as many democratization theorists analyse transitions to democracy from a position sympathetic to the desired outcome—liberal democracy—underlying this endeavour is a normative concern with improving levels of gender equality. I believe that positive gender outcomes—measured in terms of women's descriptive and substantive representation—should be a central part of transitions to democracy. As such, this book is unashamedly informed by feminist thought and scholarship as well as by some of the more dominant approaches in comparative politics and political science and it seeks to understand how positive gender outcomes can come about as a part of democratization.

But so often transitions to democracy have been seen as failing women as their outcomes do not live up to the expectations that had been generated. The questions have to be asked: Why this is the case? And under what circumstances can transitions to democracy result in positive gender outcomes? The study attempts to answer these questions in four stages. The first part of the book develops the theoretical framework through which the questions might be answered. In the subsequent three parts, that framework is applied to different aspects of the relationship between gender outcomes and democratization. The format is both thematic and comparative, using a range of case studies drawn from a number of regions. Part II looks at women's organizing. Part III examines the electoral arena. Part IV considers women's substantive representation and the state and policy outcomes of different transitions. It includes an analysis of the economic and social restructuring that has so often accompanied political transitions, but the significance of which is often ignored.

It is clear that many transitions to democracy have enhanced most women's civil and political rights. But positive gender outcomes have been easier to achieve in some areas than others. In most cases, levels of women's descriptive representation have increased over time. However, the large variations that occur between the different cases have to be accounted for. Although women's descriptive representation has increased overall, gains in women's substantive representation are often ambiguous. For example state women's machineries have been widely established, but again they vary considerably in their effectiveness. Policy change in some areas, domestic violence for example, seems easier to achieve than in others such as reproductive rights. And for many women, gains in the civil and political sphere are frequently undermined by a lack of access to social and economic rights. Social and economic rights themselves have often been undermined by the social and economic restructuring that has accompanied many transitions to democracy.

How can we explain these patterns? There are no simple answers. Causality is complex and no one factor is determining. However, it is possible to identify certain trends which allow an overarching picture to emerge. Even in cases where there have been positive gender outcomes—measured in terms of both descriptive and substantive representation—it is clear that women's mobilization on its own is no guarantee of success. Other factors—a favourable political opportunity structure and strategic organizing by key actors—are also crucial. One of the tasks of this book is to explore and assess the relative importance and interaction of these factors.

A comparative approach is therefore essential. The study uses eight countries as case studies, each of which vary in the types of transitions and democratic outcomes, the levels and types of women's organizing, and the different political opportunity structures. In all of the case studies the transitions ended with democratic outcomes, but the quality of the democracy varies considerably between countries. All the transitions took place as part of the so-called 'third wave' of democratization, and includes transitions from authoritarian rule in Latin America and from state socialist regimes in Eastern Europe. Gender outcomes were also affected by changes in the global context, including the construction of international norms about women's rights, largely as a result of the activities of global women's movements; and these were also reflected in the actions of some international and regional organizations.

Most of the case studies are drawn from two regions. The bulk of the case studies of transitions from authoritarianism come from Latin America (Argentina, Brazil, Chile, and El Salvador) and the case studies of transitions from state socialism are drawn from Eastern Europe (the Czech Republic, Hungary, and Poland), with one other country—South Africa providing an example of an insurgent transition from authoritarianism—included to increase the variation on the dependent variable (with El Salvador as its matched pair). I also make reference to two other countries—Peru and Russia—as comparator cases, as their transitions are seemingly in the 'grey zone' of those hybrid regimes that are neither fully authoritarian nor fully democratic polities.

Concurring with the claims of other democratization theorists who have undertaken this type of comparative analysis, I argue that an overarching analysis of this kind is useful for a number of reasons. An exposition that considers commonality and diversity in a range of contexts need not sacrifice empirical richness. A single (or perhaps jointly) authored study can explore major differences and similarities between cases more easily than edited collections, which tend to use separate case studies written by country specialists. It can also go beyond the sorts of analyses undertaken by monographs devoted to a single country.[1]

The empirical material for this study is drawn from both primary and secondary sources accumulated during fifteen years of research on these themes. The primary material was collected during periods of in-depth research in Chile, Argentina, Peru, and South Africa as well as during short research visits to Hungary and the Czech Republic undertaken from 1991 onwards. As will become clear in the succeeding parts, this book has also benefited hugely from the ever-growing body of work on democratization. I have drawn extensively on the valuable work on gender and transitions that has been influenced by both the gender and politics and the democratization literatures. The majority of the gender and transitions literature produced to date can be categorized as falling within two of the four streams of the comparative politics research cycle (Mazur 2002: 16). Both these—theoretically driven single country case studies and thematic edited collections that examine case studies from one or two regions—predominate (Alvarez 1990a; Jaquette 1991 and 1994; Funk and Mueller 1993; Jaquette and Wolchik 1998b; Sperling 1999; Friedman 2000; Gal and Kligman 2000; Rai 2000; Hassim 2005). Some articles also appear in gender and area studies journals and a few are found in mainstream comparative politics journals (Einhorn 1991; Gal 1994; Friedman 1998; Gaber 1999; Franceschet 2001 and 2002; Jaquette 2001; Baldez 2003). Indeed because of the interdisciplinary nature of many gendered analyses, some influential work—often focusing on the nature and identity of particular women's movements—is more closely alllied with a social movement perspective (Schild 1998).

This book aims to go beyond this existing literature and contribute to the small but growing body of work that falls into a third stream of the research cycle: hypothesis testing using two or more cases and the comparative method (Macaulay 1996, 2006; Baldez 2003; Htun 2003). It will therefore help us to discern any broad patterns that might contribute to the fourth stream of the research cycle that leads to theory building. Inevitably many of the ideas and arguments expounded here are the result of analysis and reflection I have undertaken over a long period and their development can be traced through my writings on various aspects of this topic (Waylen 1993, 1994, 1996a, 1996b, 1997, 2000, 2003, 2007). But the analysis expounded here does represent a significant extension and as well as a consolidation of this thought and research.

Two methodological assumptions therefore underpin this endeavour. First, it is possible to develop a comparative framework for the gendered analysis of transitions that is clearly situated within the discipline of comparative politics. Second, the concepts and approaches developed both within the mainstream and the gender and politics literatures can both be used in such an analysis. In this, my approach concurs with other feminist political scientists who argue that, within certain well-defined limits, gendered comparisons are not only possible but also desirable (Beckwith 2000; Mazur 2002; Baldez 2003).

As this book was completed only ten years or so after the high watermark of the third wave of democratization, it cannot be a conclusive exploration of all the major factors that should be taken into account in any study of gender and transitions. Because it focuses on eight transitions that took place before the third wave's peak and are recognized to have made the transition to some form of democracy—however imperfect—there are areas that the book does not consider. It does not explore the recent (often apparently ill-fated) attempts to establish democracy in (post) conflict situations such as Afghanistan and Iraq that result from externally imposed regime change. Nor does the book provide an extensive analysis of the 'grey zone' of hybrid regimes or electoral authoritarianism except in its use of two comparator cases: Russia and Peru. It also does not examine the 'colours' revolutions that have taken place in parts of the ex-Soviet Union. Nonetheless, while it does not address these events and cases directly, I would argue strongly that the themes and issues explored in this book are relevant to their analysis. I take up some of the wider issues pertinent to all these cases in the conclusion. Although it cannot provide definitive answers to all the questions that it poses, I intend this book to be useful to other scholars engaged in examining similar issues in these and other contexts. It is my hope that it will provoke further debate and the continuing refinement of the literature on gender and transitions.

❖ NOTE

1 I am thinking here of the work of scholars like Larry Diamond (1999) and Juan Linz and Alfred Stepan (1996).

❖ Acknowledgements

As the culmination of more than fifteen years of thought and research on gender, politics, and transitions to democracy, there are a large number of people who have contributed to this book and to whom I owe a huge debt of gratitude. Over the years this research was funded by various grants from the British Academy and the Economic and Social Research Council (ESRC). Both institutions paid for fieldwork in Chile, Argentina, Peru, and South Africa (ESRC grant numbers RES—000-22-1334 and RES—000-22-0259) at various points during these fifteen years. I am also indebted to Sheffield University for financial support granted through the various mechanisms set up to enhance our performance in the Research Assessment Exercise (RAE).

I would also like to thank all those I have interviewed over the years—too many to name individually—for their overwhelming generosity and helpfulness. I would also like to thank all those who provided invaluable help with field research over the years. They include Alan Angell, Nikki Craske, Ann Marie Goetz, Pamela Lowden, Fiona Macaulay, Marcela Rios, and Veronica Schild, as well as everyone at the Center for Latin American Studies at Stanford University, particularly Terry Karl, Phillippe Schmitter, Elisabeth Friedman, and Graciela Ducatzenzeiler who helped to make 1995–6 such as special year. I would also like to thank all those who were so helpful to me in South Africa, particularly Cathi Albertyn, Julie Ballington, Amanda Gouws, Shireen Hassim, Sheila Meintjes, and Denise Walsh. The Department of Political Studies at the University of Witswatersrand also deserves acknowledgement for making me so welcome during my stay in 2003. The Centre for Global Political Economy, Dept of Political Science, Simon Fraser University, Canada, and particularly Stephen McBride and Lynda Erickson deserve thanks for being such generous hosts while I was finishing the manuscript in 2005. Lisa Clark, Torunn Eskedal, and Beverly Bishop provided invaluable research assistance. I am also very grateful to Frances Millard, Richard Matland, Barbara Einhorn, Eva Fodor, Hana Havelkova, Alena Krizkova, and Eva Eberhardt for generously supplying information, contacts, and unpublished manuscripts that helped to fill some of the gaps on East Central Europe.

I am also indebted to a large number of friends and colleagues who over the years have also provided much needed help and support. They include Shirin

Rai, Maxine Molyneux, Ruth Pearson, Andrew Gamble, Tony Payne, Paul Cammack, Elizabeth Harvey, and Susan Franceschet. I would particularly like to thank Elisabeth Friedman for her very useful comments on the first part of the draft manuscript and Vicky Randall deserves a special thank you for her detailed and insightful comments on the whole thing.

I would also like to thank Donal O'Donoghue, Consultant Renal Physician at Hope Hospital, Salford, for helping to ensure that lupus need not put too many constraints on my life and work—over the years he has facilitated so many of my trips by finding doctors for me to visit in far flung places and has always answered all my emails, however trivial, with incredible speed and patience. Last, but certainly not least, Scott McCracken and Jessica Waylen deserve a special mention for the irreplaceable role that they play in my life.

GW

❖ Contents

❖ List of Tables

Part I ❖ Analysing Gender and Transitions

The 'third wave' of transitions from non-democratic rule has been one of the most important global political developments to take place since the 1970s. Beginning in Southern Europe (Portugal, Spain, and Greece), continuing in Latin America in the late 1970s and 1980s, and climaxing in the dramatic collapse of state socialism in East Central Europe in 1989 before continuing in parts of Africa and Asia, transitions have transformed the political landscape (Huntington 1991). Therefore while there were only 39 electoral democracies in 1974, by 1998 the figure had reached 117 and had only increased to 119 in 2005 as most transitions took place in the late 1980s/early 1990s (Freedom House www.freedomhouse.org). Some of the triumphalism evident at the height of the third wave in early 1990s has dissipated as many democracies are of a low quality and a number of states have either suffered 'reversals' or outcomes in a 'grey zone' often more akin to electoral authoritarianism than democracy. And at the same time political transitions have not brought an end to underlying social and economic problems. However despite some disillusionment with these outcomes a decade after the age of transitions was largely over, there is no denying the importance of many of these changes (Plattner 2005: 5). Inevitably the range of different transition paths and their varied outcomes has also spawned a large and diverse academic literature that has dominated the study of comparative politics for nearly thirty years.

What roles have women played within this diverse phenomenon and what has been the impact of transitions on gender relations? Although women's movements were not prominent actors in all transitions, in a significant number of cases, women organized as women did play an important part in the activities that helped to bring an end to non-democratic rule. And many women activists were keen to ensure that women's claims were taken seriously in the post-transition phase. Yet disillusionment has frequently resulted. In a number of instances, it was felt that the promise of the earlier phases was not fulfilled. There is an apparent paradox. Why is it that some of the most active women's movements were unable to translate the importance of their pre-transition activism into greater gains in the immediate post-transition period?

For example in the oft-quoted Chilean case, women organized as women played an important role in the broad movement that opposed the Pinochet regime. They were active in human rights organizations, feminist groups, and shanty-town organizations. Women, many of whom were feminists and on the left, also organized prior to the 1989 elections to ensure that their demands were included in the manifesto of the winning centre-left coalition. Hopes were high when the new government took office and a women's ministry had been established. However for the first decade after the transition, change proved more difficult to achieve than had been anticipated by many activists and commentators. Legislation legalizing divorce only passed in 2004. Indeed some feminists have been sceptical about the significance of the election of Chile's first women president in 2005, seeing it as the result of prevailing political conditions rather than as a triumph for feminism. Michelle Bachelet's candidature allowed the ruling Concertación to appear to be offering something fresh and new—a woman President—without fundamentally altering its programme or organization (Franceschet 2005, 2006; Rios 2006).[1] What were the multiplicity of factors that contributed to these difficulties and how did they interact together?

Ten years after the high-water mark of the third wave, is a good point to stand back and reflect on these questions. This book tries to explain this apparent paradox and to understand the relationship between gender and transitions to democracy more generally. Central to the argument is the notion that it is not correct just to glibly assert that transitions are bad for women. Reality is much more complicated. Transitions can provide some opportunities. But if we want to understand these opportunities and under what circumstances some women can take advantage of them, we need to broaden our horizons. To explain complex outcomes, wide-ranging analyses of transitions to democracy that do more than examine women's movements and their interaction with institutions, are necessary. This book does more than simply 'put women back in' as a corrective to the absences in the conventional transitions literature. It also shows how gender is profoundly implicated in the processes associated with transitions to democracy.

Therefore the aim of the book is not just to understand why and under what conditions women mobilize as women during various stages of transitions to democracy, a theme that has been explored extensively in much of the gender and transitions literature to date.[2] Nor is it just to explore the relatively more neglected area of the relationships of those movements with institutions such as political parties and the state during the various stages of transition. But it is also to analyse the varying nature of gender outcomes in the post-transition period. This entails looking at the ways in which the polities and policies instituted in the post-transition phase of democratization are gendered (measured for example in terms of the numbers of women in representative institutions, gender policies, the role of women activists, and political parties); and whether these are linked to factors such as the nature of the non-democratic regime and the transition path.

❖ ANALYSING GENDER AND TRANSITIONS

This book therefore moves beyond the analysis of one key variable—the role played by women's movements which is a necessary but insufficient focus for any gendered analysis of transitions—to consider a broader range of themes, actors, and institutions. This first part of the book sets up a framework with which to analyse and explain the diverse outcomes of different gendered transition paths. These outcomes will be formulated in terms of women's descriptive and substantive representation together with certain key gender policies. Descriptive representation denotes the presence of elected women in parliaments and assemblies in numerical terms and the more abstract concept of substantive representation is the expression of women's interests, particularly in policymaking both by women in elected bodies and perhaps more significantly within other institutional mechanisms and structures (Mackay 2004: 101). The rest of the book is organized thematically into three further parts that cover both the processes and outcomes of transitions looking in some detail at women's mobilizations, the conventional political arena and policy outcomes.

Because of this broad focus, we will necessarily draw our analytical tools from a range of sources. We need to isolate those elements of the mainstream literature on transitions to democracy that can ground our analysis in a thorough understanding of how and why transitions take place and with what results. But given that, in common with most political science, this literature takes very little account of gender, we will also need to draw extensively on the burgeoning scholarship on gender and politics as well as the work that specifically addresses gender and transitions. Then we can outline the frame of reference, the concepts and hypotheses that we will use to examine transitions to democracy. The rest of this first part of the book addresses these issues beginning with a discussion of the gender and politics literature focusing primarily on the scholarship that has examined the national arena.

❖ GENDER AND POLITICS

Even if the majority of the mainstream political science literature has not taken their insights on board, feminist political scientists have made enormous strides in reformulating the basic concepts and theories as well as providing new analyses that are useful for our analysis of transitions to democracy. More than thirty years ago, feminist critiques of political science began to expose the gender-blind and inadequate nature of the discipline, both theoretically and empirically (Bourque and Grossholtz 1974; Randall 1987). They demonstrated that it rested on the gender-blind assumption that it was dealing with individuals but implicitly considered only the experience of men (Carroll and Zerilli 1993). This analytical exclusion helped to establish male political behaviour as the norm and to collude with the virtual exclusion of women from the public sphere. Feminists have long argued that as a result women's political roles have often been missed, either because they were just not perceived to be such or because the dominant concepts and language could not accommodate gender difference (Randall 1991). When women were considered explicitly, it was often using crude stereotypes of female political behaviour that compared it unfavourably to the 'gold standard' of male behaviour. Institutions and policies were also seen as predominantly gender-neutral.

Early feminist work achieved a great deal in terms of putting women back into political science by collecting new data and challenging both the assumptions and the underlying basis of political theory. However for sometime it has been recognized by feminist political scientists that it is necessary to do more than put women back into political science. A gendered analysis of any political process requires a more fundamental refashioning of the discipline (Lovenduski 1998). It consists of four key elements. The first step: reformulating the concepts that underlie our analysis will allow us to have better analyses of the final three elements.

❖ The Use of Reformulated Concepts

A gendered analysis of transitions to democracy is impossible without using the reformulated concepts that underlie the study of gender and politics. First, gender difference itself must be problematized (Scott 1986). In particular it is necessary to deconstruct the false categories of men and women. The assumptions about the homogeneity of women must be taken apart to show how women are differentiated by crucial factors such as class, race, sexuality, and disability and so easy generalizations about all women are not possible. Gendered analyses therefore must take place within a wider framework of diversity. Second, we must reformulate commonly accepted notions of citizenship and rights, rejecting the false universalism of traditional theories of citizenship that has acted to exclude women (Lister 2003). This has been the case for citizenship as status—namely the rights that have often been denied to women in both de facto and *de jure* terms—as even if women have rights on paper, they have not always been able to operationalize them. It has also been the case for citizenship as practice—for example women have often been excluded from political participation. Associated with this, the rigid public/private distinction must also be challenged and rearticulated. The notion of the public sphere as the sphere of male citizens enjoying rights from which women are excluded has long been central to political theory (Pateman 1983, 1989). The 'political' is therefore implicitly masculine and women have been analytically relegated to the private sphere which lies outside the domain of the political.

However, women have never remained entirely outside the public sphere and the boundary between the public and private has not been fixed; but the distinction between the two and the roles ascribed to women in the private sphere have seriously impacted on the ways they can participate in the public sphere

(Elshtain 1981). For example the sexual division of labour within the household differentially affects men and women's access to the public sphere as women generally undertake the bulk of domestic labour. Feminists have also argued that 'private' issues such as rape and domestic violence needed to be politicized and brought into the public sphere, and that broader social and economic rights have to form an integral part of any meaningful conception of citizenship. If women do not enjoy these rights, they will be less able to access any civil and political rights that are available to them (Phillips 1991, 1993).

Finally, the definition of what counts as political must be expanded. The narrow traditional definition focused entirely on the activities of public sphere can only incorporate those formal activities within the conventional political arena. This definition excludes many of the activities in which different groups of women are often prevalent. A wider definition that incorporates informal political activity associated with communities and social movements will give us a different picture of the nature of women's political participation. Utilizing these reformulated concepts will enable us to have better analyses of the three remaining elements: (*a*) women as political actors, (*b*) political institutions, and (*c*) policy.

❖ *Women as Political Actors*

❖ *Conventional Politics*

On the whole, men and women participate in political activity, however defined, in different ways. But most of the literature on political behaviour has focused on men, even if it does not overtly acknowledge that it is doing this—much less work has looked explicitly at men acting as men, examining for example the role played by masculinity in influencing political behaviour. But there is a growing literature that examines many aspects of women's roles as political actors (Rule and Zimmerman 1994; Lovenduski 2005). Using a wide definition of the political, some of it focuses on women's activities outside the conventional political arena but it also looks at women's participation in conventional politics. Until recently its primary focus has been competitive electoral politics in the developed world.

Within the electoral arena, women have had lower levels of descriptive representation than men in formal politics whether in legislatures or executives (Randall 1987). This becomes particularly marked as you rise up through the hierarchies of political power. Women tend to vote with the same frequency as men, join political parties in relatively high numbers, but generally make up a much smaller proportion of elected representatives in legislatures, particularly national ones, and on the internal committees and executives of political parties whether in liberal democracies or state socialist regimes. Far fewer women are found in executives and even when present are often in 'soft' welfare posts of health and education, not the 'hard' posts of finance and foreign affairs.

A number of factors explain these different patterns of participation for men and women. So-called supply factors, such as the nature of women's lives, affect the numbers of women coming forward (Norris 1991). Women's roles in the public sphere are often constrained by their roles in the private sphere, as for many women, particularly the less well-off, domestic responsibilities make participation in the formal electoral arena, particularly at national level, more difficult than for many men. Women often do not have the financial or the employment background necessary to be able to launch a successful career in politics. But it is difficult to understand women's participation in the electoral arena without also considering the 'demand' side factors such as the gendered nature of the political institutions that women are involved in (Lovenduski and Norris 1993). Therefore there will be more discussion of this theme in the next part on institutions.

Feminist political scientists who focus on women's political representation have been preoccupied by several questions. First, is it important to have more women in office? Second, do women make a difference and finally, what can be done to achieve higher levels of representation? Some feminist political scientists argue that for a democracy to be fully inclusive and democratic, all groups, including women, have to be represented fairly; so larger numbers of women are important for symbolic purposes and to increase the legitimacy of political institutions (Phillips 1995). Others argue that it does actually make a difference if there are more women active in conventional politics, as once in office, women vote, behave, and legislate in distinctive ways and women voters are more likely to vote for women candidates.[3] In sufficient numbers, women legislators will make a substantive difference. Larger numbers of women will change the institutional culture by altering the masculine atmosphere and style of political interaction and debate. More controversially it has been claimed that because women legislators are more likely to take an interest in 'women's issues' such as childcare and maternity leave than their male colleagues, they will also represent the interests of women in general and promote 'women friendly' policies.

A direct link has therefore been posited between higher levels of women's descriptive representation and their substantive representation and the relationship between the two—framed in terms of how far elected women will 'act for' all women—has recently come under scrutiny (Mackay 2004). As part of this, the level of women's representation that constitutes a 'critical mass' within a legislature whereby women are no longer a token minority and can begin to act for women has preoccupied analysts. But even among the supporters of the concept there is no consensus and the levels advocated vary from 20 to 50% with 30% as a preferred figure.

However, not all feminist political scientists agree that there is a 'critical mass'. Some argue that its significance is overstated as greater numbers of women representatives do not necessarily lead to 'feminist outcomes' but simply to a greater interest in 'women's issues'. Others claim that a crucial factor is not the 'sheer numbers' of women, or where they are located but who the women are (Beckwith and Cowell-Meyers 2003). Women, just because they are women, are not necessarily going to promote 'women friendly' policies or achieve substantive change as party, class, or ethnic loyalty may take precedence. A key question is therefore how far it is necessary for women politicians to be feminists or actively promoting a progressive gender agenda in order for increases in women's descriptive representation to be translated into increases in women's substantive representation. If more emphasis is put on the nature of those women representatives, it is important to consider whether feminists in strategic locations or in alliances can play a role in achieving change. Feminist political scientists have therefore also looked at the strategies and locations that women can use to maximize their effectiveness—for example whether they should organize within women's sections and caucuses in parties and legislatures. Despite the disagreements over how far descriptive representation translates directly into substantive representation, the question of the strategies that can be employed to increase the number of women has also come under scrutiny. As we see below, the most important, and arguably the most effective measure, has been the introduction of some form of quota whether for internal party positions or legislatures.

❖ Outside Conventional Politics

Once we widen the definition of what counts as political activity, a range of women's activities outside the conventional political arena come under scrutiny. Much of the large body of research on women's movements has focused on a number of questions. Why, under certain circumstances, do women organize as women; what form do these activities take and how should these women's movements be analysed? However, if identities are complex, comprising multiple intersections of class, race, gender, and sexuality, leading individuals to react in different ways at different times, women will act politically, not simply on the basis of gender, but also on the basis of their race, class, and sexuality in a complex interaction. Therefore it is not possible to talk of *a* women's movement. And feminist movements are only one part of the diversity of different women's movements that mobilize in different ways around a range of issues. Scholars have divided women's movements up in a number of ways; for example, Molyneux (1985*a*) distinguishes between those that organize around practical and around strategic gender interests while others have made the distinction between those that mobilize around their traditional gender roles, particularly motherhood and those that mobilize around agendas that can be categorized as feminist aimed at increasing levels of women's equality and subverting gender roles. However it is difficult to make a rigid distinction between movements as many are hard to categorize in these terms and may change over time.

Beckwith (2004) proposes a broad definition in which any movement that has women actors and leaders and makes gendered identity claims is a women's movement. If we use her formulation, a whole range of different women's movements can be identified. These range from grass roots or popular women's organizations that are often active around day-to-day issues to self-avowedly feminist organizations, that can be distinguished by their goals and ideas and often comprise middle class professional women. More recently, more professionalized women's non-governmental organizations (NGOs) and wider networks or alliances often organizing around an issue on a local, national, regional, or international basis have become increasingly significant categories.

These varied women's movements use a 'wide and adaptable strategic repertoire' of different alliances and actions over multiple venues and these need to be investigated (Beckwith 2000: 448, 2004). We must look not just at the movements themselves—something that has preoccupied many analysts—but also at the ways in which many movements interact with the broader political context. Some feminist comparative political scientists have used the 'gendered opportunity structure' to conceptualize the impact of different factors on women's mobilizing (Randall 1998; Friedman 2000; Baldez 2003; Banaszak, Beckwith, and Rucht 2003). Influenced by notions of the political opportunity structure associated with social movements theorists like Sidney Tarrow (considered in more detail in Part II), scholars have looked at the wider conditions that could lead women to mobilize around their gender identities in any particular political formation. What is the relationship of different women's organizations and the state; for example, how does it vary with different kinds of state, say with authoritarian as opposed to liberal democratic ones (Beckwith 2000)? And does it vary between different parts of the state such as state women's machineries (SWMs) and finance ministries? In competitive electoral systems, the relationship between women's movements and various parts of the representative system such as political parties and legislatures as well as the women within them also becomes important. The impact of the women's movements on the political opportunity structure itself is another key question that has preoccupied scholars examining the interaction between women's movements and the political opportunity structure. How far, for example, have women's movements been able to effectively articulate gender issues, place them on the political agenda and achieve certain gender outcomes under different circumstances (Weldon 2002)?

❖ Political Institutions

We cannot understand the political opportunity structure without a gendered understanding of political institutions such as constitutions, party, and electoral systems in both long-standing and new democracies. Indeed it is impossible to comprehend the roles of women inside and outside the conventional political arena without considering how political institutions are gendered. Otherwise it is difficult to assess the opportunities that different institutions can offer women activists both inside and outside of them. To say that institutions are gendered is to imply that 'gender is present in the processes, practices, images and ideologies, and distributions of power in the various sectors of social life' (Acker 1992 quoted in Kenney 1996: 446; Friedman 2000: 35). States and political parties are predominantly gendered hierarchies with far more men than women at the top of those hierarchies and should be analysed as such. Feminist scholarship has tried to understand the mechanisms whereby institutions like political parties act to exclude women and often fail to represent women's diverse interests, as well as to examine the efforts made by women activists to increase their role and representation within those institutions.

It is useful to disaggregate this rather broad category of the institutional arena into three separate areas—the electoral, constitutional/legal, and the bureaucratic/state arenas—as each one can provide women with different opportunities and constraints even within the same polity (Chappell 2002). Women's descriptive representation is embodied primarily in the electoral arena and, as we have seen, the extent to which women's substantive representation can also be embodied there is debated. More complex characterizations of women's substantive representation that see it as the 'inclusion of women's policy preferences, concerns and interests in the policy process' which encompass institutional mechanisms and structures in the state/bureaucratic arena, are now also being used (Mackay 2004: 101). Both these elements of representation can also be embodied in the constitutional/legal arena. Once we have an understanding of women as political actors and the ways in which different institutional arenas are gendered, we can then look at policy outcomes that emerge from them.

If we examine the electoral arena first we can see that, in contrast to some of the feminist literature on the state that has been influenced by post-structuralist and Foucauldian ideas, the majority of the work on women and formal political activity in the electoral arena owes much to conventional political science approaches. A major concern has been to explore the factors that determine the varying levels of women's representation. Some studies have divided these into cultural, structural, and institutional dimensions. In keeping with supply-side notions, some scholars argue that cultural factors such as the presence of traditional attitudes about women's roles and women's leadership are crucial, while others claim that structural factors such as the level of women's participation in paid employment and professional jobs as well as levels of development play a key role (Norris and Inglehart 2001: 127).

Finally, demand-side institutional factors such as electoral rules and the role of political parties are also accorded a particular significance. Basing their arguments on evidence from liberal democracies of the first world such as USA, Britain, and Scandinavia, feminist political scientists have shown that different electoral systems can impact on the levels of women's representation: for example proportional representation (PR) systems are more likely to favour women's representation than first past the post (FPTP) systems. District magnitude, whether electoral lists are open or closed and rates of incumbency also affect the numbers of women elected—with larger district magnitudes, closed lists and low rates of incumbency favouring the election of women. There is, however, no consensus about the relative importance of each of these dimensions in general or in specific cases. Much of the literature on the advanced industrial democracies has concentrated on institutional factors but argued that cultural and structural factors are more important in other contexts.

Also central to any analysis is the role played by political parties—as one of the key mechanisms for channeling and representing interests and training leaders—in determining levels of women's representation. Parties vary tremendously. Research on Western Europe has demonstrated that parties with different ideologies tend to exhibit differences in the numbers of women in significant positions within them. Caul (1999) identifies a 'new left ideology' as a significant predictor of relatively high levels of women. Different party structures can also have an important impact on the position of women within political parties, as do different systems of candidate selection—whether centralized/local and formal/informal party systems—on the numbers of women selected (Caul 1999; Lovenduski and Norris 1993). It appears from some of the first world literature that parties with more institutionalized structures are sometimes more open to selecting women candidates as formal and enforceable rules can minimize the influence of informal networks and assert central party dominance. Recently some scholars have been hypothesizing about whether the form of party insitutionalization has a differential impact on women activists primarily differentiating between vertical (rules and hierarchical structures) and horizontal (complex and fluid networks at the base) institutionalization (Macaulay 2006). The roles that women activists can play within parties are therefore affected by the character, structures, and ideology of the party and its openness to women and gender claims.

Given that increasing the levels of women's representation is seen as a desirable goal in much of the gender and politics literature, it has investigated the relative efficacy of the different strategies used to improve women's descriptive representation as well as women's organizing inside and outside political parties to achieve it. Strategies range from affirmative or positive action, for example providing special training and encouragement to women candidates, to the introduction of quotas as a 'fast track' mechanism to increase women's representation (Dahlerup 2006). Globally, quotas have now been widely introduced particularly after the Beijing Women's Conference Platform for Action advocated institutional mechanisms to combat women's political under-representation. They can be implemented by individual parties for either internal positions and/or candidates for elections both nationally or locally. They can also be imposed through legislation or by constitutional provision. By 2006, quotas had been adopted for elections to national parliaments in around forty countries and in more than fifty other countries, political parties had voluntarily set out quota provisions (Dahlerup 2006: 3).

Quotas can be very effective. If they are appropriate to the electoral system and properly designed—for example with a placement mandate and enforced—they do achieve significant increases in the numbers of women holding office (Caul 1999; Htun and Jones 2002; Jones 2005; Dahlerup 2006; Matland 2006).[4] But despite their current popularity all over the world, quotas are controversial as a mechanism for improving women's representation (Mansbridge 2005). Critics argue that they smack of tokenism, deny equality of opportunity and can be open to abuse through croneyism. Advocates argue that as a temporary measure they are necessary to effect a change in the dominant political culture until a point is reached when they are no longer needed.

However, as Elisabeth Friedman (2000) argues, much of this work on women and conventional politics has focused primarily on increasing women's representation and leadership without always considering the ways in which the mechanisms of party politics reflect gender relations, or putting sufficient emphasis on the importance of the interaction between women's activities outside the state and formal arenas and institutional structures. The study of women in politics can therefore be an endeavour distinct from using gender as a primary category of analysis (Friedman 2000: 31).

To date, far less work has been conducted on the constitutional/legal arena as a significant site for gendered analysis and feminist interventions. But this is now beginning to change. As we will see, constitutions not only outline the structure of the electoral system but also incorporate certain civil and political rights for their citizens. In the first world the making or remaking of constitutions have provided some opportunities for feminists to ensure that gender concerns are included in institutional structures as they are formulated, thereby creating an enabling framework as part of a rights based culture (Dobrowolsky and Hart 2003). For example the process of devolution in Scotland and Wales created new structures of governance that did afford feminists—both within political parties and outside—some opportunities to embed gender issues at the outset (Mackay, Myers, and Brown 2003). Louise Chappell (2002) also demonstrates how the constitutional/legal arena provided feminists in Canada with opportunities often absent elsewhere. The Charter of Rights and Freedoms introduced in 1982 not only protected sex equality rights within it but later was used as a strategic device to challenge retrenchments under subsequent governments. Feminist political scientists therefore need to place greater emphasis on the constitutional/legal arena as a locus for shaping not only the actions of governments, but also the relationship between government and society and between social actors themselves (Chappell 2002: 119).

ANALYSING GENDER AND TRANSITIONS ❖

Finally, no gendered understanding of political institutions is complete without an analysis of the state and the bureaucratic arena. Women's substantive representation, defined terms of women's engagement in public policymaking through inclusive mechanisms such as consultative fora and mainstreaming activities as well as the incorporation of women-friendly issues into the policy process, is embodied in this arena (Mackay 2004; Mazur 2002: 38). In comparison to the amount of work on women's activities outside it, feminist analyses of the state are less plentiful but have become more sophisticated over time (Waylen 1998).[5] Although early feminist debates focused on the nature of the state and whether it could ever be a vehicle for feminists attempting to further women's interests, in recent years debates have centred around the best ways to effect the increased representation of women's interests in policy formation within the state at different levels. Initially the rather simplistic arguments were polarized between those who argued that, for women, a homogeneous state was either potentially essentially good (from a liberal/pluralist perspective) or potentially essentially bad (as patriarchal from a radical feminist perspective). Opposing strategies emerged: either keeping away from the state (as an irredeemably patriarchal oppressive institution) or engaging with it rather uncritically (Waylen 1998).

More recently there has been greater agreement that the nature of the state and the relationship between the state and gender relations is not fixed and immutable because the state is not a homogeneous entity but a collection of institutions and contested power relations. Battles can therefore be fought in the arena of the state as it is 'an uneven and fractured terrain with dangers as well as resources for women's movements' (Rai and Lievesley 1996: 1). Consequently, while the state has for the most part acted to reinforce female subordination, the space can exist within the state to act to change gender relations (Alvarez 1990a). Within this framework, the state bureaucracy becomes an area in which feminists can play an active role from within, attempting to change its structure and the ways in which it operates as well as influencing its policies at a number of different levels and areas. 'State feminism' has therefore emerged as a key strategy with which to increase women's substantive representation and the representation of their interests (however defined) within the state (Stetson and Mazur 1995). The establishment of SWMs and gender mainstreaming strategies are a central part of these initiatives.

There is now a huge amount of data and analysis of state feminism and gender mainstreaming. We have seen the diffusion of 'remarkably similar policy innovations across widely differing nation states' (True and Mintrom 2001). As a result of both the activities of women's movements nationally and internationally and global pressures expressed in international norms, many countries in both the developed and developing world established special bodies and mechanisms to achieve this increased substantive representation of women (True and Mintrom 2001). National machineries (which did not necessarily have to be part of the state) first emerged as instruments for advancing women's interests after the international women's conference held in Mexico in 1975. By the Beijing Women's conference in 1995, they had become 'the central policy co-ordinating unit within government', with the primary task of supporting the government-wide mainstreaming of a gender equality perspective in all policy areas' for example, in terms of procedures, policy formulation, and service delivery (Hassim 1999; Rai 2002: 17). Over 100 countries set up machineries between 1975 and 1997 as the international climate became more favourable towards them (Rai 2002).

There is, however, no consensus as to the general effectiveness and utility of SWMs or their ability to effectively represent women's interests in any particular context (Threlfall 1998; Rai 2002; Squires and Wickham-Jones 2002). Have states, through women's policy agencies, played a more active role in increasing women's substantive representation or have these been simply a symbolic declaration (Stetson 2001)? Stetson and Mazur (1995) claim that their effectiveness can be judged using two key indicators: policy influence and access. This requires knowledge of a number of SWM characteristics: its location/integration within the state, for example in a high or low level position or ministry; its brief whether advocacy, policy oversight or more rarely implementation; resources; its relationship with civil society; and the context within which it is operating for example whether the regime type is democratic or non-democratic. It is therefore necessary to focus not only on the institutions and structures within which the SWM operates, but also on the role of actors within the SWM and the state as well as outside. Lovenduski (2005: 15) argues that SWMs can play different roles: ranging from an insider role in which an SWM incorporates the goals of feminists and successfully genders debates to a symbolic role in which it neither advocates feminist goals nor genders debates. But any final judgement about an SWM must also look at the gendered nature of policy outcomes in any particular context. And it is to policy that we now turn.

❖ Policy

Policies often emerge from battles taking place in the arena of the state and help to construct and regulate gender relations. Scholars have taken a number of approaches to the analysis of state policies and the ways in which they are gendered, dividing them up in different ways. We can separate policy into two categories: those general policies that are ostensibly gender neutral and those policies directly concerned with gender rights and regulating relations between men and women. Policies that appear gender neutral in fact have a different impact on men and women. They can be subdivided into those policy areas linked to the public sphere and somehow seen as 'masculine' such as war and international trade, and those concerned with welfare and social reproduction (Charlton et al. 1989). Those policy areas more intimately concerned with the private sphere, for example housing, health, and education, fall under the rubric of welfare and the welfare state and are also precisely those areas affected by much of the economic and social sector reform that has been taking place at the same time as transitions to democracy.

Mala Htun (2003), looking only at those policies that regulate gender rights, argues that not all gender rights are the same. They can be disaggregated into five major areas: family and property rights, marriage and divorce laws, reproductive rights, sexuality and domestic violence, and equal rights. The actors involved in each area can vary and decision-making procedures can also vary from issue to issue. Change can therefore be easier to achieve in some categories than others. For example reforming property regimes can be seen relatively uncontroversially as modernizing outdated laws. Whereas the legalization of abortion often conflicts directly with religious principles and equal rights legislation can often be associated negatively with feminism. Actors like the Catholic Church might intervene forcefully around reproductive rights but not play a role in changes to marital property regimes. How issues are problematized and framed therefore makes a difference. For example the need for access to legal abortions can be presented in a number of ways—as a public health issue and medical problem—or framed in terms of women's rights and choice (Bacchi 1999).

How does gender rights reform occur and why it should happen in some areas of gender rights in some contexts but not in others? Blofield and Haas (2005) argue that gender rights reforms framed in terms of facilitating women to fulfil their existing roles (corresponding to practical gender issues?) are less likely to be controversial than those gender rights reforms framed in terms of improving women's rights. Lovenduski (2005) argues that activists are more likely to succeed if their 'issue frame fit' is compatible with the dominant policy discourse. Elisabeth Friedman (2006) has added an international dimension, examining the ways in which nationally based Latin American gender rights activists can utilize international and regional norms that are more developed around some gender rights such as quotas and gender-based violence than others such as lesbian, gay, bisexual and transsexual (LGBT), and reproductive rights.

Examining the processes by which reform can occur, Laurel Weldon (2002) has analysed government responsiveness to one area: violence against women in thirty-six countries classified as liberal democracies, and developed an explanation that is couched not just in terms of the nature of the state and state institutions—including women's machineries—but also in terms of their relationship with women's movements—primarily feminist ones—and their allies. Weldon (2002) argues that women's movements are always necessary for the initial articulation of violence against women as an issue and that initiatives to address violence against women are always a response by governments to demands that originate outside political institutions. But women's movements on their own are not enough to produce a government response. Allies within government are critical in placing the issue on the government agenda and therefore most policies are a result of partnerships between women's movements and sympathetic insiders. Weldon (2002) also claims that such partnerships are less effective in the absence of a women's policy machinery. Following Chappell's (2002) analysis, we need to distinguish between the electoral, bureaucratic, and constitutional/legal arenas as separate sites where different alliances and activities may be effective in achieving gender policy reform in particular cases. Positive gender outcomes are therefore achieved through complex processes in which a range of actors and institutions interact together.

A number of important general themes emerge from our examination of the gender and politics literature. For our purposes three have the greatest salience. First, we need to consider women's roles as political actors. And if we operate with a wider definition of what constitutes 'the political' than is usually adopted in the mainstream literature, we must examine women's activities within the conventional political arena and in women's organizations outside it. We need to focus not only on those women organizing as women but also on feminists organizing to promote a gender agenda. Second, we need to understand how political institutions are gendered, distinguishing between the electoral, bureaucratic, and constitutional/legal arenas. Third, the gendering of the state and policy outcomes is also an important area for analysis—how changes to gender policies come about is of particular interest (and within this the different institutional strategies to increase women's descriptive and substantive representation). This involves looking not only at institutions but also the roles of key actors both inside and outside the state in framing and articulating gender issues, placing them on the policy agenda and then ensuring that they are transformed into gender policy reform. Before we can use these insights in the gendered analysis of transitions to democracy, we need to understand the political processes involved in democratization.

❖ THE DEMOCRATIZATION LITERATURE

Despite the long-standing critiques of feminist scholars, the mainstream democratization literature has remained largely gender-blind, with very little to say about the participation of women in transitions to democracy or the gendered nature of those processes. Not unexpectedly—and as a result of its use of narrow definitions of both the political and democracy—it rarely considers either the role played by many women's activities in transitions to democracy or the question of whether women's ability to access rights should form part of the criteria for a functioning democracy (Waylen 1994; Friedman 2000). The elite focus of many of the early actor-based models compounded this tendency to ignore the majority of women's activities. However, this body of work still has much to offer a gendered analysis of transitions to democracy. Indeed, as we will see, some of the themes that are important in the gender and politics literature, such as institutional choice and the role of political parties, are important here albeit for different reasons and in rather different ways.

Therefore, rather than mounting a sustained critique of the mainstream literature, we will highlight its potential contribution to a gendered analysis of transitions using where possible empirical examples from our case study countries. We will see that the transitions literature can help us with a working definition of the supposed end state of transitions namely democracy, can suggest some of the important factors involved in transitions, and shed light on how different outcomes come about. Where appropriate we will also add a gender dimension. For example we will incorporate gender into the discussion of international and economic factors as neither area figured earlier on because to date they have not been systematically integrated into the gender and politics literature.

Any analysis of transitions must have a definition of what constitutes a democracy as otherwise it is hard to judge the outcome of the process. A great number of definitions and subdivisions of different types of democracy ('democracy with adjectives' (Collier and Levitsky 1997)) now exist within this contested area of the literature. Contemporary debates have been influenced by three conceptions of democracy. At one end of the continuum, a narrow Schumpterian approach uses a minimal institutional definition of democracy that a competitive electoral system is enough. Under this one-dimensional procedural definition, a large number of systems are democracies. Mid-range definitions based on Dahl's polyarchy are two-dimensional, as participation and the right of all adults to take part in democratic processes have to accompany electoral procedures and contestation. Countries will not meet the criteria for a liberal democracy if they lack civil rights, freedom of expression and the press and other characteristics associated with freedom and pluralism (Diamond 1999). More utopian definitions of democracy—in which citizens not only have the right but also the ability to participate unhindered by social and economic inequalities for example on grounds of class, race, or gender—are at the other end of the spectrum (Grugel 2002). Citizenship is therefore defined in the broadest sense to include social and economic as well as civil and political rights. Under this more exacting definition few, if any, countries are democracies. All these definitions incorporate different gender rights to varying degrees. Even women's suffrage is not absolutely essential to a narrow definition and although mid-range definitions include women's civil and political rights, only the more utopian definitions can accommodate women's social and economic rights.

Initially the majority of mainstream writers adopted either narrow or mid-range definitions of democracy, but over the last decade there has been more emphasis among even mainstream theorists, on the 'quality of democracy'—that elections on their own are not enough as a range of other factors, including equality and the ability to participate, have also to be considered. The need to incorporate previously excluded groups including women has been highlighted (Diamond and Morlino 2004: 20).[6] And ensuring improvements in women's rights (even quotas) has also figured as part of recent attempts to create democracy after conflict for example in Afghanistan—despite claims of instrumentalism by some sceptics. Therefore, although women's participation and rights always figured in some of the more maximalist definitions, now there is potentially more space for dialogue between feminist and mainstream scholars because recent mainstream debates on 'quality' have acknowledged the importance of women's participation and rights.

Mainstream analysts have been preoccupied with a number of other questions. Initially scholars were concerned with why non-democratic regimes break down and transitions occur. Are there any key events or actors that are crucial? Which transitions end in 'consolidated' democracies and which ones experience problems, reversals, or outcomes other than democracy? More recently attention has turned to what these new regimes are like and how we should explain and understand the different outcomes. Three major tools—actor-based models, structural models, and notions of path dependence—have been used to answer these questions of how/why does change occur, who/what are the important actors and what accounts for different outcomes. Most actor-based models see elites as the key actors in bringing about processes of change; but a few scholars, often outside the mainstream, use mass-based models that pay more attention to the role of civil society and grass-roots actors. In contrast, structural models give more weight to structures, whether socio-economic, cultural, or institutional, as important determinants of change or as preconditions for democracy. But none are sufficient on their own. Adherents of both actor and structure-based models have used notions of path dependence in their analyses. At its most simplistic, the nature of the non-democratic regime, the way it breaks down and what happens during the transition, affects the extent to which the new system will become a consolidated electoral system.

To facilitate the analysis of what are now quite long periods many scholars have divided up processes of democratization into several critical stages. Taking the pre-existing regime as the starting point; the breakdown of the pre-existing regime and the transition forms either one or two stages depending on the speed at which events take place; and finally the post-transition, sometimes called the consolidation, phase follows. Although there is often a large degree of fluidity and overlap between phases, this division allows scholars to assess the changing importance of not only different actors and their interaction with the institutional context at each critical juncture but also can give a clearer idea of exactly how a transition unfolds. As we will see certain analytical tools and approaches have been more important in the examination of specific stages.

ANALYSING GENDER AND TRANSITIONS ❖

❖ Non-Democratic Regimes

No analysis of transitions is complete without an understanding of the prior non-democratic regime as new polities in the post-transition phase do not begin with a blank slate but are influenced by the legacies of the previous regime and the process of transition.[7] A huge variety of non-democratic regimes have been identified. One very influential way of dividing them has been into authoritarian and totalitarian (with a later sub category of post-totalitarian) ideal types (Linz 1975). The term authoritarian developed in the mid-1960s to cover the broad range of military, one party and personalist regimes found in Latin America and the ex-colonies (Geddes 1999). It describes the non-democratic regimes in power in Argentina, Brazil, Chile, El Salvador, and South Africa prior to their transitions in the 1980s and 1990s. The state socialist regimes in power in the USSR and Central East Europe in the 1950s and 1960s including Poland, Czechoslovakia, and Hungary have been described as totalitarian. But according to Linz and Stepan (1996) they had become post-totalitarian by the 1980s.

Linz and Stepan (1996) argue that totalitarian (and post-totalitarian) and authoritarian regimes differ in four major ways that can have important legacies in the post-transition period. Regimes vary in terms of: the degree of pluralism (social, economic, and political) allowed, the role played by ideology, the nature of the regime's leadership and how far the regime mobilizes the people. All non-democratic regimes restrict the activities of political society. But in totalitarian and post-totalitarian regimes the single party dominates to the exclusion of all other political activities and ideologies. Pre-existing social and political organizations are suppressed. Citizens are expected to be mobilized and active in a range of party organizations but in a hierarchical, top-down, and controlled way. The all-encompassing party ideology serves an important legitimating function with its utopian world view. In post-totalitarian regimes, the dominant ideology, although still officially important, has become more of a rhetorical device and has lost much of its legitimating role. Although mass organizations linked to the single party still exist, people tend only to participate in so far as they have to. In contrast, while some authoritarian regimes use repression to prevent all conventional political activity, others sometimes tolerate a restricted amount of political activity seen as unthreatening to the regime. Fewer authoritarian regimes have an all-encompassing ideology or attempt to mobilize the population in their support.

Non-democratic regimes also vary in terms of their levels of institutionalization and the extent to which the rule of law exists. Totalitarian and post-totalitarian regimes tend to have highly formalized party and state structures and procedures, often with power concentrated in the hands of a few leaders. In post-totalitarian regimes the party leadership is still in control but it is often composed of a gerontocracy of 'men in grey suits'. Few authoritarian regimes have the same degree of institutionalization, and personalist dictatorships tend to be the most arbitrary of all with few rules and formal institutions. Under all forms of one party state and personalist dictatorships, the state apparatus is closely tied in with the regime whereas more state autonomy has existed under some military regimes.

Non-democratic regimes also differ in terms of the extent to which civil and economic society can function independently. The totalitarian (and to a slightly lesser degree post totalitarian state) regimes tolerate very little autonomous activity. Under state socialism, social and cultural life was dominated by the state and the communist party with its range of satellite organizations. Economic society was also very constrained as the state controlled the commanding heights of the economy and little private enterprise was permitted (Linz 1975). In some post-totalitarian states, however, a small degree of pluralism may be tolerated—sometimes facilitating the emergence of a dissident culture, or perhaps some limited economic or institutional pluralism within the dominant party (Linz and Stepan 1996). Authoritarian regimes in contrast tend to allow greater freedom in social and economic areas. On taking power many authoritarian regimes maintain the pre-existing economic system and allow elements of civil society such as sporting and social activities as well as religious expression to continue relatively autonomously (Linz 1975).

Non-democratic regimes vary greatly in terms of their vulnerability to collapse. Although initially surprised by the speedy collapse of state socialism, some analysts decided that although the post-totalitarian state socialist states appeared similar to totalitarian ones as the dominance of the single party, the role played by the state and the nature of the economic system appeared unchanged, they had in fact become 'hollowed out', and were characterized by low levels of mobilization, legitimacy, and ideological commitment. These changes help to explain why they were so vulnerable by the end of the 1980s as they were now more likely to be judged on their performance.

Although none of these analyses looks at gender issues, they highlight the need for us to consider the ways in which the ideologies, institutions, and the social and economic structures of different non-democratic regimes were gendered and the roles that women played within them in our case study countries. Now that we have sketched out some characteristics of non-democratic regimes, it is possible to explore their breakdown.

❖ Regime Breakdown

The mainstream democratization literature has been preoccupied with two questions in analysing this phase. First, what causes regimes to break down, and second, what forms do transitions take, particularly who initiates and controls the transition? There is a range of potential explanations. We will focus on two different kinds of actor-based explanations, as well as looking at alternative views that give more attention to the role of structures and external factors. Classic elite actor-based explanations dominated the democratization literature in the 1980s. In part fuelled by the very different circumstances of the collapse of the Soviet bloc and the breakdown of post-totalitarian regimes, other explanations came to the fore to counter the elite-based frameworks. Most analysts would now agree that it is impossible to isolate one element that is responsible for the breakdown of a non-democratic regime, pointing instead to a combination of factors.

The best-known elite actor-based explanation is expounded in O'Donnell, Schmitter, and Whitehead's four volume study, *Transitions from Authoritarian Rule*, which was based on the experience of Southern Europe and parts of Latin America and dominated the study of transitions for more than ten years after its publication in 1986. O'Donnell, Schmitter, and Whitehead (1986) define a transition as the interval between one political regime and another, delimited by the launching of the process of dissolution of the authoritarian regime at one end and at the other by the installation of some form of democracy. Tracing their lineage back to Rustow's classic study in 1970s, while recognizing the role of external factors, O'Donnell and Schmitter (1986) argued that domestic factors play the predominant role in transitions. More specifically they claimed that 'there is no transition whose beginning is not a consequence—direct or indirect—of important divisions with the authoritarian regime itself' (vol. 4, p. 19). They argued that the most important division within a regime is between the 'hardliners' (*duros*) who believe that the perpetuation of authoritarian rule is both possible and desirable and the soft-liners (*blandos*) who come to believe that the authoritarian regime (in which they have important positions) needs to create some degree of electoral legitimacy in the future but must introduce certain freedoms immediately.

If the softliners triumph, the authoritarian regime begins to liberalize often in the form of a limited political opening as was seen in Brazil and Spain. There may, for example be some consultation with civilian elites, the easing of repression and some individual rights may be allowed. The regime moves from *dictadura* (authoritarianism) to *dictablanda* (liberalized authoritarianism). This elite based explanation sees power as relatively evenly balanced between important actors and it is not inevitable that a transition to democracy will take place. As a result of this liberalization/opening, there is an increase in political activity and the 'resurrection of civil society' evidenced for example by an explosion of opposition to authoritarian rule among artists and intellectuals. But this resurrection occurs after the initial opening and is often considered dangerous, as high levels of mobilization can threaten a successful transition.

Scholars who attribute greater significance to the actions of non-elite collective actors in initiating transitions have challenged these elite actor explanations. They argue that the resurrection of civil society can occur prior to liberalization not as a consequence of it. And it can be the resurrection of civil society and the emergence of non-elite opposition that is the key factor that provokes the liberalization/opening. The role played by labour protest in the Spanish transition and of mass-based action from below, such as the huge popular demonstrations which played a part in the collapse of the Berlin Wall in 1989 and regime collapse in other parts of East Central Europe are often cited as key examples (Collier and Mahoney 1997; McFaul 2002; Bunce 2003). Others have argued that under certain circumstances non-democratic regimes can be fundamentally undermined by the actions of insurgents such as guerrillas (Wood 2000). But rarely in any of this literature have women's movements or the actions of organized women been mentioned except in passing.

Structural factors, particularly economic ones, also play an important part in the breakdown of many non-democratic regimes (Haggard and Kaufman 1997). Both economic crisis and economic growth have been seen as undermining non-democratic regimes but most analyses have focused on economic crisis. Przeworski and Limongi (1996) for example have shown that non-democratic regimes are less likely to survive crises than democratic ones. In their exploration of the relationship between economic crisis and transition Haggard and Kaufman (1995, 1997) have focused on the ways in which economic conditions influence the timing and terms of democratic transitions and post-transition political alignments. They make a distinction between transitions that occur in the context of economic crisis and non-crisis transitions that occur when economic performance is strong. Economic crises undermine the 'authoritarian bargains' that exist between authoritarian rulers and key socio-political groups. As a result authoritarian regimes become vulnerable to defections from business communities and to protest 'from below'. Regime breakdown becomes more likely, reducing the old regime's capacity to have an impact on the transition and its aftermath; and increasing the likelihood of political fragmentation in the post-transition period (Haggard and Kaufman 1995).

Other analysts stress the role of external/international events in catalysing the breakdown of non-democratic regimes. Two important factors have been isolated. The first is conflict, particularly defeat. For example Argentina's defeat by the UK in the Falklands/Malvinas conflict of 1982 prompted the military to handover over power. Post-conflict efforts to promote democracy from outside can also fall within this category. Second, the withdrawal of external support can weaken a non-democratic regime if it has been sustained in power by a hegemon. The satellite states of East Central Europe were weakened after Gorbachev introduced the 'Sinatra doctrine', modifying Soviet foreign and security policy. From then on the USSR was no longer prepared (or able) to keep the Eastern bloc and Warsaw pact together through force, in contrast for example to their response to the Prague Spring in 1968. After the end of the cold war, the USA too was no longer prepared to support anti-communist authoritarian regimes regardless of their activities. As a result authoritarian regimes in El Salvador and Guatemala were put under pressure to move to systems that at least appeared to be more democratic.

❖ *Transitions*

Once a non-democratic regime has broken down, the subsequent transition can take many forms. Much of the democratization literature has been preoccupied with analysing different transition paths and who controls the transition itself. A pacted transition was initially seen as the path most likely to result in the con-solidation of democracy (O'Donnell, Schmitter, and Whitehead 1986). It typically occurs after a gradual opening/liberalization when elites from the non-democratic regime make a pact with the moderate civilian elite opposition. Together they negotiate nature of the transition and the new system, deciding for example who is allowed to participate and the fate of the old non-democratic regime. Liber-alizing from a position of strength, elements of the non-democratic regime play an important part in shaping the transition and its outcomes. This influence can constrain the new government limiting for example its ability to deal with human rights abuses of the previous regime. Two of our case study countries, Brazil and Chile (as well as Spain) are cited as classic examples of pacted transitions. But these have also taken place after periods of insurgency and civil war as demonstrated in the South African and El Salvadorean cases. Bargains were also made between outgoing communist elites and the emerging new democratic elites in some of the transitions in East Central Europe such as in Poland and Hungary (Elster et al. 1998; Bunce 1999).

The collapse or hurried exit of a non-democratic regime in a 'crisis' transition provides a direct contrast to a gradual pacted transition. Often in a weak position, for example after a military defeat, the old regime is less able to impose conditions either on the nature of the new system and who can take part in it, or gain impunity from investigation for human rights abuses. It is also less likely to retain a significant degree of influence over the new government. Many of the transitions in East Central Europe, such as that in Czechoslovakia that took place relatively quickly after a short period of mass mobilization catalysed by the removal of Soviet support fall into this category.

In the absence of economic crisis, authoritarian rulers are more likely to retain the support of parts of civil society even as they withdraw. This support can allow them to impose an institutional framework (the terms of transition) that maintains their privileged position but can also favour their political allies and restrict their opponent's activities. Haggard and Kaufman (1995) use two of our case study countries—Argentina and Chile—as contrasting examples of crisis and non-crisis transitions. In Argentina the military withdrawal took place in the middle of an economic and military crisis, as the regime failed in its attempt

❖ ANALYSING GENDER AND TRANSITIONS

to recapture the Malvinas/Falklands as a distraction from the regime's economic problems. The military lost the support of all sections of the population and as a result had very little control over the transition, allowing the opposition some freedom of manoeuvre. In contrast the Pinochet regime in Chile withdrew amid high rates of economic growth as Chile was heralded as the 'tiger' economy of Latin America. The military regime still had the support of important sections of the population including business. Pinochet could therefore set the terms of transition. The post-transition political system that favoured the right was established according to the 1980 constitution designed by the military. All mainstream politicians felt constrained to pledge their support for the regime's free market economics. As a result the winning centre-left coalition maintained the military regime's economic policies tempered with extra social spending. The nature of the pre-existing regime, whether a military regime, personalist dictatorship, or state socialist state, timing and the way it breaks down can therefore have an important impact on the subsequent transition path.

❖ *Post-Transition Outcomes*

In the 1990s scholars' attention shifted from achieving transitions to the outcomes of those transitions: whether they were consolidated democracies displaying certain characteristics associated with functioning democracies, or fell within the 'grey zone' of hybrid regimes, such as competitive or electoral authoritarianism, that had some of the trappings of electoralism but were not democracies. Initially analysts were preoccupied with a number of questions: what is a consolidated democracy, what factors are likely to prevent consolidation from occurring, and what needs to be done to achieve it.

Definitions of consolidation varied. In some minimalist procedural conceptions the willingness of important groups to surrender power after an electoral defeat is the key characteristic. For mid-range analysts democracy has to be the 'only game in town' as behavioural and attitudinal factors are also central (Linz and Stepan 1996; Diamond 1999). Some of the debates about consolidation have been framed in terms of stability versus quality. Is a consolidated democracy, one that endures, appears institutionalized and does not break down or are there broader criteria? At first analysts focused on stability and endurance and on the type of institutions that would achieve them—asking whether parliamentary or presidential systems were more effective; what kind of political parties are desirable and whether concurrent economic reform programmes were also needed.

However, an emphasis on procedural issues—such as the presence of institutionalized elections—to the exclusion of other factors can obscure a number of problems—the 'faultlines of democracy' (Agüero and Stark 1997). Early on Guillermo O'Donnell (1994, 1996) argued that many new democracies were democracies in the sense that they fulfilled the criteria for Dahl's polyarchy and were enduring, but they were not consolidated. He claimed that the fixation on institutionalization obscures the presence of informal rules and procedures such as nepotism, clientelism, patronage, as well as delegative tendencies that he terms particularism. These 'delegative democracies' are often strongly majoritarian, with populist presidents governing using executive decrees and often without the backing of a political party (O'Donnell 1994).

However, once democracies appeared established, concern with their overall quality increased. The need for a whole ensemble of democratic institutions, rights, and characteristics associated with liberalism was now emphasized. The rule of law to guarantee the rights of citizens, free speech, the freedom of association, participation, accountability, and a vibrant civil society have all been identified as essential components of any democracy (Diamond 1999; Diamond and Morlino 2004).

By 2000 scholars' concerns widened further as the full extent of outcomes—other than consolidated democracies—had become evident. It was even claimed that the transition paradigm was over as the early optimism about the prospects for transitions to democracy was not born out by events (Carothers 2002). The emergence of the 'grey zone'—regimes that are not democratic but are also not conventionally authoritarian in ways that we understood them in the past—was one feature of this late period of the third wave (Diamond 2002). At certain times both our comparator cases, Peru and Russia, have been placed in this category. Regimes in the 'grey zones' do not fit easily into any of the usual categories of authoritarianism, such as military regimes, personalist dictatorships, or one party states, as new forms have developed. Despite the presence of elections, these 'hybrid regimes' fail to meet the substantive tests of democracy (Diamond 2002). For example 'competitive authoritarianism', in which despite restrictions, the possibility that the opposition might win exists, has increased hugely (Levitsky and Way 2002). At various times, Russia, Zimbabwe, Iran, and Kenya have been categorized in this way. 'Electoral authoritarian' regimes, such as Pakistan, Egypt, and Uganda, in which electoral processes exist but are largely a facade, have also increased in number. The changed international environment provides much of the explanation for this phenomenon as the end of the cold war and the triumph of Western liberalism has increased the pressure on all states to adopt electoral procedures even if they remain authoritarian in essence.

The third wave of democratization has also corresponded with a rise in nationalism and ethnic conflict. Granting and/or extending citizenship is part of the process of democratization and it has often been accompanied by the assertion of various national, religious, and minority rights which had been repressed by the previous non-democratic regime. This has been seen in East Central Europe and the ex-Soviet Union, as well as in parts of Latin America and Spain. As a result analysts have asked whether conflicts are more likely to emerge during transitions or in new democracies, or in poorer less stable democracies and whether certain institutional set-ups are more likely to promote conflict.[8] Indeed it has led to a reappraisal of Rustow's argument (1970) about the necessity of national unity as a key precondition for establishing democracy. Again few transition scholars have considered the ways in which these national and ethnic conflicts have been gendered for example with women often portrayed as the mothers of the nation. But as Racciopi and See (2006: 18–19) argue, this dimension has also been under-theorized in the gender and transitions literature to date.[9]

Despite Rustow's influential (1970) early argument that one of the prerequisites of successful democratization is the existence of an undisputed territorial unit in the form of a state, analyses of democratization have often neglected the importance of statehood, both in terms of state capacity but also in terms of the state as a coherent territorial unit. The nature of the state—whether it is weak and dismantled or relatively strong and well organized—is also crucial (O'Donnell 2003). Incomplete state building is now recognized as very problematic for democratization (S. Friedman 2003). Indeed scholars like O'Donnell (2003) have begun to speculate about the relationship between the nature of the non-democratic state and the way the regime (as a different entity to the state) collapsed, and the transition and post-transition outcomes. He asks whether stronger states leave a better inheritance after the collapse of non-democratic regimes than weaker dismantled ones.

Therefore the relationship between different transition paths and these varying outcomes is hotly debated. Although there is no agreement about the specifics, most analysts agree there is some connection between the nature of the non-democratic regime, the way in which it breaks down, the transition path taken and eventual outcomes. Outside political society and the state, the role of civil and economic society and the extent to which they had an independent existence prior to the transition can also have a significant impact on outcomes. Their absence is more likely under totalitarian regimes or personalist dictatorships. Non-democratic regime breakdown—whether it is a crisis or non-crisis transition, precipitated for example by external events, economic collapse, or military defeat—will also have an impact on the speed of the transition and the likelihood that it is negotiated or pacted. All of these factors will affect the institutional legacy inherited by the new regime. The nature of the transition, for example whether it is pacted, has an impact on the institutional set-up that is chosen. The continuing influence of non-democratic elites (variously called authoritarian enclaves or reserved domains (Valenzuela 1992)) can constrain the manoeuvrability of the new civilian government, for example, with regard to dealing with human rights abuses of the previous regime.

Some scholars have been preoccupied with the differences between transitions from authoritarian regimes in Latin America and state socialist ones in East Central Europe, questioning how far a literature that was initially based on the experience of Latin America can be relevant to the transitions from state socialism. They have disputed whether pacted transitions in East Central Europe and the ex-Soviet Union have the same consequences as in Latin America and Southern Europe. In contrast to the dominant wisdom drawn from the analysis of prior cases elsewhere, Bunce (2000, 2003: 174–9) has argued that it was those transitions in East Europe with high levels of popular mobilization and that made a sharp break with the past that were more likely to become sustainable and full-scale democracies. In contrast those that combined pacting with demobilized publics were most likely to result in the continuation of non-democratic rule. McFaul (2002) echoes this theme when he argues that mass mobilizations played a greater role in East Central Europe and that the outcomes of pacted transitions are different. Relatively evenly balanced pacted transitions, favoured in Latin America, are less likely to end up as democracies than the transitions in which actors from below—such as occured in the Czech Republic and the Baltic states—hold most power. The relatively balanced transitions are more likely to lead to unstable outcomes such as happened in Russia. And ones where the ancient regime is more powerful can lead to new forms of authoritarian rule (e.g. Belarus and Kazakstan). There has been some conjecture that, contrary to expectations, transitions in East Central Europe have proved easier, more rapid, and more thorough than in Latin America and Southern Europe (Schmitter 2003). This issue will be taken up in gender terms in the rest of this book.

In general the establishment of the procedures and institutions associated with electoral democracy has proved easier to achieve and has, in many cases, been more durable than had initially been thought possible. But, at the same time, it has been claimed that electoral democracy has been less meaningful and of a lower quality—characterized by poorly performing institutions and high levels of inequality—than had been anticipated (Karl 2003). Leading Karl (2005) to argue that, although agency is important in processes of transition, structures (institutions and preconditions) are more important in influencing outcomes and consolidation. In order to more fully understand the range of different outcomes, we will now explore in more detail some of the central themes of the post tran-sition phase: institutional choice, political parties, economic reform, and external factors (leaving the key theme of the role of civil society to Part II as to date its consideration in the majority of the mainstream democratization literature has been minimal).

❖ *Institutional Choices*

During the transition and post-transition phases, actors are faced with decisions about the nature of the institutional set-up to be (re)established. Mirroring the debates in the gender and politics literature on the institutional set-up most likely to result in higher levels of representation for women, the institutional form most likely to sustain democracy and build a legitimate political system has been investigated. Some analysts like Przeworski (1991) believe that the creation of suitable institutions is the key factor in ensuring a successful transition but others argue that these choices are only the result of other factors. The first choice to be made is around the constitution. Should the new polity continue to use the non-democratic regime's constitution (perhaps with some modifications), revert to a previous one, or design a new one? All these routes have been taken by our case study countries. Spain, Brazil, and South Africa are probably the best-known examples of countries that adopted new constitutions designed by constituent assemblies as part of their transitions. These processes often involved battles over the nature and extent of the rights to be included within them. Each route has different implications for the vision of citizenship, rights, and participation in the new polity embodied within it.

But it is the choice of the electoral system and governmental structures that has provoked a bigger debate among political scientists. Should, for example, it be an FPTP or a PR system and with what size of constituency? The choice between a presidential and a parliamentary system of government has been seen as the most crucial.[10] Latin American countries such as Chile, Brazil, and Argentina have tended to adopt presidential systems, East Central Europe has a mixture of parliamentary and semi-presidential systems (of the premier presidential variety) and the ex-Soviet Union has mainly semi-presidential systems (of the presidential parliamentary variety). Linz (1990), later backed up by the quantitative analyses of Stepan and Skach (1993), has descried the perils of presidentialism, arguing that parliamentary systems outperform presidential ones and break down less often. They are more likely to have majorities to implement their programmes, to have political experience, to lead to power-sharing and coalitions and less likely to rule at the edge of the constitution and abuse their power. In contrast, presidential systems are overly rigid, face problems of legislative deadlock and dual legitimacy, and are vulnerable to many of the problems, such as populist outsider presidents ruling without party support in a manner, reminiscent of O'Donnell's 'delegative democracy' (1994).

However, others have disputed whether the case against presidentialism is so clear-cut. Mainwaring and Shugart (1997) argue that it does have some advantages, such as greater choice and accountability for voters and that the contrast between parliamentary and presidential systems is not always as marked as Linz alleges. For example not all presidential systems allow presidents to issue decrees and the 'winner takes all' scenario can also occur in parliamentary systems with disciplined parties and large majorities. Many of the problems associated with presidentialism are actually due to other factors both inside and outside the political system. Presidential systems are more likely than parliamentary systems to be found in poorer and larger countries, where there are already a number of other obstacles to democracy. Other characteristics of the political systems, such as the instability and fragmentation of party systems, will, for example, facilitate the election of presidential outsiders. The combination most likely to lead to instability and failure is a strong president together with extreme multi-partism as disciplined parties are necessary for a presidential system to work (Mainwaring and Shugart 1997). It is much harder for a president to cooperate with party leaders if parties are weak and fragmented. Finally, they claim that some of the problems that have been associated with presidential systems can be ameliorated.[11] Institutional choice is therefore more multifaceted and complex than some commentators would claim. It must take into account the related issue of the functioning of political parties and party systems which we now turn to.

❖ *Political Parties and Party Systems*

As we have seen in our discussion of gender and politics, political parties play a central role in democratic systems contesting elections, articulating interests, aggregating demands, and integrating and recruiting citizens into politics and therefore are essential for any well functioning polity. The ability of political parties to play these roles in many third wave democracies has been undermined by a lack of institutionalized and stable parties and party systems (Mainwaring and Scully 1995; Randall and Svasand 2002*a*, 2002*b*). Mainwaring and Scully (1995) argue that weakly institutionalized party systems are a significant handicap to democratic consolidation. Polities with weakly institutionalized party systems have high levels of electoral volatility (Mainwaring 1998). People do not vote in stable and consistent ways from one election to the next so there are a large number of floating voters. As a result there are huge fluctuations from one election to another and parties come and go. This makes outcomes erratic and uncertain. Weakly insitutionalized parties lack stable roots in society—there are low levels of party identification, many people have no preferred party and do not trust political parties. Voters may split their ticket between the presidential and legislative elections and therefore is it likely that a president may end up without much support in the legislature. Often polities have a large number of parties, many of which are very recent.

In weakly institutionalized systems, parties frequently have low levels of organization. They are often poorly financed and lack organizational structures and formal procedures such as for candidate selection. Factionalism is common within parties as is party switching and weak party discipline. It is therefore relatively easy for individual parties to become personalistic vehicles for leaders. Weak party systems often exhibit high levels of personalism as it is easier for personalist and non-party candidates to win. In a context where political competition does not have to be channelled through parties or where people do not have great loyalty to parties, voters will be more likely to support candidates, such as Yeltsin and Putin in Russia or Fujimori in Peru, without a clear party label. Politics therefore becomes personalized and populist as candidates get support on the basis of their personality. Finally, there is a low level of legitimacy and trust in parties and elections. Voters are often unperturbed by the dissolution of parties as they do not necessarily see institutional processes as the only way of channelling and resolving political conflicts.

However, different cases and regions do not all exhibit the same characteristics. The role of political parties can vary according to whether the transition is a democratization or re-democratization and whether it is quick or slow, pacted or unpacted. In East Central Europe there were very few political parties in existence at the point of transition. No political parties apart from the communist party had been allowed under state socialism and the subsequent speed of the transitions meant that few parties had time to emerge. As a result social movements and broad opposition fronts, such as Solidarity in Poland and Civic Forum in Czechoslovakia, were initially the key players. But the unity of these movements dissipated relatively soon. Lewis (2001) has argued that the transformation of broad fronts into new political parties was a key moment of the transition. Subsequently, party systems in East Central Europe have had low levels of electoral participation in terms of voting and activism. Political parties have relatively weak structures with small memberships and underdeveloped national organizations. Because many of them are new, they have shallow roots in the electorate. Parties, therefore, do not play a role as agents of mobilization and integration, but this is not necessarily linked to a lack of legitimacy (Lewis 2001). Because of their greater longevity, many reformed communist parties have stronger structures and more developed national organizations than other parties and they have enjoyed electoral success. However, multiparty systems have not had long to develop. As a result Lewis (2000: 17) claims that ten years after the collapse of state socialism it was doubtful whether the party systems of East Central Europe were even as formed as those of Latin America which are themselves considered to be relatively undeveloped in comparison to Western Europe.

In Latin America many parties that predated non-democratic regimes reformed and therefore almost inevitably have a greater longevity than the majority of parties in East Central Europe. In Chile, for example, parties re-emerged that conformed to the old division between the right (that supported the military), the centre, and a new centre–left umbrella party to get round the remaining restrictions on the Left. The centre Christian Democrats (CD) joined up with the centre-left to form a successful alliance that won subsequent elections. In Argentina, the Peronists (initially a populist worker's party) and the Radicals (a more middle class party), who had been the most important parties prior to military rule became key players again. In Brazil the parties created by the military regime continued to operate. However, new political parties have also been formed. Most spectacularly the PT, the Workers Party in Brazil, emerged from the trade unions and social movements around Sao Paulo. Overall, Latin

American party systems display varying levels of institutionalization (Mainwaring and Scully 1995). Chile has one of the most long-standing and institutionalized party systems. But other party systems suffered virtual collapse. In Peru the main long-standing parties became discredited after they performed badly in the 1980s. The 1990 presidential election was contested by two outsiders and won by Fujimori. South Africa demonstrates an example of a different phenomenon. A one-time revolutionary party, the African National Congress (ANC), transformed itself into a political party, participated in a pacted and negotiated transition and then won subsequent elections. But most other insurgent groups, for example in Guatemala and El Salvador, did not win elections after they had become left-wing political parties.

Unstable parties and inchoate party systems can therefore contribute to the problems faced in the post-transition period. As a consequence, Mainwaring (1998) has claimed that one of the important tasks of consolidation is to ensure that party systems become institutionalized. Following Huntington, Mainwaring (1998) argues that: (*a*) party systems need stability in the rules and nature of inter-party competition with parties that are also relatively long-lasting and stable; (*b*) political parties need to have roots in society and to have captured the long-term loyalty of some social groups; (*c*) major political actors need to accord legitimacy to political parties and electoral processes and see them as the means of deciding who governs; and (*d*) parties need to have organizations that matter, namely have institutionalized structures that are not controlled by a few personalities, with party discipline in legislatures and party elites that are loyal to those parties.

However, not all commentators are agreed that strong institutionalized parties and party systems are always positive. Matland and Taylor (1997), examining Latin America, have argued that long-established parties are not necessarily democratic actors just because they are traditional and long-lasting. They are likely to have acted in undemocratic ways in the past, both in terms of their internal practices and their commitment to the electoral rules of the game. The key to their behaviour now is how they were treated under the non-democratic regime. If badly treated, they are less likely to behave undemocratically after a return to competitive electoral politics (Matland and Taylor 1997). In Part II we will consider the potentially demobilizing impact of the (re)emergence of strong political parties on civil society and social movements, including women's movements, who then may not play such an important role in the post-transition phase as they did in the breakdown of the non-democratic regime. The importance accorded to political parties in the mainstream literature therefore reinforces the lesson drawn from the gender and politics literature that any gendered analysis of transitions must focus on their role, investigating for example the gendered implications of institutionalized or inchoate party systems and the role of women within them.

❖ ANALYSING GENDER AND TRANSITIONS

❖ Economic Reform

Academics and policymakers have focused a great deal of attention on the relationship between economic and political reform. Although the timing has varied most countries undergoing political transitions have also undergone some form of economic transition. At one extreme, the countries in East Central Europe and the ex-Soviet Union embarked on a far-reaching transformation from state socialism to some kind of a capitalist system. Many Latin American, African, and Asian countries have also undertaken extensive programmes of economic reform closely associated with the neo-liberal doctrine of rolling back the state and allowing the free market to rule. The policy prescriptions flowing from these ideas—the so-called Washington consensus, also known as 'first generation reforms'—dominated the thinking of international financial institutions (IFIs) and economic policymaking in many parts of the world in the 1980s and most of the 1990s (Haggard and Webb 1994).

Reform policies, claimed to be the only way to end economic crisis and achieve sustained economic growth, focused on fiscal discipline, the liberalization of trade and investment regimes, the deregulation of domestic markets, and the privatization of public enterprises. As part of the imposition of first generation reforms, frequently at the behest of the IFIs, huge cuts were made in the state provision of social services to reduce fiscal deficits (as the demands of macroeconomic policy won out). This was combined with an ideology that advocated transferring social service delivery from the state to the market and private sector often on a decentralized basis.

Much of the developing world saw a huge increase in poverty as a result of economic crises and the imposition of structural adjustment programmes (SAPs) inspired by the neo-liberal ideas of the Washington Consensus in the 1980s and 1990s. At the same time as welfare provision was reduced, there was an increase in hardship far greater and far more enduring than that anticipated by policymakers with a concomitant increase in demands for welfare services. The ranks of the needy were swelled by the 'new' poor, such as downsized civil servants, who were seen as more potentially destabilizing than the demobilized 'old' poor (Graham 1995).

Although not discussed in the section on gender and politics, feminist scholars began to analyse SAPs soon after the implementation of first generation reforms. Critiques of the gender-blind models underlying SAPs demonstrated that they did not take the reproductive economy or women's unpaid labour into account while at the same time assuming its elasticity (Palmer 1992; Bakker 1994; Sparr 1994; Elson 1995). SAPs also ignored the sexual division of labour, for example, assuming the mobility of labour from industrial jobs typically done by men to service sector jobs typically done by women. They also ignored the particular constraints on the mobility of female labour both from discrimination outside the household and from men and women's very different roles within the household (Collier et al. 1994). In contrast to the individual focus of these models, feminist economists argued that adjustment was also a household and community process and individual responses were made in a household and community context (MacDonald 1998).

Second, a number of empirically based case studies demonstrated what these factors meant in practice. They examined the impact of cuts in welfare services and subsidies in the context of high levels of unemployment, inflation, and falling wage levels on gender relations and women's paid and unpaid labour in both the productive and reproductive spheres (Moser 1992; Tripp 1992). Women play different roles from men in the provision and consumption of social services, therefore they are differentially affected by both economic crisis and any changes in social service provision. It is women who generally have responsibility for ensuring household well-being and liaising with health, education, and other welfare services. It is also women who make up the majority of teachers, nurses, and care workers. The cuts in welfare provision that frequently accompanied SAPs therefore increased women's unpaid provision of welfare services in the household as women took up the slack left by the reductions in service. At the same time cuts reduced the employment opportunities for women in state sector welfare services. Some studies also examined women's responses to economic crisis and the resulting increase in poverty that took place in the absence of effective state services in many parts of Latin America (Valdes and Weinstein 1993; Blondet and Montero 1995; Barrig 1996). A variety of survival strategies (both individual and collective) and other forms of 'making ends meet' were adopted by poor women. Feminist scholars therefore highlighted the ways in which different groups of women contested the impact of structural adjustment on both individual and collective bases.

The levels of poverty and hardship associated with first generation reforms proved to be far greater and more long-lasting than had been anticipated. The perception became widespread that fragile new democracies had to be protected from the potentially destabilizing short-term consequences of economic reform to ensure that reform policies and newly elected governments were not derailed by widespread opposition. As a consequence, both academics and policymakers advocated the introduction of an interconnected package of measures to ensure the sustainability of economic reform—primarily building coalitions to support reform and providing safety nets such as poverty alleviation programmes to protect those groups hardest hit by reform processes (Graham 1994). The aim was to include new and hitherto excluded groups, such as the poor, ethnic minority groups, and women, in political processes and to institutionalize distributional conflicts by absorbing them into the political arena so that populations would 'own' the reforms rather than feeling that they had been imposed from above (Haggard and Webb 1994). However, initial fears proved unfounded as the expected backlash against economic reform did not materialize in the short term (Mainwaring 1999). Few elected governments in the 1980s and 1990s were destabilized by populations suffering the consequence of severe economic recession. But the disquiet about the impact of reform did not dissipate.

By the end of the 1990s it was widely felt that 'first generation' reforms had failed to bring promised levels of growth, resulting instead in widening inequalities and continued high levels of poverty. Therefore a 'second generation' of reforms, that would maintain the market orientation of the first generation with a commitment to free market capitalism, was needed (Pastor and Wise 1999). But they should tackle the distributional and institutional questions that the first generation had ignored (in part because policymakers had not anticipated that the distribution of income would worsen in the medium- to long-term). According to Pastor and Wise (1999) this new generation of reforms was to undertake three tasks: complete the market reforms left over from first generation, tackle the issue of inequality, and ensure good governance. As reform programmes were not necessarily internally consistent and could have contradictory implications, they had to be implemented by savy politicians governing with support of the people (not simply using technocrats and presidential decrees as was possible with the first generation).

Although still situated within the same paradigm, the 'Post-Washington Consensus' did signal a change of focus. The post-adjustment policy package placed more emphasis on the role of the state and institutions (broadly defined as 'rules') and on the potentially deleterious effect of both high levels of inequality and the widespread lack of participation on economic reform and ultimately on rates of growth and development. Citizen participation and a constructive dialogue with civil society, including women's organizations, were now valued. Because of this emphasis on participation and properly functioning institutions, some of the debates about second generation reforms resonate with discussions about the quality of democracy. And institutions such as the World Bank also began to advocate the somewhat contentious 'business case' for gender equality and adopted gender mainstreaming. However, although second generation reforms paid more overt attention to gender and gender equity within their frameworks, the social policies emanating from this new push to tackle poverty and inequality often have negatively gendered implications as again their implementation is dependent on women's unremunerated labour (Molyneux and Razavi 2005). Therefore the complex relationship between political and economic transitions also needs to be understood in gendered terms.

❖ *The International Environment*

Democracy is now seen as a global norm to be legitimately promoted by a range of international actors. As we have seen, many non-democratic regimes now find it

34

hard to resist the pressure to adopt the trappings of electoral processes. Therefore the spread of democracy as a global norm has also contributed to the rise of competitive authoritarian regimes. However, until recently, most theories and accounts of democratization have focused primarily on the national context. But within comparative politics the need to incorporate the international context as an explanatory variable in its own right into theories of democratization has now been recognized (Grugel 2003). Huntington's concept (1991) of the third wave was one of the first suggestions of the significance of the international context as it analysed democratization as a global phenomenon linked by processes such as contagion and diffusion and spread by the global media in an era of mass communications. Processes of globalization have also contributed to the creation of greater political, economic, and cultural links between countries, weakening the capacity of states. Insulation from global processes is therefore more difficult to achieve and, as a result, the impact of globalization on transitions to democracy has to be taken more seriously (Grugel 2003).

This change of emphasis has also been mirrored in the gender and politics literature and the importance of external factors on the national context has been increasingly recognized. The third wave also coincided with the spread of second wave feminism and the development of influential global women's movements that had a substantial impact on both the global and many national contexts. But its influence and the extent of international norm change varied over this time frame (Jaquette and Staudt 2006). After a period of growth, the high water mark occurred in the early 1990s towards the end of the 1985–95 Decade for Women. A backlash had begun by the time the Beijing women's conference was held in 1995 and the period since the mid-1990s has been one of retrenchment as religious fundamentalisms and the political right became more influential, campaigning particularly around reproductive rights trying to limit women's access to abortion and even contraception. Domestic gender policy change and norm diffusion cannot now be seen in isolation from international influences.

We can examine the multiple links between international factors and transitions to democracy in terms of key actors and ideational processes. Three main actors stand out: states, international organizations, and transnational NGOs. Over the period of the third wave the main role played by superpowers has been as external hegemons, for example keeping non-democratic regimes in power during the cold war and conversely helping to bring about their collapse. Some states, particularly the USA, have also played a role in promoting regime change/democratization through methods that range from pressure (with varying degrees of formality/informality) at one end of the spectrum through sanctions, conditionality for example for bilateral loans, financial support for NGOs, and opposition groups, to outright force at the other end. Indeed imposed democratization has become more significant recently (Whitehead 2003). International and regional organizations have also played a part in promoting democracy and regime change.

❖ ANALYSING GENDER AND TRANSITIONS

They, too, have used international regimes such as human rights conventions to put pressure on non-democratic regimes and mandated international sanctions against some non-democratic regimes. International and regional organizations have also used conditionality for loans particularly around good governance, participated in international peacekeeping and reconstruction operations. The role played by transnational NGOs in supporting processes of democratization has been increasingly lauded. A number of NGOs such as Amnesty International have been long-standing campaigners against human rights abuses of non-democratic regimes and supported groups opposing authoritarianism. More recently, international NGOs have played roles in supporting new democracies by building civil society and election monitoring.

Gender concerns have become more prominent for states, international organizations, and NGOs (and have even been cited as one aim of imposed democratization). In part, this is due to the activities of international women's movements that have become prominent global actors. Their activities, for example around the international women's conferences that took place in Mexico in 1975, Nairobi in 1985 as well as Beijing in 1995, raised the profile of gender issues such as women's political representation and the need to incorporate a gender dimension into security and post-conflict operations. International women's organizations and networks of gender activists advocating improvements in women's rights framed many of their arguments to fit the new global norms of human rights and democracy (Clark, Friedman, and Hochstetler 1998; Keck and Sikkink 1998; E. Friedman 2003). As a result women's citizenship rights and human rights—expressed for example in the right to bodily integrity free from gender-based violence—have now become a more accepted part of international norms and international human rights regimes have had to take gender on board (Friedman 2006).

The major international ideational process identified in transitions to democracy has been diffusion—defined as the spread of knowledge and ideas that are gradually internalized by domestic actors. Opposition elites from non-democratic regimes often absorbed new political ideas in exile which they then utilized when they returned home. Diffusion has not just been confined to ideas about democracy. Many women (often left-wing) activists, for example, were influenced by the Western feminism they came across in exile. Later during transitions, institutional models used in other contexts have been adapted for new situations. For example the South African Truth and Reconciliation Commission was modelled in part on the Rettig commission established to investigate human rights abuses in Chile. The global spread of certain gender norms was also significant in facilitating this process of institutional diffusion. State feminism, quotas, and gender mainstreaming have all become widely accepted and adopted by both a range of national and international actors. When deciding upon their own strategies and goals, feminists involved in a range of transitions looked at the institutional models adopted elsewhere when advocating state women's machineries, constitutions, or quotas.

At the same time as external factors can have a significant impact, they do not impact equally or in the same ways in all contexts. Geopolitical location makes a huge difference. Pressures to democratize are, according to Levitsky and Way (2003), much greater in those states with close linkages to the West for example through geography and the connections of civil society actors. Greater prominence is then given to human rights abuses. If this is combined with a high degree of Western leverage, democratization becomes more likely (Levitsky and Way 2003). The possibility of EU accession has affected political and policy developments in many ex state socialist states in East Central Europe with important implications for gender norms and relations. The international context has also changed considerably over the last twenty-five years. The end of the cold war, the advent of the war on terror, the conservative backlash, and the changing fortunes of the global women's movement have all altered the international environment in ways that impact differently on different regions and cases (Jaquette and Staudt 2006).

Despite its gender blindness, a number of themes stand out from this now huge literature on democratization that are particularly important for our analysis. First, it is useful to break up the analysis of transitions into a number of critical phases. Any gendered analysis must begin with an understanding of the non-democratic regime differentiating between two ideal types of authoritarianism and state socialism. It is then possible to look at regime breakdown, and, mindful that phases are sometimes simultaneous or overlapping rather than easily distinguishable and discrete, at the transition and post-transition periods. Second, any study must consider both the role of different actors, whether elite or mass, and structures, such as the institutional context, as well as the interaction between them at different stages of the process of transition. It will then be possible to see how all these factors impact on different transition paths and their various outcomes. Transitions vary considerably in their speed, whether they are pacted, the role played by external factors, and the nature and significance of the institutional legacy of the prior non-democratic regime. In the post-transition context, different institutional choices, the roles played by political parties and economic reform are all important considerations. As a consequence of analysing the complex interaction of all these factors, it is possible to understand the range of different outcomes that emerge. Several themes figure in both the mainstream and the gender and politics literatures. Central to both is the analysis of the role of certain elite and mass actors, political parties and party systems and the impact of institutional choice. Both increasingly recognize the centrality of economic and external factors. A number of questions emerge. Which definition of democracy works for a gendered analysis? What is the connection between the nature of the non-democratic regime, the way in which the regime breaks down, the transition path, and gender outcomes? Are there significant gender differences between transitions from state socialism and authoritarianism? And, is there a relationship between poor quality democracy and poor quality gender outcomes? But as we have seen, without some modification, the mainstream literature cannot provide the answers to these questions. We are now in a position to bring together the relevant elements of the gender and politics literature and the transitions literature to create a framework that can take our analysis forward.

❖ THE FRAMEWORK
❖ *The Approach*

In order to answer the questions outlined above and account for different gender outcomes that result from transitions to democracy, this book examines not only different women's roles within various stages of transitions but a range of other factors that can help us to understand how the different gender outcomes come about. Central to any attempt to understand the gendered nature of transitions to democracy is an ability to deal with 'complex and varying causal patterns'. This cannot be done through the generation of a general model that can be applied universally but by hypothesizing about causal regularities using comparative analysis set within a theoretically informed comparative framework (Skocpol 1992: 39). This is no easy task and needs to be done with care and precision.

This study will use a comparative macro-historical analysis (influenced by the work of scholars like Theda Skocpol (1979, 1992) to try to explain and understand variations in the gender outcomes of transitions. It will unite two major elements of macro-historical analysis—path dependency and historical institutionalism—with feminist analyses. Historical explanations that highlight the importance of causal sequences in the past therefore play a key role in this study. Some scholars argue that this is enough to constitute a path-dependent analysis while others, like Mahoney (2000), argue that path dependence needs contingent events (that cannot be explained on basis of prior events or initial conditions) that set in motion institutional patterns or event chains that have deterministic properties. Whether it is termed path dependence, causal sequences, such as the sequence of events set in train during the breakdown and transition must be investigated in any gendered analysis of transitions.

The book also draws on institutional approaches to politics that see the configuration of governing institutions and political party systems as shaping the relationships among political actors and the possibility for policy change (Skocpol 1992; Thelen and Steinmo 1992). Political struggles are inevitably mediated by the institutional context in which they take place. The ways in which institutions can shape not only actors' strategies and their outcomes but also their goals therefore need to be investigated (Thelen and Steinmo 1992). Bringing together the analysis of structure and agency in this way will encompass the roles played both by key actors and by their institutional contexts. As a result we will be able to explain why it is that in some contexts women's movements that played an important role in the breakdown and transition stages do not necessarily appear to be able to achieve such positive outcomes in the post-transition phase, in contrast to other situations where women's movements have been less active and organized but outcomes have not been significantly worse.

This endeavour concurs with Valerie Bunce's (2000: 15) stance that if certain conditions are met 'the comparative method—or controlled comparisons among a limited number of cases—can be powerful in uncovering causal relations'. Comparative political scientists agree to some extent on the conditions that are necessary for this type of analysis to work: the question under investigation must be well specified and the cases must be well chosen and justified (Skocpol 1992: 44). We will now specify our key question in more detail and elaborate both the variables and the actual cases that will be used to determine the answers.

As already elaborated, the fundamental question is: under what circumstances can transitions to democracy result in positive gender outcomes? The dependent variable—positive gender outcomes—is defined as measurable improvements in women's descriptive and substantive representation and gender policy reform in the post-transition period. As the gender status quo in force at the breakdown of non-democratic rule and the institutional legacies vary from case to case, they need to be investigated. Positive gender outcomes are therefore contextual and relative rather than necessarily absolute. They will be measured in terms of a change from the previous situation within a particular case study country rather than by universal criteria. But we will also make some broad comparative judgements to set any changes in context.

Indeed some limited general benchmarks for descriptive representation can be set. Levels of women's descriptive representation (in the lower house of legislatures) can be divided into three categories: low (up to 10%); moderate (between 10 and 25%) and high (above 25%) with a figure of 25% or above signifying a positive gender outcome. A number of factors account for the figure of 25%. It is significantly above the global average (16.3% in early 2006), so its attainment marks an achievement. Second, it was chosen with some regard to the literature on what constitutes a critical mass of women legislators (for many scholars 30% is an important benchmark). But third, it does not set the barrier so high that almost no cases could be included. Any higher than 25%, the level of representation within the legislature would exclude virtually every country, but a lower figure of say 20% would be too low to be considered a positive outcome. In 1997, just after the peak of the third wave, only 12 of the 120 countries surveyed by the Inter-parliamentary Union (IPU) achieved this figure of 25% in their lower or single house, but this number had increased to 30 by 2006.

❖ ANALYSING GENDER AND TRANSITIONS

We can evaluate a positive gender outcome in women's substantive representation (defined as the expression of women's interests, particularly in policymaking) in a number of ways. The extent to which women legislators act for women is one. The existence of effective SWMs is a second way to judge the representation of 'women's interests'. An SWM's effectiveness can be assessed in terms of its position within the state, its resources and capacity namely Stetson and Mazur's category (1995) of policy influence and access. Finally, we can evaluate positive gender outcomes in policymaking by examining a number of key areas of gender rights reform within the constitutional/legal arena. As we have seen, gender rights are not one homogenous category but are a number of different categories often governed by different legal regimes (Htun 2003). In addition to the implementation of electoral quotas enacted to enhance descriptive representation, we will consider outcomes in three areas: divorce, reproductive rights particularly abortion, and domestic violence. These three areas have been chosen for a number of reasons. First, they have all been key issues for feminist movements in a range of different contexts.[12] But although they are all 'strategic' gender issues, they nonetheless vary in terms of their contentiousness; the ways in which they have been framed; and the extent to which favourable international norms have been constructed around each issue. For example abortion—and reproductive rights in general—has been one of the most controversial of the gender rights, particularly if framed in terms of women's autonomy and right to choose, and the area where there has been the greatest disagreement in the international arena.

As our interests are broader than simply the civil and political dimensions of women's citizenship embodied in the various dimensions of representation, we are also concerned with the social and economic rights that facilitate civil and political ones. Therefore we also need to consider the implications of broader social and economic changes such as the economic and social sector reform that has accompanied many political transitions as part of our analysis of gender outcomes. This will encompass concerns such as welfare provision and employment sometimes categorized as women's practical gender interests.

What independent variables are we going to use in our analysis? Based on the preceding discussion of both the mainstream democratization literature and the gender and politics (including the gender and transitions) literatures, a number of factors must be included. A gendered analysis of transitions has to consider both actors and institutions. Using a broad definition of the political, the first task is to isolate the key actors that can contribute to positive gender outcomes. Much of the democratization literature now emphasizes the role played by civil society and organized women's movements are central actors in most analyses of gender and transitions to date. No study could therefore fail to include their activities and the extent to which they were able to articulate gender issues in transitions. However, we also saw from some of the gender and politics literature that certain women activists and small issue networks, who are often feminist, have played important roles within first world political arenas as well as in some gendered analyses of transitions (Caul 1999; Franceschet 2005; Waylen 2007). As we have seen, much of the democratization literature highlights the role of elite actors in transitions. The activities of key women activists therefore must be analysed separately from broader women's movements. We must look at activists' strategies and tactics, the alliances they have made as insiders and outsiders as well as their ability to place gender issues on the agenda of the transition.

But any analysis has to consider not only the key actors, but also the institutions with which they interact together with the broader context of the transition. For example, we have seen from the gender and politics literature that the nature of the electoral and party systems and even SWMs can have an important impact on levels of women's representation and their effectiveness. If we divide up the institutional arena into the electoral, bureaucratic, and constitutional/legal arenas we need to examine the relative openness of each of these three arenas to actors pressing gender concerns in different contexts particularly in the post-transition period.

There are a number of other important contextual factors. The institutional legacy of the previous non-democratic regime provides us with another variable. We need to examine the differences between state socialist and authoritarian gender regimes and how far these different regimes leave different institutional legacies. The nature of the transition from non-democratic rule—its timing, whether it is a slow or quick, pacted or unpacted one and its openness to gender claims—is another important factor. Do different paths offer women actors different opportunities? The external context forms the final factor. As we have seen from the democratization literature, the external environment has now been recognized as an important dimension to be considered in any analysis of transitions. With a few exceptions, there is, as yet, little analysis of it in the gender and transitions literature (Alvarez 2000; Baldez 2003). Despite this, it is clear that a number of elements—such as the impact of international women's movements and networks; international organizations, conferences, international norms and legal regimes such as CEDAW; the role of other states such as the USA and regional organizations such as the EU; and the diffusion of ideas, policy, and funding; and how they have changed over time—all need to be incorporated. We will then be able to assess how far their impact varies in different contexts.

Because transitions to democracy and their outcomes are the result of the complex interaction of a large number of different factors, it is not possible to have a more parsimonious analysis with fewer variables. Of necessity our framework will be complex but it will enable us to reach more nuanced conclusions. Before we can begin the investigation of the interaction of all these factors, assessing how far certain gender issues could be articulated, placed on the policy agenda and then translated into positive gender outcomes in a range of transitions to democracy, we need to specify our case selection.

❖ ANALYSING GENDER AND TRANSITIONS

❖ *The Case Studies*

In order to avoid some of the pitfalls of comparative analysis—particularly too few cases and too many variables—the wide-ranging analysis of gender and transitions envisaged in this book has to build on more than just two or three country case studies.[13] Intra-regional and cross-regional comparison that can encompass different types of non-democratic regime—particularly authoritarian and state socialist regimes—and transition paths is one important way of providing enough suitable cases with a sufficient range of variables and outcomes. But cross-regional comparison itself has not been uncontentious. In an early exchange in the mid-1990s Valerie Bunce (1994) argued against the cross-regional comparisons favoured by Terry Karl and Philippe Schmitter (1994, 1995), claiming that analyses undertaken within regions are more valuable and avoid 'conceptual stretching'.

There are however good methodological arguments in favour of comparing cases across regions. Cross-regional analysis highlights the importance of contextual variables and allows analysts to better specify theories with regard to those contextual variables (Huber 2003). Indeed in a seeming reversal of her earlier position, Bunce (2003: 192) later argued that the cross-regional analysis of democratization can be particularly useful where regions are very different, for example in terms of their culture, historical development, and relationship to the international system, as it can contest and complicate both the underlying assumptions and analysis. It also minimizes the possibility that the cases chosen will reduce the variation in the dependent variable and determine the conclusions drawn. Therefore the addition of more regions allows the introduction of new variables and issues and can challenge common assumptions, approaches and arguments. Bunce (2003: 169) also argues that it is necessary to expand the number of dependent variables—and if possible 'restrain the universe of causes'—that can be done by widening the analysis. However, she (2003: 192) warns that region should not employed as a variable in its own right—it is not just a summary of factors that have taken on geographical form—it is necessary to specify those variables that characterize regional patterns (Huber 2003).

In that spirit, this book is premised on the assumption that comparing cases across and within regions is both possible and useful for this kind of endeavour. It enables us to widen the analysis from the transitions from authoritarianism that formed the bulk of the Latin American examples and which initially also dominated study of gender and transitions. The analytical centrality of transitions from authoritarianism represented by the Latin American cases had a significant impact on the underlying assumptions and approaches of the gender and transitions literature. It reinforced its early focus on the analysis of women's movements that had been active within civil society for relatively long periods. Broadening the range of cases to transitions from state socialism and insurgent transitions will help this book move away from that dominance.

We also need a relatively large number of case studies because we are dealing with a large number of variables. Eight countries that are commonly recognized to have made a transition to some kind of democracy will provide us with a big enough range of both independent and dependent variables, but will still be a small enough 'n' to allow for sufficiently in-depth qualitative analysis.[14] And even within these eight, some features of each country will inevitably be explored in more depth than others. We will also refer to two other comparator cases—Peru and the USSR (and Russia as one of its successor states)—chosen primarily because they exhibit outcomes within the grey zone and can supply some interesting contrasts and useful comparisons.

The full-scale cases comprise three Latin American, one Central American, three Eastern European, and one African case study. The countries (in alphabetical order) are Argentina, Brazil, Chile, Czechoslovakia (and one of its successor states—the Czech Republic), El Salvador, Hungary, Poland, and South Africa.[15] They are therefore drawn predominantly from two regions: Latin America and Eastern Europe, in part because these are the two areas that have been most widely researched and analysed within both the mainstream and gender and transitions literature. But more importantly each region also had very different non-democratic regimes that provide us with case studies of authoritarianism and state socialism. Less usually, South Africa will also be considered. It provides an important additional case study as it gives variation in both the independent and dependent variables. In many ways its gender outcomes are the most positive of all the cases, and its transition path is somewhat different to most of the others. Therefore it is not included as the representative of another geographical region namely Africa. And, as will be explained below, El Salvador another 'insurgent transition', although in some ways an outlier, has been included as its matched pair. Including a case study from Southern Europe such as Spain or one from Asia would have introduced too many regions and variables. The German Democratic Republic might also have made a potentially interesting case study but because it was absorbed into West Germany in the aftermath of the transition, its outcomes are unusual.

In all the case study countries the breakdown of their non-democratic regime and subsequent transitions occurred as part of the third wave of democratization. Indeed, most went through these processes in the late 1980s and early 1990s and none after the high point of the third wave in 1995. For most cases our analysis will concentrate on the breakdown of the non-democratic regime, the transition and first ten to fifteen years after the first competitive election. All the case studies could be categorized as semi-peripheral middle income countries, with the majority falling into the upper middle income category (Argentina, Brazil, Chile, Czech Republic, Hungary, and Poland) and only two in the lower middle income category (El Salvador and South Africa) together with the comparator cases of Russia and Peru. The pre-existing regime in three of the cases was state socialist

(Czech Republic, Hungary and Poland) with the USSR as a comparator case. And in the other five it was some form of authoritarian regime—either military or military dominated (Argentina, Brazil, Chile and El Salvador) or racially exclusive regime (South Africa)—with Peru as an authoritarian comparator case. For full socio-economic details of all the case studies see the appendices.

The countries have therefore been chosen to provide a sufficient number of cases of transitions from both state socialism and authoritarianism to enable us to come to some firm conclusions about the importance of the different forms of non-democratic regime as well as identify some differences within these broad categories. Indeed, to avoid over-homogenization, Linz and Stepan (1996) make distinctions between various post-totalitarian regimes to take account of the differences between state socialist states—classifying them as early, frozen (in which hardliners were unable to liberalize (GDR and Czechoslovakia)) and mature (in which reformists were willing to liberalize and reform (Hungary)). Poland they classify as being in many ways closer to an authoritarian regime than a totalitarian one, as the regime allowed some social pluralism and felt forced into a military takeover in the early 1980s. The military regimes in Latin America also exhibit differences. Regimes in power in Argentina and Chile in the 1970s both followed a neo-liberal model to some degree, whereas the regime in Brazil (and Argentina in the 1960s) was more closely associated with bureaucratic authoritarianism and the Peruvian regime was seen as relatively reformist. El Salvador was ruled by a military civilian alliance prior to the transition, and the authoritarian regime in South Africa was somewhat unusual because of the overwhelming salience of race.

The cases vary in terms of the importance and range of women's movements, feminist activists and networks active at different stages of the transition. They range from cases with very significant movements at one end of the spectrum (Chile, Brazil and South Africa) to virtually non-existent ones at the other end (Hungary and the Czech Republic). They also followed a range of transition paths from the quick 'crisis' transition (Argentina, Czechoslovakia) to slower negotiated ones (Chile, Brazil, and South Africa). The importance attributed to civil society in initiating the transitions also varies between countries. Some of the cases have been seen as transitions from below where mass mobilization played an important role in toppling the non-democratic regime (Poland and the Czech Republic). Both El Salvador and South Africa had 'insurgent transitions' in which left-leaning opponents of the non-democratic regime played a key role in its demise. In the South African case the insurgents took power but in the El Salvadorean case they failed to win subsequent competitive elections. The transitions in Brazil, Chile, South Africa, El Salvador as well as Poland, and Hungary were pacted ones in which key decisions were taken during negotiations between members of the non-democratic and opposition elites.

The cases not only exhibit different transition paths but also display a range of different institutional legacies from these non-democratic regimes, and different outcomes in the post-transition period. Most of the case study countries have made transitions to reasonably stable electoral democracies even if the quality of those democracies varies somewhat. After a period of increasingly presidential rule, Argentina experienced severe political and economic crisis in the late 1990s and early 2000s. There are also fears that a dominant party state is emerging in South Africa. Both South Africa and Chile have been constrained by the institutional legacy of non-democratic regime. The Czech Republic, Poland, and Hungary are considered to be three of the most successful post-state socialist transitions undergoing the fastest and most organized move to liberal democracies and the quickest and smoothest transition into the EU (Fodor 2004). Our two comparator countries—Peru and Russia—have been identified as part of the 'grey zone' at different points. Different scholars have classified them both as poor/non-democracies, or sometimes as displaying the characteristics of competitive/electoral authoritarian regimes and personalistic rule particularly Peru under President Fujimori and Russia under President Putin.

The case study countries vary in their post-transition institutional structures, namely their constitutions, party, and electoral systems. For example at one extreme the comparator cases demonstrate many of the characteristics of inchoate party systems whereas at the other the Chilean party system appears much more stable. The external context within which the case study countries operate has had some different implications in different cases. State socialist regimes were very differently positioned in the cold war to many authoritarian regimes such as El Salvador and Chile that could count on US support as bulwarks against communism. In the post-transition context accession to the EU has been an important factor for Poland, Hungary, and the Czech Republic helping to determine the nature of constitutional change and certain policy outcomes.

As we will see, the gender outcomes vary considerably between the cases. There is some initial evidence to support the common contention that the majority of transitions have been disappointing in gender terms. Women's descriptive representation was low almost everywhere immediately after the majority of transitions in Latin America and East Central Europe. Women formed an average of only 8.8% of the representatives elected at the first elections in East Central Europe (a huge drop from the levels under state socialism) and figures were even lower in Latin America. Initially many countries either maintained the constitution designed by the non-democratic regime or returned to the previous one. Although many states did create SWMs, they were often weak tokenistic bodies established from the top down. Finally, most transitions brought few improvements in key areas of gender policy such as reproductive rights. Indeed in El Salvador and Poland there has been retrenchment. However, this pattern is not universal. Overall, gender outcomes appear more positive in some transitions than others and some gender outcomes appear easier to achieve than others so simple generalizations cannot be made.

❖ ANALYSING GENDER AND TRANSITIONS

In order to explore these different patterns, gender outcomes must be dis-aggregated. A number of positive ones can be identified. For example levels of descriptive representation have been high in both Argentina and South Africa. New constitutions that contained gender equality measures were introduced in South Africa and Brazil. SWMs were set up with the active involvement of fem-inists in South Africa, Chile, and Brazil. Improved measures against domestic violence have been introduced in many of our Latin American case studies and finally reproductive rights, in the form of access to abortion, have been improved in South Africa. Indeed South Africa has been seen as one of the most successful transitions in gender terms.

In order to account for these varying gender outcomes and explain the rela-tive success of the South African case, we will now embark on a wide-ranging analysis of transitions that is genuinely comparative rather than individually or regionally based. The analysis in the rest of the book will continue on a thematic rather than a simply geographical or chronological basis but it will be attentive to the critical phases of transitions. It examines the processes by which gender issues can be articulated, placed on the agendas of transitions, and translated into policy outcomes in three parts: looking first at women's organizing, then at the electoral arena, and finally at the state and policy outcomes. Each part is organized chronologically charting developments over time in that arena.

Part II deals with the role of women's movements and key women actors oper-ating in civil society outside the conventional political arena—in part because this has been the focus of so many of the gendered analyses of transitions to democracy to-date but also because women's movements can play such a key part in the initial articulation of gender issues. The varying roles of different women's organizations will be examined in non-democratic regimes, regime breakdown and transition, and post-transition outcomes. This part also considers how different women's organizations interact with the changing political opportunity structure at differ-ent stages of transition. Part III examines how the conventional political arena—as a key dimension of the institutional context—is gendered during transitions to democracy. It will focus particularly on the impact of political parties as well as electoral systems on the varying levels of women's descriptive representation seen in post-transition contexts. Lastly, Part III will consider how far women representatives act for women. The final part of the book examines women's substantive representation. It will complete the analysis of the institutional arena by looking at the ways in which constitutional/legal and state/bureaucratic arenas are gendered at various stages of transitions to democracy. The discussion will focus first on constitutions and SWMs—examining their potential to improve women's substantive representation. It will then move on to look at the policy outcomes that have emerged in different post-transition contexts. Varying gen-der policy outcomes with regard to divorce, domestic violence and reproductive rights will be considered, before analysing the gendered consequences of the social and economic reforms that have so often gone hand in hand with the political reforms.

By the end of the book it will be possible to reach some conclusions about the relationship between different transitions and gender outcomes. An analysis that not only looks at women's movements but also considers the institutional context within which various actors operate as well as the impact of differing transition paths and institutional legacies, will give us a more sophisticated understanding of the opportunities and constraints that different transitions can provide. We will understand how and why gender issues were articulated, placed on the agenda, and then translated into gender policy outcomes during any of the transitions we are looking at. We can use this approach to explain the outcomes of different gendered transition paths through an analysis that looks at the interaction of key actors and the institutional contexts. And we will draw some conclusions about why in some contexts where women's movements have played an important role in the breakdown and transition phases, they have not necessarily achieved such positive outcomes during the post-transition phase in comparison to some other contexts where women's movements have been less active and organized. But we must, at the same time, remember that changes to women's civil and political rights and the enactment of gender reforms on paper do not necessarily lead to the improvement of all women's day-to-day lives. The ability to access rights depends on a number of other factors such as the social and economic consequences of transitions both in terms of government's capacity to implement change as well as citizens' capacity to exercise new rights. We will start with the role of women's organizing in various stages of transitions to democracy.

❖ NOTES

1 Marcela Rios (2006) argues that because the Chilean Concertación government (in power for 15 years), although successful in economic terms, had become seen as distant change was needed. Therefore although a Concertación defeat was always unlikely, Bachelet as a female candidate could be seen as a break with the past, possessing desirable qualities of openness, uncorruptability and closeness to the people, reinvigorating its support, and appealing to groups hitherto marginal to electoral processes. Rios does however admit that the campaigns of feminists for the last three decades to increase the representation of women in politics were significant in facilitating her candidature. And that women, especially poor women, who traditionally voted in greater numbers for the right were responsible for Bachelet's increased margin of victory compared to her immediate prede-cessor the socialist Ricardo Lagos.

2 This work has been predominantly concerned with two themes. First is the role of organized women in the breakdown of non-democratic regimes and the subsequent transition to and consolidation of competitive electoral politics. This is fairly well-worn ground as much of the early work on Latin America focused on the role and internal characteristics of women's movements. However, it was sometimes overly voluntaristic,

tending to privilege the actions of women's social movements and women's mobilizations without always considering their interaction with different institutions sufficiently. Second, some examined women's movements' interactions with the changing political context.

3 S. Thomas, *How Women Legislate* (Oxford 1994) for a study of the USA.

4 A placement mandate determines where on electoral lists women candidates must be placed.

5 For a longer discussion see Georgina Waylen (1998) 'Gender, Feminism and the State: An Overview', in V. Randall and G. Waylen (eds.), *Gender, Politics and the State*. Routledge, pp. 1–17.

6 For evidence of this see the articles in a special section on the 'Quality of Democracy', in *Journal of Democracy*, 15(4): 2004). Plattner (2005: 6) too argued that in 2005 the three leading areas for scholarship were: the 'grey zones', post conflict democracy building, and the 'quality of democracy'.

7 But some analysts, often influenced by rational choice analyses like Pzerworski (1991), have argued that there is a blank slate.

8 Political scientists have advocated several potential solutions. Disregarding options such as secession, assimilation, and coercion, institutional solutions are the main format for diffusing and managing ethnic/national conflict as institutions have both symbolic value and can alter the distribution of power. The two main forms of institutional set-up are consociationalism and federalism.

9 Feminists have long argued that nationalism and ideologies of nationhood are heavily gendered. Men and women play different roles in nationalist projects. Men are often defenders of the nation while women are often primarily mothers to populate the nation and hold the virtue of the nation. An emphasis on 'the nation' can also hide inequalities within it particularly around gender and keep women's roles subordinate and private (Yuval-Davis 1997). Feminists therefore disagree about the extent that nationalism and its discourses can be a progressive force for women.

10 And more recently between these and the hybrid option of a semi-presidential system.

11 For example the rigidity of presidential systems can be reduced by shortening term lengths, allowing for re-election and even early elections in certain circumstances. The legislative powers of presidents, such as the power to issue decrees, can be limited. Concurrent elections for the president and legislature reduce the likelihood of a president without strong support in congress. And measures such as high electoral thresholds can reduce extreme multi-partism.

12 There are some strategic issues such as property rights/land rights that, although a central concern in some contexts such as many parts of Asia and Africa, have not been included because they do not have the same salience everywhere. This is not to devalue their importance.

13 There are a number of different criteria that we could use to select our cases. We need to decide on the most appropriate number and location. Should they be chosen on a most similar or most different systems model (Landman 2000: 29) or selected on the dependent or independent variable (Bunce 2000)? We could combine both the most similar and most

different systems design and select on both the dependent and independent variable. We also need to ensure that our choice of cases avoids the pitfalls of too few cases and too many variables, selection bias and establishes equivalence—namely that the same concepts and categories work in different situations.

14   The definition of democracy used here is a mid-range one that uses institutional and procedural criteria as well as civil rights such as freedom of speech, etc.

15   Only the Czech Republic and not Slovakia is considered in the post transition period as any extra case studies would have made the analysis too unwieldy.

Part II ❖ Women's Organizing

The first substantive part of this book examines women's organizing during the different stages of transitions to democracy. This theme, seen by some feminist scholars as not only the most important variable in any analysis but the key to the achievement of positive gender outcomes, has been the focus of much of the research on gender and transitions to date. But women's organizing has also been a source of disappointment as many of the expectations generated during the breakdown of some non-democratic regimes were not fulfilled in the immediate post-transition period. To explain how gains can be made in the aftermath of transitions, we must look at more than just women's movements. But even if a comprehensive analysis of gender and transitions has to examine a broader range of factors than women's organizing, that organizing must be our starting point.

We need to understand how women mobilize, under what conditions and with what results. But we cannot do this without differentiating between different kinds of women's organizing. We need to examine the aims, tactics, and strategies of a range of organizations and of the key actors within them. However, we cannot focus just on the internal characteristics of different movements and organizations. We must also examine how women's movements interact with their context—both national and international—over the different stages of a transition, assessing the significance of the different types of non-democratic regime—whether authoritarian and state socialist—and different forms of transition—whether negotiated, rapid, or slow—before we can examine how a range of women's movements have fared in the new conditions of the post-transition period. This analysis will form one part of our assessment of the extent to which different women actors could articulate gender issues, place them on the agenda of the transition and subsequently translate them into policy outcomes in our eight cases.

To help structure this analysis of women's organizing, we will begin by considering the little the democratization literature has said about any mass organizing— not just women's movements—in transitions to democracy. We will then look at the civil society and social movement literature, even if it too has engaged in 'surprisingly little interrogation of the relationship between gender and civil society' (Howell and Mulligan 2003: 157).

❖ Democratization, Civil Society, and Social Movements

In Part I, we saw that initially the predominantly elite focused democratization theorists rarely considered civil society. If they did, either they did not see it as a key actor in the breakdown of non-democratic regimes or they deemed it to be too active and as such a potential threat to a successful transition (O'Donnell, Schmitter, and Whitehead 1986). But recently, civil society has come under more systematic scrutiny, prompted by a number of factors. Popular mobilization was important in the rapid collapse of many state socialist regimes. Analysts, concerned with the quality of democracy, have begun to use broader notions of what constitutes democracy which entails looking at all forms of participation, not just at the nature of institutions.[1] And now there is virtual unanimity among policymakers and scholars (even among those theorists who hold the narrowest views of what constitutes democratization) that a vibrant civil society has a positive role to play in the creation and deepening of democracy. But apart from the normative consensus over its desirability, there is dissension about almost every other aspect of civil society. There is no agreement about what it is and what role it should play (Van Rooy 1998). Is it, for example, an actor, taking the form of differing types of organizations, or is it a space in society between the state and the market? We can divide these diverse views into two broad groupings: liberal and radical approaches. Each has a different understanding of the role of civil society in transitions (Grugel 2002).

In the liberal view, civil society is the associative life that is separate from family, the state and the market.[2] It is a space for action between the private sphere and the state within which a huge range of organizations—from chess clubs to professional NGOs—can operate. This classic view has its roots in political economy and De Tocqueville's thesis that a dense network of civic engagement is a key feature of a healthy democracy (Putnam 1993). Civil society, in this somewhat conservative and static view, plays a key role in supporting democracy and the free market (Whitehead 1997). And it is this broad liberal approach that has tended to inform those democratization theorists that have considered civil society. Linz and Stepan (1996: 7) argue that civil society is one of the five arenas necessary for democratic consolidation. Diamond (1999) also sees it as a sphere that can help to effect a transition, promote democratic consolidation, and play a role in deepening democracy. Within this liberal perspective, although civil society is not significant in bringing about transitions, it does play a role in maintaining a democracy, even if, as Diamond (1999) believes, ultimately it is political institutionalization and the political sphere that are the key to democratic consolidation. However, although a thriving women's associative life is part of a successful liberal democracy, this liberal view can offer limited insights into the oppositional roles played by women's organizations in transitions.

❖ Women's Organizing

In the contrasting radical vision, inspired by the ideas of Gramsci and Habermas, civil society is an actor, playing an anti-hegemonic, anti-state, and oppositional role in both democratic and non-democratic systems. As such the radical view offers more potential for the analysis of the oppositional activities of women's movements and their role in regime breakdown and transition. Although this approach to civil society has, not unsurprisingly, been ignored by most of the democratization theorists that we have considered so far, it was espoused and developed by activists and intellectuals who contributed to the collapse of communism in East Central Europe. It also influenced some Latin American scholars who developed a broad definition of democracy that highlights building social citizenship through activities and struggles that expand democratic practices and strengthen the culture of citizenship (Jelin and Herschberg 1996). Civil society plays a role in the transformation of state institutions helping to redefine what counts as political (Jelin 1996). And it is social movements that are one of civil society's central and most vital components within this radical perspective.

Indeed we cannot consider women's organizing without looking at the huge and diverse literature on social movements. Both the 'European' and the 'American' variants have something to offer the analysis of women's movements in transitions to democracy. The European variant that dominated the 1980s fits most easily into the radical view. It focuses on identity, identity formation, and the internal characteristics of social movements, particularly the 'new social movements' that emerged in established liberal democracies from the 1960s onwards. Much of the literature of the 1970s and 1980s 'praised their putative eschewal of institutional politics, their defense of absolute autonomy and their emphasis on direct democracy' (Alvarez, Dagnino, and Escobar 1998: 13). However, because of its concern with internal characteristics of movements rather than their interactions with their context, the European approach is not enough.

The US variant focuses more directly on how social movements operate and interact with their context. One branch, resource mobilization theory, sought to break with what its proponents saw as the grievance-based conceptions of social movements and examine instead how actors mobilize, their strategies and organizational resources (McAdam, McCarthy, and Zald 1996: 3). But in keeping with American social science traditions, it has often employed narrow and instrumental concepts of rationality and strategic choice to explain actor's decisions. Despite criticisms that it too ignored the wider context and was only relevant to professional social movements or interest groups in America, it did draw attention to the strategies and tactics utilized by social movements (Tarrow 1998: 16).

As we saw in Part I, the second branch—the political opportunity structure model—can deal with the social and political context by looking at resources external to movements. The political opportunity structure includes state institutions and national political traditions that provide both opportunities and constraints for social movements. It therefore conditions the emergence, strategy,

WOMEN'S ORGANIZING ❖

and the likelihood of success of a social movement. And a movement's rise and fall is, in part, a response to changes in the political opportunity structure. Social movement activity often follows a cycle of protest or contention, expanding and contracting as the political opportunity structure changes (Tarrow 1998: 25). Social mobilization increases when new external political opportunities facilitate it and peaks after more movements have joined around a 'master frame' of shared goals. General mobilization then declines as differences over content and tactics emerge between participants. Social movements will not re-emerge until the political opportunity structure is conducive to the start of a new cycle, even though the previous cycle may have left its own legacy such as new institutions.

Over the last decade a synthesis has emerged that, although dominated by the American perspective, also contains elements of the European emphasis on identity. It sees three broad sets of factors—political opportunities, mobilizing structures, and framing processes—as important in both the emergence and development of social movements: (McAdam, McCarthy, and Zald 1996: 2). The inclusion of framing processes—the ways in which participants collectively understand and define what it is they are doing—is a recognition of the importance of the ideational—that without shared and socially constructed meanings and identities—it is unlikely that people will undertake collective action.

But, in common with the civil society literature, very little of the diverse social movement literature engages with gender (Beckwith 2000: 458). Despite this silence, feminist scholars have identified women's movements as a subset of social movements (Beckwith 2000: 458; Beckwith 2004: 4). And increasingly some feminist scholars, often based in North America, have used the synthetic approach to understand under what conditions women mobilize by looking both at the movements themselves and the context in which they are operating (Baldez 2002). We, too, will use the concepts of opportunities, mobilizing structures, and framing processes to structure our discussion of women's movements in the various stages of transitions to democracy. If we accept that, under certain circumstances, women's movements can have an impact on the context within which they operate, and that they and their activities are shaped by that context (e.g. in terms of their opportunities, conditions, and constraints), we need to incorporate that institutional context and its impact into the analysis.

Prior to this, we must develop our discussion of what is meant by a women's movement begun in Part I. As we saw, Karen Beckwith (2004: 3–4) has argued that women's movements have women actors and leaders and that they organize around women's gendered identity claims. Therefore women's movements comprise women explicitly mobilizing as women but because they represent different identities, interests, and issues they can take a variety of forms (Baldez 2003: 253). In our analysis of women's organizing in transitions, we need to disaggregate the different components of the category of women's movement according to their type, character, and activities.

❖ WOMEN'S ORGANIZING

Feminist organizations, rather than being seen as synonymous with women's movements, are only one subset. Not all women's movements are feminist and feminist movements are identifiable by their particular goals and ideas (Beckwith 2004: 5). But although they all believe that women are in a subordinate position and that something should be done about it, they vary in their explanations as to why this is so and in the solutions advocated to ameliorate the situation. Therefore feminist groups also cannot be assumed to be homogeneous. Not only must we identify differences between women's movements, but we must also ascertain the importance of different feminist groups within these broader women's movements. Indeed we need to investigate under what circumstances feminist organizations, and key actors within them, can play significant roles. Second, we need to look at the internal characteristics of any women's movement, assessing its strength, as evidenced by its influence, its cohesiveness, and its autonomy from other organizations. Third, we must also look at its activities—in particular its engagement with different parts of the transition process—and its relationships with other groups and institutions.

As a result we can understand the complex interactions that determine the effectiveness of women's movements during transitions to democracy—measured in terms of their ability to articulate gender issues, put them on the agenda, or even to shape policy outcomes. To see whether we can discern any overall patterns in women's organizing, we will proceed chronologically, dividing Part II into three further sections: the non-democratic regime and its breakdown, the transition itself, and the post-transition period, each corresponding to a critical phase in the overall process of transition.

❖ WOMEN'S ORGANIZING IN NON-DEMOCRATIC REGIMES

When considering the extent and nature of women's organizing under non-democratic regimes, we need to distinguish between authoritarian and state socialist regimes. As we saw in Part I, there were important differences between these regime types in terms of the role of ideology, levels of economic, social and political pluralism, their leadership, and the extent to which they mobilized people. We need to explore how all these factors impacted on women's organizing and on broader opposition movements. We also need to take account of other contextual factors, such as the varying degrees of openness to international influences and organized religion. Our choice of case study countries will also allow us to investigate differences within these categories as well as between them.

❖ *Authoritarian Regimes*

As we saw earlier, the category 'authoritarian' includes a range of institutional set-ups. Despite their differences, many authoritarian regimes shared some

54

characteristics—similar political beliefs, repression, and the suppression of the conventional political arena—that had particular and often contradictory gender implications. Although they did not share one overarching ideology, the majority of authoritarian regimes, including military dictatorships, were relatively right-wing. Even if they did not have an ideological programme, most military regimes advocated right-wing 'traditional values' including fairly traditional notions of women's roles that were more (as in Chile) and less (as in Brazil) adhered to. 'Western Christian family values', that included support for family, god, and the elevation of motherhood as women's proper role, were easily subsumed into the doctrine of national security adhered to by much of the military in Latin America in which it was the duty of the state to protect the country against the threat of communist subversion.

For example General Pinochet, leader of the very ideological Chilean regime, made pronouncements about the position of women in Chilean society, stressing the important role played by women in transmitting and defending the spiritual values of the nation (cited in Munizaga and Letelier 1988: 540, quoting from Pinochet's pronouncements in the press). He stressed that 'the most important labour of women is motherhood', arguing that the Chilean woman is beautiful, an indomitable defender of her home, an unselfish, self-sacrificing, and a loyal wife. Her nobility and dignity are not obscured by poverty and are enhanced by hardship' (quoted in Chuckryk 1984: 235). The Chilean military government elevated motherhood as women's primary task, stressing women's charitable and self-sacrificing role in both public and private sphere. Together with Pinochet's government, women were positioned in a special role as defenders of the moral order.

A smaller number of authoritarian regimes attempted to organize and incorporate women on the basis of these designated roles on a semi-formal basis. In Chile autonomous Right-wing women's organizations, such as *Poder Femenino* (PF), that had been active immediately prior to the coup, were demobilized and absorbed (Power 2002). Two other government controlled women's organizations were then used to incorporate women. The first, the National Secretariat for Women (SNM) was created in October 1973 soon after the Junta took power and headed by Pinochet's wife. It was a highly ideological state organization, made up primarily of volunteers acting to promote Pinochet's vision of society, particularly with regard to women, and to provide welfare to the poor. The volunteers were mainly middle and upper class, often wives of members of the armed forces and committed to supporting the regime and maintaining the image of the 'patriotic self-sacrificing mother'. It has been estimated that between 1973 and 1983 the activities of the SNM involved two million women (Bunster 1988). It worked closely with the second organization, the Mother's Centres (CEMAs). They had been set up by a Christian Democrat government in the 1960s to help poor women gain the means to generate income and become involved in community affairs. CEMAs were taken over by the military regime and used to incorporate mainly poor women into a framework which supported the government often in competition with the more oppositional organizations established under the auspices of the church (Agosin 1988). In 1983 CEMA Chile had around 230,000 members, 6,000 volunteers, and over 10,000 centres throughout the country.

Most authoritarian regimes were underpinned by varying degrees of repression. Prior to the end of the cold war, the doctrine of national security justified repression against civilians as part of the 'total war' against subversion and many regimes received support, particularly from the USA, to prevent the spread of communism (Waylen 1996). As a result human rights abuses were played down or ignored by powerful allies, allowing some regimes a relatively free hand. For a number of regimes high levels of repression, resulting in torture, death, and disappearances, was one of their defining features. In Argentina the notorious 'dirty war' led to the disappearance of thousands of people and both the Pinochet and the apartheid regimes as well as the El Salvadorean military were widely condemned for their human rights abuses. Paramilitary death squads and extra-judicial killings were therefore a feature of many authoritarian regimes.

Women were not immune from this repression. It is estimated that in Argentina, women formed 30 per cent of the disappeared and 3 per cent of them were pregnant (Fisher 1989: 105). Ximena Bunster-Burotto (1985) has identified two main groups of women who were singled out by the military regimes. First, women were targeted for their own activities. In Chile many women with prominent public political roles as union leaders, academics as well as political activists were arrested. Second, women were detained because of their relationship to men: partners, sons, and fathers. While in detention, women were brutalized and tortured in the same ways as men. But there is also evidence that women were treated in gender-specific and sexualized ways. Bunster-Burotto (1985: 304–5) describes family torture, where women were tortured or raped in front of their children, or their children beaten in front of them. A variety of forms of sexual assault and rape were commonly used, paralleling the ways in which rape has been used as an instrument of war. In 2004 the Valech Commission on torture reported that around 12 per cent of the Chilean torture victims were women, almost all of whom had been victims of sexual violence (*Guardian* 30 November 2004).

To varying degrees, authoritarian regimes also suppressed the conventional political sphere, often banning trade unions and political parties (particularly on the left) and closing congresses (although the Brazilian, South African, and El Salvadorean regimes did allow some limited and very strictly controlled political activity). The repression or the limiting of the conventional political arena meant that it could not be the locus of political activity. However although there was little political pluralism, a greater degree of social and economic pluralism was tolerated. As a result parts of civil society, for example some community and church based organizations, could still function. A community rather than an institutional basis (in the form of a trade union, political party or workplace) often then became the focus for activity. Women often find it easier to participate in this context than in more formal institutional arenas. Indeed the identification of women as apolitical and therefore their activities as not being political, sometimes allowed women certain initial room to manoeuvre, which was unavailable to men, before their activities were seen as subversive (Waylen 1993).

Paradoxically the repression of the conventional political arena and the fracturing and emasculation of political opposition therefore could create the 'political space' and with it the opportunities that allowed women's activities to achieve a relatively high profile outside it. As we also see in Part IV, often this coincided with severe economic hardship caused by the impact of the debt crisis and structural adjustment packages which also pushed women into adopting collective survival strategies (Safa 1990). Despite the attempts of military regimes in Latin America to depoliticize society, the late 1970s and 1980s saw the emergence of strong and heterogeneous women's movements operating outside the conventional arena, in part a result of the combination of authoritarianism and economic recession (Jaquette 2001).

Different groups of women created a range of mobilizing structures in response to authoritarian regimes. We will look first at those movements that emerged under the military dictatorships in Chile, Argentina, and Brazil, with some reference to Peru, before highlighting some contrasting features of the South African and El Salvadorean experiences. Three major types of oppositional women's movements have been identified, although their sometimes shifting boundaries makes clear delineations difficult (Waylen 1993). Two of these, human rights groups and urban popular movements, had women as the majority of the members and pressed primarily social and economic demands. Important human rights groups protesting about the disappearance of their relatives and demanding their return emerged in those countries most affected by repression, disappearances, and torture.

The best known human rights protestors are the Madres of the Plaza de Mayo formed in Argentina in 1977, but the Agrupaciones de Familiares de Detenidos-Desaparacidos (AFDD) and the CoMadres were formed in Chile and in El Salvador respectively (Schirmer 1989, 1993). The Madres used traditional notions of motherhood as the pivot of their protest, arguing that the disappearance of their children prevented them from fulfilling this role and forced them into the public sphere to search for them. The symbolic, ethical, and non-negotiable nature of the Madres' demands was an effective tactic in a context where bargaining was not on the agenda. This discourse also gave them a certain (limited) protection from repression. The Madres often used innovative forms of protest. Their weekly demonstrations on Thursday afternoons in the Plaza de Mayo, the main government square in Buenos Aires, were well known. They would march in a circle wearing white kerchiefs embroidered with the names of their missing children and grandchildren, later carrying their pictures, and demanding their return. The CoMadres and the AFDD used similar tactics of taking to the streets (Fisher 1989). The attitude of the Catholic Church to these organizations varied from country to country. In Argentina the Church was broadly sympathetic to the military government and unsympathetic to the Madres. In contrast the Chilean Church (particularly in Santiago) did provide help to the AFDD, and in El Salvador, where the Church had embraced liberation theology to a much greater degree, as well as supporting groups such as the CoMadres, it played an important oppositional role in its own right (Schirmer 1993).

In many instances the emergence of popular organizations was catalysed by the economic hardship experienced under authoritarian rule. These movements grew up primarily in poor urban neighbourhoods and focused on the 'politics of everyday life'. Many organizations were funded from abroad and operated under the auspices of the Catholic Church and NGOs in the face of both repression and recession. In Brazil the Communidades Eclesias de Base (CEBs), heavily influenced by liberation theology, provided an important, if not unproblematic, space in which women could mobilize (Alvarez 1990b). The majority of members of popular movements were women, indeed Corcoran-Nantes (1990) estimated that 80% of those involved in Brazil were women. The activities that movements engaged in were largely social and economic in orientation and often focused around consumption issues. Some popular organizations pressured the state for improved services. For example the favela movement and the daycare and health movements are representative of a large number of important popular movements that emerged in Brazil in the 1970s (Corcoran Nantes 1993).

Other popular organizations implemented collective survival strategies either through the collective provision of necessities or through income generation. Communal kitchens are probably one of the best-known examples of the collective provision of food. The Ollas Comunes (communal soup pots) in Chile dealt with the most immediate needs, through women collectively providing a large number of families with meals, often with the help of the Church (Fisher 1993). Artisanal workshops such as bakeries and craft workshops producing goods and services for exchange in the market also played a significant role (Hardy 1985).

These activities were carried out predominantly by poor women from the 'popular sectors' acting in their roles as mothers, household providers, and managers as class and gender identities interacted. However, to see them as simply economic, underestimates their significance. First, they have to be seen as political. In part because some authoritarian regimes began to see them as subversive and therefore as political and so the women involved came to see them in the same way (Fisher 1993). Second, the experience of collective organizing in the public arena brought about a sense of empowerment and a different understanding of gender issues for many of the women involved (Alvarez 1990a).

58

There has been considerable debate about the framing and meaning of the activities of human rights groups and popular organizations. In Latin America a discourse of maternalism was important in both types of organization and increased the effectiveness and mobilizing potential of both. The attempts to abolish political activity in the public sphere increased the politicization of the private sphere and helped to break down the barriers between the public and the private. Women entered the public sphere in the basis of the politicization of their social roles as mothers and household providers. However, feminist commentators have debated how far the gendered politicization of motherhood actually extended (Waylen 1992*a*). How far is it 'progressive', laying the ground for a new politics of identity based on an 'ethic of care'? Or does it simply reinforce traditional notions of women's proper roles even if women do enter the public sphere in ways that they have never done before (Craske 1999; Bouvard 1994).

The third kind of oppositional women's organizing that (re) emerged under authoritarianism can be broadly termed feminist. Heterogeneous movements of women organizing together as women to press gender-based demands were active in Argentina, Chile, Peru, and Brazil. Many countries had had predominantly middle class suffrage movements earlier in the twentieth century that had disappeared after women got the vote. Chile, for example, had entered what Julietta Kirkwood called a period of 'feminist silence'. In the 1970s and 1980s feminist groups, active around women's inequality and subordination, emerged (Sternbach et al. 1992). A number of factors prompted this development. Alvarez (1990*a*) has claimed that the greatest space for the development of feminist movements existed where authoritarian regimes had pursued state-led development at some time, such as happened in Brazil and Peru. The resulting expansion of educational opportunities and the increase in professional and technical employment for middle class women provided a spur for the re-emergence of feminist organizing. Some authoritarian regimes therefore played an unwitting role in the development of feminist movements in the 1970s and early 1980s. The international context became more favourable. The experience of exile and contact with feminism in Western Europe and North America was an important influence for many women, particularly those on the left. The growth of international feminism—expressed in the women's decades, the first of which was inaugurated in Mexico in 1975 and the development of influential international women's movements, also contributed. The emergence of regional *encuentros* (meetings) also enhanced this process, facilitating the diffusion of ideas and the development of regional networks and campaigns.

The diversity within feminism was reflected in the activities that feminists engaged in. Some, like the Circulo de Estudios de la Mujer founded in Chile in 1977, concentrated on the analysis of women's subordination through discussions and seminars; others set up women's centres such as the Flora Tristan centre in Peru; ran workshops and courses on themes such as sexuality and health;

organized theatre groups; campaigned around issues such as sexual violence and pornography; and produced feminist publications such as Brasil Mulher founded in 1975 and Nos Mulheres founded in 1976 which together became the principal voices of the growing feminist movement in Brazil (Jaquette 1989). In the 1980s feminism in Brazil also began to recognize issues connected to the private sphere and more identified with radical feminism such as domestic violence and reproductive rights and finally had to also take on issues of race and sexuality (Alvarez 1994). Umbrella organizations also formed to coordinate the diverse activities of the various groups into bodies resembling a national movement such as the coordinating committee established in the late 1970s in Peru (Jaquette 1989).

The growing feminist movements had to deal with two key questions during the 1980s: first their relationship with the left and second, their relationship with the movimiento de mujeres (popular women's movements) (Alvarez et al. 2002). As we will see neither was straightforward. Many of those women who became feminists had been active on the left and experienced marginalization and gender discrimination within left-wing organizations that had provided an important catalyst for the emergence of feminist organizations (Valenzuela 1998). Feminists developed analyses that went beyond the parameters of class and imperialism favoured by the left and began to point out the connections between authoritarianism and patriarchy. They linked authoritarianism in the home with that in wider society, hence the slogan of the Chilean movement 'Democracy in the country and in the home' (Chuckryk 1989a). As a result, socialist feminism, particularly in the 1970s and early 1980s, became a prominent strand within feminism as a whole. Some feminists maintained ties to left-wing organizations, engaging in a *doble militancia* (double militancy) that led other feminists to distrust their commitment to feminism. Known as the 'autonomy versus integration' debate, *feministas* disagreed with *políticas* over how far feminists could ever work within organizations like left-wing parties. By the mid-1980s the debate had faded somewhat and a compromise position of 'engaged autonomy' had been reached (Alvarez et al. 2002: 543). But for feminists (and many other women's groups) a troubled relationship with the left did not end (Chuckryk 1989b). The relationship between feminism and the left is a theme that will crop up again—not only when we examine the electoral arena in Part III—but also when we look at the insurgent transitions in South Africa and El Salvador in which the left-leaning opposition played a key role.

Although feminism is often identified as a predominantly middle-class phenomenon, a popular feminism also emerged during this period. It grew out of the experience of working class and poor women organizing and campaigning self-consciously as women in the community organizations described above. Through their experiences of organizing around consumption issues and collective survival many women began to organize around issues like reproductive rights, sexuality, and domestic violence, more often identified with feminism and set up women's centres in poor neighbourhoods (sometimes set up after taking up these more controversial issues had alienated them from their previous backers, the Catholic Church (Alvarez 1990*b*)). In Chile a number of organizations emerged like the Domitilas and MOMUPO (Movimiento de Mujeres Pobladoras) that initially refused the title 'feminist' but declared itself to be so in 1985. But this popular feminism saw itself as distinct from the feminism of the affluent middle class that prioritized gender at the expense of issues of class, race, and economic survival.

These different groups of women were sometimes linked by the activities of new feminist NGOs. Often funded by international donors keen to support women's projects and operating under the auspices of the Catholic Church, NGOs became an important medium through which middle-class feminist and professional women worked with poor women. According to Veronica Schild (1998), they had a two-pronged approach to women's empowerment. As a response to women's everyday survival needs, social workers, health and education professionals supported the activities of organized women such as soup kitchens and artisanal workshops. They also had an educational component that some commentators have termed a 'feminist curriculum' (Valdes and Weinstein 1993: 196). Feminist professionals organized workshops that often engaged in *conscientización* (consciousness raising) as well as leadership training and sessions on sexuality and women's legal rights. These feminist NGOs were important in the development of women's movements under authoritarian rule but tensions sometimes existed feminist NGOs and popular women's organizations around issues of class, race, and the meaning of feminism.

The development of women's organizing in other authoritarian regimes followed different trajectories to the ones outlined above. In both South Africa and El Salvador the nature of the broader opposition struggle against authoritarian rule profoundly shaped the opportunity structure for women's organizing and influenced their activities. In contrast to the often-fragmented opposition that existed under many authoritarian regimes, a more coherent opposition dominated the political opportunity structure. In El Salvador there were two phases of women's organizing in the period prior to the establishment of negotiations that marked the beginning of the transition in late 1991 (Stephen 1997). In both phases, the impact of the twelve-year civil war (1979–81) and the dominant role played by the five largely left-wing groupings that came together to form the FMLN in 1980 was very significant. Between 1975 and 1985, some women's organizations such as the human rights group CoMadres emerged as part of broader grass-roots opposition movements and as a response to repression. They mobilized around economic issues, survival in war and human rights issues. But the opposition coalitions and therefore almost all the women's organizations were not autonomous but linked either directly or indirectly to one of the revolutionary political parties that were fighting against the government. The first major women's organization established during this period, the Asociación de Mujeres Progresistas de El Salvador (AMPES), was set up in 1975 by women from the communist party, and was followed by more than half a dozen more party-linked organizations. With the exception of one organization, this first generation of women's organizations died out in the mid-1980s as a result of government repression (Hipsher 2001: 138).

In South Africa, despite the often high levels of repression, there was history of mass organizing against apartheid that included significant organizing by women from all races that had a lasting impact on women's organizing. The longevity of the formal and informal networks among South African women was an important and necessary antecedent to later organizing. Best known are the activities of the Federation of South African Women (FSAW), a self-avowedly multiracial umbrella women's organization whose federal structure brought together women from a number of ethnically based organizations (Walker 1982: 172).[3] FSAW drafted a Women's Charter that saw women's equality as part of national liberation. It also organized mass resistance to the extension of the pass laws to black women culminating in the march of 20,000 women in Pretoria in 1956 (Walker 1982: 153–88). The political opportunities provided by the struggle against apartheid conditioned the emergence and mobilization of the women's movement. The framing of the women's movement's demands and the means of articulating them were shaped by the importance of the discourse of Rights and citizenship within the opposition to apartheid. The Women's Charter campaign was part of a campaign that was linked to the Rights-based Congress alliance whose creation in the 1950s was a key moment in the development of the multiracial opposition (Kimble and Unterhalter 1982). In 1955 the Congress Alliance produced the Freedom Charter outlining the conditions for a non-racial South Africa, using a discourse of rights and equal citizenship. Women organizing as women had therefore long been part of the opposition to the racially based apartheid regime, arguing that women's equality was part of the struggle for national liberation and equal rights and citizenship for all (Gaitskell and Unterhalter 1989).

Therefore, despite often-ferocious levels of repression, many authoritarian regimes offered opportunities for diverse forms of women's organizing to emerge in an international context that from the mid-1970s offered increasing support. Jaquette (2001: 117) has claimed that in Latin America these disparate but also overlapping women's groups could come together to form women's movements that were also united by the possibility of creating the opportunity to conduct new kinds of politics based on solidarity and self-help. These movements had therefore begun to articulate gender issues as part of the broader opposition to authoritarian rule. However, the nature of the relationships of these organizations to that broader opposition, particularly to the left, ranged from closeness to antipathy. The degree to which these heterogeneous women's movements included those who saw themselves as overtly feminist also varied considerably.

62

❖ *State Socialist Regimes*

Women's organizing under state socialism offers a marked contrast. There were few opportunities for autonomous women's organizing in any of the state socialist regimes. As we saw in Part I, little social, economic, or political pluralism was allowed and the regimes were relatively isolated internationally. The communist party was the only political organization functioning in these one-party states and the state owned and controlled all major economic assets. The control that communist parties exercised over the political and economic systems extended into civil society. Few autonomous organizations were permitted outside the wide range of communist-sponsored ones. Even in Poland where the regime was forced to tolerate the Catholic Church's activities, allowing it to publish newspapers and teach religion in schools, other institutions were highly constrained in what they could do.

However, all state socialist countries claimed to be committed to women's equality and had even declared that the 'woman question' was solved. But their notions of women's emancipation were limited, based on a 'selective canonization' of the works of Marx and Lenin (Molyneux 1981). In the official, economistic analysis, women were emancipated primarily through their participation in the labour market and their liberation from the constraints of the traditional social order. Emancipation therefore came from above. Rights were 'given' rather than fought for and as a result were taken for granted (Einhorn 1991). But as we see in Parts III and IV, despite some important legal gains such as divorce legislation, instituted as part of what Dolling (1991) has termed 'patriarchal-paternalistic' policies, women were faced with a double (if not triple, if one counts attending meeetings and being active in the public sphere) productive and reproductive burden in societies that gave little priority to providing the population with labour-saving consumer goods. In the face of 'emancipation from above' which made entering the labour market obligatory for women, the family and private sphere were often a haven from the demands and interference of the state and a site of resistance, a place of autonomy and creativity in the absence of a full-fledged civil society.

The control that communist parties exercised over civil society also constrained the emergence of women's movements operating outside state control. Indeed in countries like Poland and Czechoslovakia where women's organizations had flourished in the interwar period, they were suppressed when the communists came to power (Fuszara 1991: 128; Haskova and Krizkova 2003: 46). Autonomous feminist movements were deemed unnecessary and part of bourgeois society. Independent women's organizations were not tolerated. Indeed campaigns around issues like equal pay were considered irrelevant in a society that was already constructed around principles of equality, despite the evidence of gender disparity in earnings (Watson 1997). The role of the state in providing welfare and social care also meant that opportunities for organizing informal networks around the provision of services such as childcare within communities were severely constrained (Einhorn 1993). Finally, in the face of pressure to maintain solidarity within the private sphere as the only alternative to state power, there was little opportunity to organize around issues like domestic violence (Einhorn and Sever 2003).

The only women's organizations that could exist—like the Czechoslovak Women's Union, the National Council of Hungarian Women (which replaced the Hungarian Women's Democratic Alliance in 1970), the Women's League in Poland and the Soviet Women's Committees, and Women's Councils in the USSR—were sanctioned by the state and part of the communist party apparatus. In addition to monitoring women's position in society and publishing statistical surveys, these organizations functioned to mobilize women in support of the party and transmit party policy to women rather than to actually represent women. As such, despite nominally large memberships, they were never genuinely mass organizations and became increasingly moribund and despised.

However, Einhorn and Sever (2003) warn us not to fall for one of the 'myths of transition' that although officially politically equal, women were politically inactive lacking a space within civil society to exercise any control. They argue that in fact the private sphere was a place of political action and informal networks could exist alongside official state-run groups. As a result, family, community, and kinship networks acted like civil society elsewhere and within these networks women played central and powerful roles (Einhorn 1993). Julia Szalai (1998) has argued that women in Hungary were central to the networks that developed around the informal sector activities that grew as a result of liberalization introduced by the relatively reformist regime. Einhorn and Sever (2003: 170) conclude that the women's movements that could exist under state socialism have been obscured on two levels. First, the organizing was not around the women's issues as they had been established by women's movements in the West; and second, because the state denied it a political language and the legitimacy to articulate objectives and programmes, the civil society activity that did occur was hidden.

Despite the efforts to minimize dissent, some opposition to the regimes did emerge prior to the late 1980s and women were active within these groups. The most long-standing and organized opposition developed in Poland. Three strands—the workers and trade unionists, the intelligentsia, and the Catholic Church—with a range of views on gender relations—came together in the Solidarity movement formed in 1980. The Gdansk Accords reached between Solidarity and the government after the strikes of 1980 mentioned improving women's reproductive roles through improved provision of maternity leave and childcare. Although cited as evidence that the early Solidarity movement supported gender rights, it has been claimed that its support for family orientated policies came from its conservative vision of women's roles, not its support for gender equality (Reading 1992). Some dominant elements within Solidarity shared the Catholic Church's desire to restrict reproductive rights. But, as in other dissident movements, women played active roles within Solidarity. They coordinated its underground cells and ran the leading dissident newspaper (Einhorn and Sever 2003). Indeed there is some evidence to suggest that, after the virtual military coup of 1981, women played a more prominent role in reconstructing Solidarity's activities when it went underground than they did later (or that they are given credit for) (Matynia 2003).

Barbara Jancar (1985) has analysed the role of women in two very different opposition movements: Solidarity, as a mass movement of both workers and intellectuals (with ten million members at its peak) and Charter 77, formed in the 1970s by a small group of intellectuals and writers in Czechoslovakia. Former Charter 77 member Jirina Siklova has pointed out that one fifth of the signatories of the 1977 Charter and a third of its spokespersons were women (Siklova 1993: 77). However, according to Jancar (1985), despite the very different character of both movements, 'women in the opposition appear more marginal to the organizational structure of the opposition movements, with visibility in leadership depending on male endorsement'. Jancar (1985) also notes that women were less likely than men to get elected to leadership positions. Although they constituted about half the rank and file members of Solidarity, women made up only 7% of the delegates at the first Solidarity Conference in 1981. Of the approximately 400 documents produced by Charter 77, none made many mention of gender issues.[4] Similar findings have also been reported in Hungary (Einhorn 1993: 160). Therefore no women were in significant leadership positions in dissident movements in any of our three case study countries (Fodor 2004a). However, women did play major roles in other peace, environmental and human rights movements such as the Independent Peace Association in Czechoslovakia and the Dialogue and the Danube Circle in Hungary (Einhorn and Sever 2003: 169). Significantly most women active in opposition groupings did not see themselves as feminists, or as organizing around gender issues, but as protesting more generally about social and human rights issues.

There are a few notable exceptions to this pattern where women did organize primarily as women. Perhaps the most successful was the women's peace movement that emerged in East Germany in 1982. But there are also a few examples of women organizing overtly as feminists. The Polish Feminist Association was established in 1980 by a small group of women and was set up to counter the male dominated structures of Solidarity. In 1979 an independent feminist group in Leningrad published a samizdat, *the Almanac: Women and Russia*, but the group was soon accused of producing anti-Soviet propaganda and forced to disband (Waylen 1994). However, these were exceptions. In the fifteen years before 1985, few avowedly feminist organizations emerged. Except perhaps in the GDR, women in East Central Europe had few contacts with international feminism. There were relatively few opportunities for women to organize autonomously as women under state socialism. Any structures that did emerge could not be highly developed as they had to be very informal if not covert. State socialism also militated against the emergence of overtly oppositional feminist organizations because ideas of women's emancipation had been captured by the regimes themselves and so were discredited as they were associated with the old order (Molyneux 1991).

Therefore the political space for varied and vibrant women's organizing that existed in many authoritarian regimes was largely absent under state socialism; where although women were often active within informal networks associated with family and community and some participated in opposition organizations where they existed, there were fewer opportunities for women to organize autonomously as women. Under authoritarian regimes, women organized around a range of issues, some more associated with economic survival and human rights abuses and others with a more overtly feminist agenda. In many authoritarian regimes, a discourse of maternalism brought some women into the public sphere but there are partial exceptions to this pattern such as South Africa. The Catholic Church and the left could also play both a constraining and facilitating role in different contexts. The Church tended to be more supportive of human rights and economic organizing but wary of and even hostile to anything that smacked of feminism. The left had a sometimes close but also very difficult and often antagonistic relationship to feminism. International feminism, the experience of exile as well as external funding had an important influence on many women activists and groups. More isolated from outside influences, feminism and women's emancipation were negatively associated with state socialism in East Central Europe and the majority of women who organized outside the official organizations did not do so explicitly as women or around gender issues.

❖ WOMEN'S ORGANIZING IN THE BREAKDOWN OF NON-DEMOCRATIC REGIMES

As we saw in Part I, the role of mass opposition in regime breakdown is contested. But whether it was critical, mass opposition to non-democratic rule was often more significant than elite theorists would admit. Indeed it frequently peaked prior to the transition proper and individual women were part of it. However, as a result of the differences outlined above, the extent to which women *organized as women* could play an active role in the breakdown of non-democratic regimes and make gender claims visible within the opposition varied considerably. Using the examples of Chile, Brazil, Poland, and East Germany, Baldez (2003) has argued that, if certain conditions were fulfilled, women's mobilization could peak during the period of regime breakdown and women could come together across class and party lines to demand women's equal participation in any future democratic government. For this to occur, women's movements need organizational resources in the form of pre-existing formal/informal networks and movement discourse has to be framed so that women see the issues in gender terms (which can for example result from the diffusion of international feminism). Finally women have to feel excluded from the agenda setting process within the opposition. Although Baldez's formulation (2003) is rather narrowly focused and can oversimplify the complex array of conditions that contribute to gender mobilization, it does alert us to the need to think about the circumstances under which women will organize, not only to articulate gender issues, but also to get them on to the agenda of the transition.

If we broaden the analysis to include the ways in which non-democratic rule broke down, we can see that it affected women's organizing. A relatively drawn out period of political liberalization, such as occurred in Brazil, could act as a catalyst to the development of new forms of women's organizing as well as a spur to the continued growth of existing forms. Even in the Soviet Union, some women's groups, including avowedly feminist organizations, were among the large number of official groups that emerged in the late 1980s as a consequence of the liberalization associated with perestroika (Sperling 1999: 18).

In East Central Europe as a whole, however, despite the reopening of the 'women question' and the liberalization associated with glasnost in the late 1980s, few feminist groups were among the organizations that emerged as part of 'resurrection of civil society'. Because autonomous women's groups did not already exist, women organized purely as women did not play a key role in the relatively rapid and partly externally catalysed transitions, even though women were active participants in the mass demonstrations and broad movements that contributed to the collapse of state socialism. Few women were in leadership positions within the opposition movements. The association of women's emancipation with state socialism also militated against organized women attempting to put gender issues on the agenda of the transitions. Indeed much of the opposition to state socialism was either dismissive or actually hostile to feminism. For example the Czech dissident leader Vaclav Havel's publicly espoused traditional views on gender roles (Eisenstein 1993).

In contrast, in parts of Latin America, women's movements, comprising a range of different organizations, both feminist and non-feminist, were significant and visible actors in the broad opposition coalitions that contributed to the breakdown of authoritarian rule (Jaquette 2001). For example the Madres who engaged in one of the first open protests against the Argentine military government, helped to bring about the 'end of fear' and achieved a high profile both nationally and internationally. The celebrations held to mark international women's day in Chile in 1978 were one of the first mass protests against the Pinochet regime (Chuckryk 1989a, 1989b). As we have seen feminists saw their struggle as one against both authoritarianism and patriarchy. The first Paulista Women's Conference attended by almost 1,000 participants in 1979 was according to Sonia Alvarez (1994: 28) 'a unique contribution to the struggle for a democratic Brazil, proclaiming that power relations in the family, in daily life, in civil society and not just in the state and political society, must be democratized'.

Some women's organization became players in wider opposition politics in Chile (Chuckryk 1989*b*; Valenzuela 1995, 1998; Waylen 1998). Between 1983–6 diverse women's movements had a high profile in the period of mass mobilization against the dictatorship. At the same time, the political parties reformed and coalesced into two groups, the moderate Alianza Democratica (AD) which increasingly favoured a strategy of negociación (negotiation), and the left-wing Movimiento Democratico Popular (MDP) which advocated ruptura—the violent overthrow of the military dictatorship. Women's organizations tried to remain unified in the face of a divided political opposition through broad umbrella movements such as MEMCH 83 and Mujeres por la Vida. In 1984 MEMCH 83 developed the Plataforma de la Mujer Chilena, but despite attempts to avoid factionalism, it became more associated with the radical MDP strategy of mobilization and many feminist and centrist groups left (Molina 1989). Mujeres por la Vida, founded by a group of sixteen women, many well-known political figures, played a more moderate role. Over 10,000 women attended its first meeting in 1983 to demonstrate that unity could be achieved in the face of political sectarianism (Baldez 2000). It also participated in the Asamblea de la Civilidad, a broad and moderate opposition front formed in 1986 to oppose the dictatorship. A Pliego de las Mujeres (a women's petition) was included in the Demanda de Chile, a document submitted to the military government in 1986 and the feminist and socialist Maria Antonieta Saa sat in the Asamblea as the women's representative. Although middle-class women, feminists, and political activists became more integrated into national politics, some popular women's organizations felt that Mujeres por la Vida did not represent them in the assembly (Angelo 1990). But these women's movements did position women as political actors in their own right and help to associate their activities with the broader concerns of citizenship, rights, and democracy.

In South Africa and El Salvador women's organizations also played important roles in the breakdown of the non-democratic regimes. In El Salvador the second phase of women's organizing corresponds to the breakdown of the authoritarian regime (Stephen 1997). The number of women's organizations exploded after a limited liberalization between 1985–9. However, by the final guerilla offensive in 1989, most were still linked to one of the politico-military organizations of the FMLN and had been formed to support the revolutionary movement (often taking advantage of foreign funding) (Hipsher 2001: 141). Although they increasingly took up gender issues such as sexual violence and began participating in international and regional women's organizations, many groups were unwilling to use the term feminism. Therefore, when the peace negotiations began, a large number of women's organizations existed, but were still dominated by their links to the left-wing organizations that had promoted and constrained them with their sometimes ambivalent attitudes to feminism. As some women's organizations focused more on gender issues these contradictions increased.

In South Africa vibrant women's organizations at both community and regional level reemerged in the upsurge of opposition generated by the ill-fated programme of 'conservative modernization' that marked the beginning of the breakdown of the apartheid regime in the 1980s. Most organizations allied themselves to UDF, a broad opposition grouping within South Africa that was substituting for the banned ANC (Beall et al. 1987; Kemp et al. 1995; Seekings 2000; Wood 2001). A vibrant black women's movement developed and three broad regional women's organizations began organizing against apartheid in which individual women came together on a cross-class cross-racial basis for the first time (Geisler 2004). At the end of that decade women in South Africa were beginning to organize more self-consciously around gender issues even if they did not use the term feminism overtly. By this time a synergy existed between the internal activists and left-wing ANC women in exile in terms of their activities and debates (Hassim 2002a: 175). They came together at the Malibongwe conference convened in January 1990 to discuss how to achieve gender equality in the new South Africa and the need for a national women's movement. Significantly the word feminism was used in the final document. Therefore although women's organizing was shaped by the nature of the opposition struggle, many women activists recognized the need for a more autonomous strong mass women's movement that could fight for gender claims and that a strategic intervention into the transition was necessary of women were to ensure that some of their basic demands were to be achieved.

Levels of women's organizing therefore varied considerably at the point when different non-democratic regimes broke down. At one end of the spectrum were organized women's movements, containing feminist actors. These movements, and key actors within them, that were active in the breakdown of the non demo-cratic regime, wished to ensure that gender issues remained on the agenda. We saw this in Chile, South Africa, and Brazil. At the other end of the spectrum were cases where few women were organized as women and no women's organizations had a significant impact on the breakdown. This was particularly true of the collapse of state socialism in much of East Central Europe. Lying in the middle of these two positions were cases where women's organizations had played a role in the regime breakdown but for various reasons, they had not come together in order to put gender issues visibly on the transition agenda. Argentina and El Salvador would fall into this category.

But although organized women could play significant roles in the breakdown of authoritarian regimes, there is a fundamental difference between playing a role in regime breakdown and ensuring that gender issues remain visible and on the agenda of the transition. Playing a role in the breakdown is no guarantee that the latter will occur. We will consider this key theme in more detail in our next section to ascertain what conditions must be fulfilled in order to ensure that gender issues remain on the agenda of the transition. We need also to explore how these forms of pre-existing organizing fared during the subsequent transition phase.

❖ WOMEN'S ORGANIZING IN THE TRANSITION PHASE

Once a transition is underway, the political opportunity structure alters as the political initiative and activity shifts towards the conventional political arena. It is often claimed that women's movements are more important in the breakdown and early stages of a transition than in the later stages as party politics and conventional political activity have a negative effect on women's organizing. All social movements, including women's movements, are faced with decisions about the tactics and strategies to pursue under the new conditions. Women activists adopt different strategies and goals based on their own beliefs and the opportunities afforded by different institutional contexts. The classic dichotomy, between autonomy—remaining aloof from the new political institutions risking marginalization—or integration into these new processes and risking co-optation, recurs.

Our task in this section therefore is twofold: first to explore what happens to those women's movements and forms of organizing already identified, and second to assess their roles in the period between the breakdown of the non-democratic regime and the first or founding election. We will examine the strength, effectiveness, and activities of the different organizations. If we examine the interaction of different forms of organizing with different transitions, we can also discern how transitions impact on women's organizing and assess the opportunities for organized women to influence political processes within different transition paths. We must also assess the impact of any participation by organized women in those political processes and the extent to which gender issues were placed on the transition agendas. Since there are very few cases where women did impact on the unfolding transition process, we will examine those cases in more detail to understand the significance of the contextual factors. As we saw in Part I, mainstream writers have identified two major characteristics that contribute to different transition paths: the speed of the transition and whether it is negotiated or pacted. We will divide our analysis accordingly.

❖ *Rapid Transitions*

Rapid transitions are often catalysed by a crisis and subsequent collapse of the previous regime. They often result in a quick hand over of power and, as a result, the surviving elements of the non-democratic regime have little influence over the transition path and outcomes. In order to have some influence over a rapid transition from either state socialism or authoritarianism, it appears that women have to be organized as women already as a speedy transition does not offer many opportunities for new and effective women's organizations to emerge. The

Czechoslovakian case appears to confirm this view. The frozen post-totalitarian regime collapsed very quickly after ten days of demonstrations in November 1989 in part because there were no influential reformist moderates who might favour negotiations within the hardline regime. And the dissidents who formed the core of the opposition—although a great moral presence—had no desire or organizational capacity for strategic and tactical negotiations (Linz and Stepan 1996: 321–2). Large numbers of women took part in the demonstrations that brought down the regime and some leading women dissidents were beaten by the police. Women were also involved in the formation of Civic Forum (a broad anti-communist opposition front) in November 1989 in Prague and Public Against Violence, its sister organization in Bratislava that went on to contest and win the founding elections held in June 1990. But they played mostly secondary roles, primarily in service rather than policymaking or deliberative activities (Wolchik 1998: 159). As a result, although a broad opposition grouping like Civic Forum contained women, they did not play prominent roles or organize around gender issues. No other significant autonomous women's organizations existed and none could emerge during the short period between the collapse of the old regime and the founding elections.

In Argentina, although women's organizations existed prior to the transition, they, too, had little influence over the rapid transition from authoritarian rule. Soon after its defeat in the Malvinas in June 1982, the military announced that elections would be held shortly and they took place in October 1983. A withdrawal in the mid of economic crisis and military defeat constrained the influence of the armed forces over the transition. The political parties could refuse the overtures of the military in the unpacted and free Argentine transition and as a consequence few restrictions were placed on the political system (Linz and Stepan 1996). But despite the relative openness of the transition, the influence of women's groups was limited. A number of feminist organizations such as the Movimiento para Liberación Femenina and the Asociación de Mujeres Argentinas that had emerged in the 1970s were not in a strong position to influence events because of their small size, strategies and loose organization (Feijoó 1998). They were accustomed to working in small groups in consciousness raising and self-reflection and saw politics in terms of individuals rather than groups (Feijoó and Nari 1994: 118).

The Madres were potentially more influential as their human rights protests had helped to bring about the end of fear and delegitimize the military government internationally (so much so that Alfonsín used their rhetoric and slogan 'We are Life' in his presidential campaign). However, as we will see in the post-transition period, a number of factors undermined their continued influence in the new environment. Bargaining was more effective in the new political context, but the symbolic, ethical, and non-negotiable nature of the Madres' demands for the return of their children made it hard for them to bargain. In addition, 'the determined, charismatic, and single-minded leadership' needed under military rule was often inappropriate in the new political conditions (Brysk 1994: 24). The Madres announced before the elections 'that come what may, who even wins [the elections], their children must appear alive and those guilty of crimes against the people must be punished' (quoted in Feijoó and Gogna 1990: 89). Therefore although important women's organizations existed under authoritarian rule, they did not strategize together to affect the transition and the context of the transition itself did not facilitate it.[5]

❖ *Pacted Transitions*

A gradual liberalization associated with the longer breakdown and transition from a non democratic regime can offer opportunities for activists, including women's organizations, to develop strategies in response to unfolding events. We will try to determine under what conditions liberalization during a transition can provide women's organizations with opportunities. A significant proportion of drawn-out transitions were pacted—based on elite-level negotiations initiated after splits in the non-democratic regime allowed some elements to negotiate with the moderate opposition. We will examine a number of pacted transitions with varying levels of women's organizing to see how far organized women could have an impact on the period between the breakdown of the non-democratic regime and the founding election.

If we look first at the pacted transitions where there was little women's organizing, we see that they were typified by low levels of autonomous women's organizing prior to the regime breakdown. This is true of the pacted transitions from state socialism that took place in Poland and Hungary. In both countries low levels of women's organizing can be attributed to the nature of the pre-existing regimes and the opposition.

Solidarity and the Catholic Church had dominated the Polish opposition after 1980. Having begun negotiations with the regime in 1988, Solidarity's domination continued until the first fully free elections of autumn 1991. Few autonomous women's groups existed outside this opposition bloc and organized women played no role in the transition, except around the issue of abortion. The legislative attempts to ban abortion supported by Solidarity during this period spurred the growth of new women's groups—some of them feminist and most of them single issue—united in their support for women's reproductive rights (Einhorn 1993: 191). The battle over abortion also contributed to the demise of the Solidarity Women's section that had been formed in the autumn of 1989 as a result of pressure from the International Confederation of Free Trade Unions (Watson 1996: 220). Run by young women who had contact with feminists abroad, it expressed support for a women's right to abortion as well as gender equality. After a dispute with the Solidarity leadership over these issues it was dissolved in the spring of 1991 (Hauser, Heyns, and Mansbridge 1993: 263). As a result women organized as women played a minor role in the Polish transition. Therefore although Linz and Stepan (1996) argue that many of the characteristics of the pacted transition in Poland resembled Chile and Brazil—in part because the Polish regime was the closest to an authoritarian regime—women's organizing during the transition does display a somewhat different pattern.

Similarly, no more than a handful of feminist groups formed in the predominantly anti-feminist climate of the less constrained Hungarian transition that followed soon after (Einhorn 1993). Women, organized as women, did not play a role in opposition groupings such as the Hungarian Democratic Forum (HDF) founded in 1987 or the Alliance of Free Democrats (AFD) set up the following year that subsequently played a key role as political parties in the negotiated transition. As a result organized women had little impact on the Hungarian transition (Fodor 1994).

If we turn to examine the four cases where women's organizations were active during the transition to democracy and did attempt to influence it, we can see that in all cases, because of a more favourable political opportunity structure, women's organizations already existed prior to the transition. Both the organizations and their capacity to impact on the transition processes varied considerably. At one end of the spectrum women's organizations in Brazil were fractured by the new political context and rendered relatively ineffective. In El Salvador and Chile, women did organize to influence the first elections but in differing ways with differing results. At the other end of the spectrum, organized women in South Africa were able to intervene into the negotiations that designed the new institutional set-up prior to the first non-racial elections.

First, we will look at the transition with the least input from organized women. The Brazilian transition was the longest and one of the most constrained of all our case studies. Linz and Stepan (1996) argue that it began in 1974 with liberalization and increasing party competition and ended in 1990 with the first directly elected president. But Alvarez (1990a) argues that the transition ended with the inauguration in 1985 of the first indirectly elected president (and the first civilian) since the military took power. We will use Alvarez's (1990a) delineation as the governments in power between 1985 and 1990 were significantly different. During the 1970s most women's movements were uninterested in institutional politics and remained aloof from the newly liberalized party competition taking place between the two government created parties. But new parties were formed when the political opposition fragmented after a multiparty system, intended to reduce the power of opposition party, was installed in 1980–1 and from the early 1980s onwards opposition state governments were elected.

Women trying to advance a gender agenda had to decide whether to adopt a new strategy of integration in this new era of more genuinely competitive multiparty politics or maintain their autonomy. Popular women's movements often remained more marginal than other women's organizations. Those opting for integration had to choose between different parties. The PT and PMDB were the two most popular options. But this choice debilitated and demobilized the politically heterogeneous women's movement in Sao Paulo and women's movements could not maintain their unity. By 1982 they had become fractured and demobilized by the new political context and less able to influence transition outcomes (Alvarez 1990a: 159). In fact the influential thesis that the reconstitution of party politics can disempower and demobilize women's movements originates in part from the Brazilian transition. But as we see in parts III and IV, independent feminists could impact on a number of the state governments and political parties that they entered.

In El Salvador organized women did attempt to influence the first competitive elections that marked the end of the transition in April 1994. The El Salvadorean transition got underway when UN supervised peace negotiations began between the government and the FMLN and resulted in the Peace Accords signed in January 1992. The negotiations and increasing liberalization coincided with a huge expansion in the number of women's organizations in 1990 and 1991. Many were still linked to the different parts of the FMLN that were keen to benefit from the international funding available to women's organizations. But feminism now figured far more prominently. Exiles, influenced by feminism abroad, returned, and women's organizations increased their participation in international and regional feminist activities (Hipsher 2001: 143). Tensions between these increasingly feminist organizations and the parties increased. As a result most women's groups had disassociated themselves from the FMLN by 1993. The history of Las Dignas (Women for Dignity and Life) illustrates 'this journey of separation' (Hipsher 2001: 145). The organization was founded in July 1990 by Resistencia Nacional (RN), one of the constituent groups of the FMLN, but as it became increasingly feminist, it became more critical of the RN and its attitude towards Las Dignas and finally it became autonomous in 1992 (Stephen 1997: 71). Therefore, the familiar issues of 'autonomy versus integration' and *doble militancia* were keenly felt by many feminist groups as they struggled to become more autonomous from those organizations that had been instrumental in their foundation.

Despite the proliferation of increasingly feminist women's organizations, the Peace Accords of 1992 did not include a gender perspective and female combatants did not get equal treatment when fighters were demobilized (Luciak 2001: 39). As a result women activists wanted to ensure that gender issues were not marginalized in the forthcoming elections. Although some umbrella meetings and organizations, such as the Concertación de Mujeres por la Paz, la Dignidad y la Igualidad, had already happened in 1991, an important period of coalition-building among different women's organizations began in the following year (Stephen 1997). Three main groupings (plus a large number of other organizations) came together in January 1993 to form Mujeres 94 specifically to influence the political process in the run-up to the elections. After eight months of preparatory work, the Mujeres

94 coalition produced a women's platform of fourteen demands that included an end to sexual violence, and to laws that discriminate against women, 50% of all leadership positions, and reproductive rights. The platform was presented to all the political parties in August 1993 in a public ceremony and was eventually endorsed by the two main contenders: the left-wing coalition (that included the FMLN) and the right-wing party ARENA (Kampwirth 1998).

Although Mujeres 94 successfully articulated gender issues at the national level, the coalition could not get its demands taken seriously by all the political parties. Despite endorsing the women's platform, it was not reflected in ARENA's electoral platform (Kampwirth 1998). However, the FMLN, the largest party in the left-wing coalition, did partially recognize some demands at its 1993 convention and in an election leaflet aimed at women, outlined seven ways in which the FMLN would make women's lives better framed similarly to the women's platform demands. But the FMLN did not command sufficient electoral support and the right-wing ARENA won the election. At the same time, Mujeres 94 was dogged by sectarianism and embroiled in controversy about its relationship with the political parties on the left. Las Dignas, for example, argued that party militancy was incompatible with maintaining autonomy as an activist in the women's movement, while another influential group, the Melidas (Movimiento de Mujeres 'Melida Anaya Montes' or MAM) claimed that it was possible to be both a representative of the women's movement in Mujeres 94 and a party militant (Luciak 1998). Therefore, although women's organizing did grow during the transition period and feminist activists came together to articulate gender issues during the run-up to the elections, their ability to get them on the agenda of the transition was ultimately constrained.

In Chile, the transition period was the high point for women's organizing (Frohmann and Valdes 1993). Women attempting to affect the political processes focused most of their efforts on one political grouping—the Concertación—a centre-left alliance contesting the founding elections. These elections were set in train when Pinochet lost a plebiscite on his continuing presidency in 1988 after the opposition gained 56% of the vote after uniting in a successful 'no' campaign (Linz and Stepan 1996: 206). Chile is a classic example of a non-crisis negotiated transition in which the military regime played a key role in the construction of a new system designed to ensure that the right was favoured and its vision, embodied in the constitution of 1980, would be maintained. As the parties of the centre and centre–left had become committed to a transition achieved through negotiation and accommodation with the military regime, they accepted the system constructed by the outgoing regime. In the period between the plebiscite and the elections, some terms were renegotiated. For instance the number of elected senators was increased and the centre–left opposition moderated its position on human rights abuses, prioritizing truth over justice (Barahona de Brito 1997: 104). Once it had become obvious that the opposition was likely to win the forthcoming election,

Pinochet put in place further measures to constrain any incoming elected government (Linz and Stepan 1996: 210). For example the wife of the head of the armed forces, rather than the president's wife, was to remain as head of CEMA–Chile.

Women's movements, although they did not impact on the closed process that determined the new polity, were affected by the dynamics of the political processes that were underway. The question of what role they should play in relation to upcoming elections became pressing. These developments, in combination with their previous experience of the Asamblea, reinforced the belief of some feminists that more than ever it was necessary to enter the political process, while others decided to remain outside (Molina 1990). Much of the feminist movement reorientated itself and debated the ways in which women should 'do politics' (*hacer política*), the alliances they should make and the aims they should have. Some organizations, such as La Morada, remained sceptical about the benefits that a formally democratic government would bring to women in terms of any real shift in the balance of power between the sexes (Molina 1989). Meanwhile others argued that the experience of the Pliego and the Asamblea demonstrated several things: the shortcomings of women's politics, the difficulty of articulating women's demands in formal politics, and the lack of receptivity of political parties and social organizations to women's demands.

The conclusion drawn by many was that, while the pressing task was to enter the political process, there was a need to preserve autonomy at the same time. To move away from simply denouncing gender discrimination to placing feminist demands on the agenda of the transition, the Feminist Movement issued the Demandas de Mujeres a la Democracia in 1988. They included proposals for an executive-level state agency to devise policy on women and a 30% quota for government and parliament (Franceschet 2004). At the same time some feminists increased their efforts to enter formal politics and, as we see in Part III, made some headway within the political parties of the Centre and centre–left. Old tensions that had existed between the *feministas* (feminists) and *políticas* (female activists within political parties) were reduced as many *políticas* became more sympathetic to the feminists' aims.

Perhaps the best-known and most effective attempt to place feminist demands on the agenda of the transition was the creation of the autonomous Concertación Nacional de Mujeres por la Democracia in 1988. The major impetus for its formation was the perception of women's continued lack of influence in the run-up to the 1988 plebiscite and the selection of very few women candidates (around 5% of the total) for the subsequent elections. It was formed by a group of women active in the range of parties of the Concertación together with independent feminists (including academics and activists, many of whom were middle-class professionals). Marcela Rios (2003: 265) has claimed that contrary to the 'official story' the women's Concertación did not represent all the women's movement.

The women's Concertación had three aims: to raise women's issues on the national political scene, to work in the presidential and parliamentary campaigns on behalf of the Concertación, and to formulate a programme for women for a future democratic government. It only attempted to influence the agenda of the centre-left Concertación, dominated by the Christian Democrats. According to Maria Elena Valenzuela members of the women's Concertación assumed that the newly elected government (and by implication the state) would be a gender-neutral tool that could be used in gender-based ways. Namely that engaging the state would be a relatively straightforward process to bring about an expansion of rights and democratic procedures through which women could also be incorporated as citizens.[6]

The women's Concertación proposals, including one for the institionalization of women's interests in the state through a women's ministry, were presented to the Concertación as demands and most of them were incorporated into its electoral programme (Montecino and Rossetti 1990). The activities and visibility of women's movements during previous phases of the transition, combined with the activities of feminists within the centre-left parties, meant that those political parties felt unable to ignore the demands of the women's Concertación. The Concertación committed itself to 'fully enforce women's rights considering the new role of women in society, overcoming any form of discrimination', while 'enforcing the measures required to adequately protect the family'. These goals were to be achieved through: legal changes that improved women's legal position; social participation and the incorporation of women into the political system and labour market; and the creation of national machinery at state level that would propose policy and oversee its implementation by other ministries (Waylen 1998: 158).

The women's Concertación therefore grew out of a history of efforts by organized women to influence the political agenda. The Concertación's adoption of its proposals resulted from a strategy of direct engagement by parts of the Chilean feminist movement with the political process in the form of the main opposition coalition. And it is highly unlikely that, without this pressure, the Concertación would have adopted these ideas. However, as had been the case with some of the earlier attempts to create a united movement, some women active in the popular organizations felt that the Concertación did not represent their interests (Angelo 1990). Furthermore groups outside the political process, such as the predominantly female human rights groups (*agrupaciones*) like the AFDD, had far less influence over the transition. While they maintained critical support for the centre–left opposition, they disagreed with the dropping of the call for the abrogation of the amnesty law and were unhappy with the 'political contingency' that emphasized reconciliation and prioritized truth over justice, making the trial of all those accused of human rights abuses impossible (Barahona de Brito 1997: 121). Although the transition was severely constrained by the influence of the military and the processes by which the new institutional set-up was designed were largely closed to women, gender issues were placed on the agenda of the winning centre–left coalition as a result of the efforts of a group of organized women (Waylen 2000).

Finally, in South Africa an alliance of women organized to influence the actual negotiations that decided the shape of the new institutions. The pacted transition began with the release of Nelson Mandela and the 'unbanning' of the ANC in February 1990 and ended with the first non-racial elections held in April 1994. In the face of a worsening structural crisis and stalemate both sides realized that neither side could win outright and that only a negotiated settlement could provide a long-lasting solution (S. Friedman 1993*a*). The elite multilateral and bilateral negotiations, dominated by the ANC and the National Party, were to design the political and constitutional set-up for the new South Africa with the understanding that the economic system would remain intact. Women activists who had been organizing as women, increasingly around gender issues and as feminists, were determined to ensure that women's claims for equality, put on the agenda as a legitimate part of opposition demands, were not excluded from the transition. Links already existed between feminists inside and outside the ANC and both groups wanted to ensure that they were involved in the processes of constitution-building. There was widespread agreement that there was a strategic need for a broad women's movement from which to press gender claims (Geisler 2004).

The formation of a broad alliance, the Women's National Coalition (WNC) was the most important development in women's organizing in this period (Hassim 2002*b*). Although the WNC was set up on the initiative of the ANC Women's League (ANCWL), it was an independent organization that could articulate its demands independently of the ANC. By 1994 it consisted of ninety organizations and thirteen regional coalitions and negotiated diversity through coalition politics rather than in one organization (Cock 1997: 313). The WNC had a twofold role. Its first function was to contribute to the building of a national women's movement through a grass-roots campaign to draft a charter for women's equality. Its second aim was to influence the political processes. The charter campaign was to be a mobilizing and educating process to be achieved through an ambitious programme of participation and consultation. The charter was also meant to provide the basis for intervention into the constitutional negotiations, but it took so long to produce that it was too late to be included. It ultimately did not succeed in building a broad-based grass-roots women's movement. In fulfilling its second aim, the WNC played a key role in facilitating the intervention of organized women into the transition process and the creation of a 'triple alliance' of women activists, academics, and politicians.

Women's lack of influence in Conference for a Democratic South Africa (CODESA), the first stage of the negotiating process, was one immediate spur to the formation of the WNC (Albertyn 1994). The WNC then identified three tasks it had to undertake in the second stage, the Multi-Party Negotiating Process (MPNP): to secure the inclusion of women in the party negotiating teams, to ensure the inclusion of non-sexism in the constitutional principles, and to secure the inclusion in the constitution of an equality clause that would override customary law. The first aim was achieved relatively easily (Geisler 2004). One delegate from each party and government negotiating team was to be a woman. Women activists organized around the second and third aims and the WNC helped the triple alliance to gain more influence over the MPNP than over CODESA. It set up a monitoring team to advise the cross-party women's caucus and to monitor the technical committees and the Negotiating Council. The WNC also lobbied and protested on its own account, particularly around the equality clause that was fiercely resisted by the traditional leaders who saw it as a threat to inheritance, property, and marriage laws that favoured them. We will see in Part IV that after up-to-the-last minute negotiations, the dispute was resolved in favour of the women's lobby. As we see again in Parts III and IV, despite difficulties in influencing the process, the WNC did achieve a surprising unity and influence, contributing for example in one of the most gender-sensitive constitutions in the world (Geisler 2000: 614).

A range of women therefore came together during the transition to form the WNC. It was a broad independent women's umbrella alliance that had feminist activists playing key roles within it, but it also had close links to a number of political parties, particularly the ANC. The ANCWL played an important role within the WNC but could not be dominant within it, and, as we see in Part III, needed a women's movement to help it to strengthen its own, sometimes uncertain, position within the ANC. The WNC acted on its own account but also facilitated the emergence and success of a strategic alliance of women academics, politicians, and activists, many of whom were feminists. The synergy of this triple alliance allowed some strategic interventions into the MPNP which none of partners could have achieved on their own. Successful intervention into the constitutional negotiations was possible even although the negotiations were elite and party-focused. As a result organized women ensured that a broad commitment to gender equality on the part of the dominant opposition grouping was translated into a constitutional form.

The large variations in women's organizing—ranging from virtually no women's organizing of any kind to broad-ranging women's movements that influenced the transition itself—were determined by a number of factors: the levels of pre-existing organization, the characteristics of the movements themselves, and the extent to which feminists played a key role within them. But the broader context and how a movement interacted with it was also crucially important. The character of the transition itself—its speed, and if pacted, the openness of the processes that decide on the institutional set-up of the new polity—was central. It is impossible to understand the variations we have seen without understanding the relationship between organized women and a number of other actors within the electoral arena, particularly the (opposition) political parties and any feminist actors within them. The overall character of the opposition, namely the extent to which it was fragmented or united, its ideology, and openness to gender issues (themes which all recur in Part III) were important. These differences help to account for the presence and absence of women's organizing and for the variations in the success of those women who organized to influence transitions in placing gender issues on transition agenda—whether in an election manifesto or in a transition settlement such as constitution. In the remaining section of Part II we consider women's organizing in different post-transition contexts.

❖ POST-TRANSITION WOMEN'S ORGANIZING

For many commentators, the post-transition period has seen the demobilization of social movements as their visibility and importance declines and protest levels fall to one of their lowest points in the cycle (Tarrow 1998). Opposition movements often won the founding elections and the conventional political arena became the primary focus for political activity. The conventional wisdom is that women's organizing also declines during this period. But competitive electoral politics and the control of the state by an elected government offer women's movements the possibility to forge new relationships with governments, political parties, and some parts of the state—particularly with new state women's machineries where they are established. Often movements have to contend with the consequences of dual transitions, both political and economic, as the (re)institution of competitive electoral politics was often accompanied by economic, restructuring. These changes have had huge implications for civil society and its social, economic, and political role. Different women's movements reacted in different ways to the new situation. The relationship of women's organizations with different parts of the state and the political system and its potential rewards and hazards is an important theme in the post-transition period. We will trace what happens to the women's organizations we have already observed and the extent to which new forms of organizing can emerge in different contexts. To judge the effectiveness of women's movements, we must examine not only the extent to which women's movements could articulate gender issues and get them on to the political agenda, but also their roles in achieving positive gender outcomes (or preventing the implementation of negative ones)—in the making and implementation of policy to improve women's descriptive and substantive representation.

We will begin by examining what happened in those cases—primarily transitions from state socialism—where few women's organizations existed at the time of the founding elections. In none of these cases have large and influential women's organizations emerged in the post-transition period. Many commentators have remarked upon this phenomenon, focusing primarily on the absence of significant feminist movements. But Einhorn and Sever (2003) argue that, as a result, the variety of women's organizations that have developed since the collapse of state socialism has been ignored. A significant number of women's NGOs now exist and women are often prominent in the NGO sector. Gal and Kligman (2000: 15) claim that the term NGO is preferred, because 'civil society' is part of a discourse that is now too associated with the opposition to state socialism.

Many of these NGOs have received support and funding from outside, as part of externally driven efforts to build a vibrant and functioning civil society after the demise of state socialism. Donors have included international organizations, the EU, Western governments like the USA and foundations such as Soros. Sundstrom (2005: 428) found that 67% of the 60 women's NGOs she looked at in Russia received some foreign funding and 42% were primarily foreign funded. In the Czech Republic, the communist women's organization transformed itself into an important women's NGO gaining EU funding (Haskova and Krizkova 2003: 47). Einhorn (2006) claims that as a result, foreign donors keen to develop civil society have promoted NGOs at the expense of more grass-roots-based organizations.

Many women's NGOs are active at the local level and around a particular issue or set of issues such as the provision of a women's shelter or a hotline. As we see in Part IV, they have often stepped in to fill the gaps left by the reduction in state welfare provision. Einhorn and Sever (2003), citing a UNICEF report, describe four main areas of NGO organization in the 1990s: activism against violence, social services such as health care and education, the promotion of business and professional activities, and political participation. For example they estimate that the 600 women's NGOs that existed in Russia between 1997–8 were operating in all of these four areas. Chimiak (2003: 15) cites a Directory of Women's Organizations and Initiatives published in 2001 that lists 116 women's organizations in Poland, active in a range of locations both within and outside Warsaw and in spheres spanning unemployment, lesbian rights and self-help groups. Wolchik (1998: 171) points to the emergence of a similar pattern in the Czech republic. By 1994 thirty-four women's organizations existed, ranging from an association for women entrepreneurs to housewives' organizations. And by 2005 fifty-nine entities were listed in the register of women's organizations (Eberhardt 2005a). In the same year 350 organizations claimed to be actively involved in women's issues in Hungary (Eberhardt 2005a). The majority of these groups do not see themselves as political and are unlikely to define themselves as feminist even if they deal with issues such as domestic violence often associated with a feminist agenda. Indeed Eberhardt (2005a) claims that fewer than ten of the Hungarian organizations can be identified as feminist.

It is this perceived lack of feminist movements that has preoccupied many western commentators, provoking a number of articles with titles such as 'The Feminist Movement in Poland: Why so Slow?' (Bystydzienski 2001). But as Einhorn and Sever (2003) note, the reality is complex. As we have already seen, anything to do with women's emancipation was negatively associated with the discredited old regime and this association extended to feminism, seen as just another 'ism' (Jaquette and Wolchik 1998: 9). Many Eastern European women have stressed that feminism has different meanings in East Central Europe and Russia (Zhotkhina 2005). Matynia (2003) for example argues that because liberalism never flourished in Poland, a feminism that is based on liberalism is not relevant. As a result 'Western feminism' has been rejected as an alien import. Many women do not define the issues that they are active around in those terms arguing instead that they face different constraints and so feminism takes different forms (Zhotkhina 2005).

But a small number of avowedly feminist groups did emerge in the post-transition period. They included newly formed women's studies centres in universities across the region. For example the Centre for Gender Studies was founded in 1991 by a groups of women including ex-dissident Jirina Siklova (Wolchik 1998: 172). It has now evolved into Gender Studies, the most important women's NGO in the Czech Republic with six part-time workers, a library and is active around issues like domestic violence.[7] In Russia, feminist groups, that often had roots in groups that were founded during the period of glasnost, came together at two independent women's forums that were held in 1991 and 1992 (Sperling 1998). A small feminist network of ten women was established in Hungary in the early 1990s by women academics and produced the only feminist publication. An offshoot continued in the form of an organization active around domestic violence.[8] In Poland, feminist organizations such as the Warsaw Women's Rights Centre and Oska centre were also established and have remained active around gender issues.

Many feminist groups, like Gender Studies in the Czech Republic, have also received funding and assistance from Western donor organizations and from women's groups elsewhere as part of their attempts to build civil society. This involvement has contributed to the establishment of regional organizations such as the Karat coalition and the Network of East West Women (NEWW), initially established by feminists from the USA and the former Yugoslavia that now links more than forty countries with its headquarters in Poland. Some of the scepticism about western feminism evident in the early 1990s appears to have diminished over the subsequent decade (Einhorn 2006).

The extent of women's organizing—particularly feminist organizing—varies between our case studies. Some feminists and commentators have talked most optimistically about the developments in Poland. Matynia (2003) for example argues that feminist discourse is now more mainstream as a cohort of women publish about and debate gender issues. She cites the example of a letter of protest that was sent to the European Parliament by dozens of prominent women about EU accession and its implications for women's rights. But she too admits that women organizing around gender issues have not yet had a huge impact on government and policymaking. And there is less evidence of feminist organizing in Hungary compared to Poland or even the Czech Republic.

Although few women would see themselves as part of a coherent women's movement, there are examples of groups, both feminist and non-feminist, coming together around particular issues. For example in Hungary there have also been campaigns around domestic violence, prostitution, and attempts to restrict maternity provision. But the responses to attempts to restrict women's access to abortion, particularly in Poland in the early 1990s, have been the most notable. Although ultimately unsuccessful, the campaign to stop the legislation included demonstrations and the lobbying of parliament and was waged by a large number of groups. Indeed Fuszara (1993: 251) has argued that in Poland 'paradoxically, the antiabortion draft helped women to create women's organizations and a women's movement in defense of their rights'. Even if, according to Einhorn and Sever (2003: 177), the campaign against the abortion ban was fought as a socio-economic problem not as a women's rights problem. Sundstrom (2005) has argued that women's NGOs in Russia have been less effective than soldier's rights movements. But women's NGOs active around domestic violence and appealing to universal norms against bodily harm have been more effective than those active around gender discrimination that appeal to notions of gender equity particularly in the labour market. The effectiveness of women's NGOs therefore depends in part on the issue they are active around.

Indeed in much of East Central Europe there has been little contact between women's NGOs and the state. Many organizations do not see it as part of their role to attempt to change government policy. Matynia (2003) argues that women's NGOs in Poland are like 'fenced playgrounds' within which women can do what they want but cannot graduate from. However, as we see in Parts III and IV, women's organizations often lack sympathetic insiders within the government, legislature, and bureaucracy with whom to liaise. Governments are often unsympathetic to gender issues and even when they are more sympathetic, the lack of institutionalized political systems and resulting frequent changes in government means such favourable interludes may be short-lived.

If we examine the fate of women's organizing where women's movements already existed—a situation that was more common in transitions from authoritarianism—we see that in the post-transition period most women's movements could no longer regard themselves as unequivocally oppositional as they had done under the non-democratic regime. Some organizations chose engagement with the political arena and others remained aloof. In previous sections we divided those women's organizations active during transitions from military regimes into three major categories: human rights movements, popular organizations, and feminist movements.

If we look first at human rights movements, we see that the trends that were visible during the transition period intensified in the post-transition period as human rights organizations had to decide on their strategies in the new era of electoral politics. Faced with the dilemma of how to deal with the human rights abuses of the previous non-democratic regime, many of the new civilian governments, for example in Chile, Argentina, and South Africa, opted in the first instance to prioritize truth over justice. In the quest for reconciliation and constrained by the nature of the transitions themselves—they chose to discover what had happened, which often entailed offering abusers freedom from prosecution in return for their testimony—rather than prosecuting all those guilty of human rights violations. In the face of outcomes that would not match up to their demand for justice, human rights groups could choose one of two options. They could either keep their demands as non-negotiable and preserve their absolutist ethical stance or they could engage with the political system which would entail bargaining and a willingness to compromise some of those demands (Waylen 2000).

As we have seen, prior to the elections in 1983 the Madres in Argentina had demanded that all those who had disappeared should come back alive and all those who were guilty would be put on trial. The Madres (barring exceptions like Graciela Fernandez Meijide who later became a presidential candidate) then refused to participate in the National Committee on Disappeared Persons (CONADEP) established by the new government of Alfonsín as its ambit fell short of the retribution demanded by the Madres. They were also very critical of the limited nature of the trials for human rights abuses. As a result of their decision to stay outside the judicial processes the Madres were soon in confrontation with the new civilian government (Feijoó and Nari 1994). In 1986 it led to a split within the Madres over goals and strategies. At stake were issues such as whether the remains of their children should be forensically identified or whether to accept compensation from the state for their deaths thereby admitting that the demand that their children should be returned to them alive would never be fulfilled. The breakaway Linea Fundadora and the Abuelas (grandmothers) opted to involve themselves in the political system while the remaining Madres did not (Waylen 2000). So the Madres objected to the exhumations of unidentified bodies, arguing by this time that they already knew who was dead; what they needed to know was who killed them. The Abuelas cooperated as they wanted to discover the identities of the female victims and whether they had given birth in order to trace any surviving children and secure their return.[9] The Abuelas subsequently set up a DNA bank to help with tracing children of *desaparacidas* (disappeared).

In Chile, the first two Concertación governments observed the amnesty proclaimed by the Pinochet regime in 1978 and apart from a few high-level cases, did not bring significant actions against actions of the military implicated in human rights abuses (Loveman 1991). The emphasis of government was on the 'whole truth and justice as far as possible'. Disappearances were investigated primarily to ascertain what happened through the work of the Rettig commission and the families of victims were compensated (Barahona de Brito 1997). In the face of government attempts to close the issue of human rights abuses, the AFDD maintained their activities, demanding justice not prudence. The AFDD adopted tactics similar to the breakaway Linea Fundadora, by critically engaging with the political system: dealing with political parties, testifying to the senate, and accepting compensation; as well as demonstrating outside the presidential palace on the anniversary of the coup and even hunger striking.[10] By 2004 the issue of human right prosecutions was still ongoing as the attempts to prosecute Pinochet continued, but a government-created commission reported on the estimated 35,000 victims of torture and the socialist president Lagos announced compensation from the state in the form of life pensions. The AFDD had remained active and although the report was welcomed by its vice president Mireya Garcia who argued that it was a historic step that recognized political prisoners, the compensation deal was denounced as inadequate.[11]

Therefore, even in the case of human rights groups that were prepared to engage with the system, the nature of the (often pacted) transitions meant that civilian governments have been constrained in the extent to which they could prosecute human rights abusers in the short-term. Human rights groups are therefore unlikely to achieve their other demands unless they are prepared to give up one of their most fundamental ones for justice (Waylen 2000). Some movements choose to broaden the range of issues that they are involved in. In El Salvador the CoMadres began to consider women's rights as human rights in the 1990s and started to campaign around issues like domestic violence (Stephen 1997).

Popular movements also had to adjust to the new era of electoral politics. Many social movements had been historically wary of connections with political parties, fearing manipulation and control through clientelistic structures. With a few exceptions such as the PT in Brazil, the parties themselves were often ambivalent about popular mobilization and uninterested in the movements. The restoration of conventional political activity was accompanied by the seeming exclusion and demobilization of many grass-roots social movements including women's popular organizations (Foweraker 1995). The indirect effects of economic crisis and neoliberal economic policies also impacted negatively on popular organizations as the state increasingly withdrew from welfare provision, leaving activists with less time and energy for mobilization as they had to spend more time in daily survival. These trends were intensified by a number of other factors.

First, the Catholic Church that had previously supported many popular movements, modified its stance. The Vatican's move away from the relatively progressive tenets of Vatican II had repercussions on the work the church could do in Latin America (Drogus and Stewart-Gambino 2005). In Brazil the increasingly conservative church abandoned its commitment to grass-roots activism. This change contributed to the decline in the activities of the CEBs that had played such an important role in promoting women's activism under the dictatorship (Drogus 1999). A similar trend also occurred in Chile. Opus Dei, the right-wing catholic organization became increasingly influential as progressive priests were replaced and the church withdrew from its social commitment to focus on '*evangelización*' (Schild 1998). Second, the return to competitive electoral politics led to a reduction or redirection through the government of much of the funding from bilateral agencies, private foundations, and international NGOs that had supported the work of so many popular organizations. In Chile an estimated one billion dollars in international aid was channeled through the Concertación government. The national state therefore became both an increasingly important source of funds and a gatekeeper for funds from abroad (Schild 2002). These tendencies were exacerbated by the redirection of donor funding from Latin America towards Eastern Europe after the collapse of state socialism.

As a result of all these developments, the number of popular organizations declined after the return to civilian rule. In Chile, prior to the Concertación government taking office, there were forty-four *talleres productivas* (workshops) in existence in the central zone of Santiago, but by the end of 1993 the number had fallen to eight (Rios 1994). The survivors were also encouraged to alter and diversify their activities. As we see again in Part IV, many civilian governments adopted development strategies that emphasized primarily economic solutions—particularly access to the market—as the solution to poverty. As a result, OEPs and some *ollas communes* in Chile came under pressure to become *microempresas* (micro-enterprises) gaining contracts from government agencies to supply school meals in their areas. Many Latin American feminists expressed scepticism about the economic viability and the distorting effects that the transformation into micro-enterprises brought about.[12]

However, some other well-known examples do not conform strictly to this pattern. In Peru, our comparator case, popular organizing actually peaked after the return to civilian rule in the 1980s. But it coincided with economic crisis, political chaos, and the withdrawal of the state from what little welfare provision it had previously engaged in. Two main types of popular women's organization, organizing around day-to-day survival in poor urban neighbourhoods mushroomed in what was one of the largest mobilizations of poor women. It is estimated that by 1991 720 Comedores Populares (communal kitchens) provided one and a half million meals per day in Lima, a city with a population of 7 million (Barrig 1998). They were autonomously organized by women federated into neighbourhood, district, metropolitan, and national organizations. They used foreign aid to provide much of the foodstuffs and were supported by the church and feminist NGOs who offered training and support (Blondet and Montero 1995). The Vaso de Leche (glass of milk) programme was established by the left-wing mayor of Lima and in 1986 organized nearly 100,000 women to distribute 1 million glasses of milk a day in 7,500 neighbourhood programmes (Blondet 1995).

Despite their acknowledged success in the provision of basic needs and in enhancing the lives of many poor women by increasing their autonomy and self-esteem, these programmes did experience problems. In common with many popular movements, their relationships with political parties and the state, both local and national were fraught, as they tried, not always successfully, to avoid co-optation and clientelistic relations. The Comedores maintained a greater distance than the leaders of the Vaso de Leche programme who had close political ties from the beginning, but this lessened the ability of the two groups to work together. Once the organizational structures became larger and more centralized, gaps opened up between the higher echelons of leaders who negotiated with donors and public officials and the grass-roots members. As a result the popular organizations were not well placed to resist the hardship of the severe economic crisis of the early 1990s and the assault of Sendero Luminoso (Shining Path) on the leaders of popular organizations, accusing them of corruption and even assassinating them. Therefore, although women's popular organizations initially increased after the return to civilian rule, they too found it hard to negotiate relationships with political parties and state institutions that were either increasingly ineffective, corrupt, or authoritarian (Barrig 1998; Blondet 1995).

If we look at our third type of organization, we can see that while the visible presence of many feminist movements declined in the post-authoritarian transition period, the range and heterogeneity of feminist organizations increased. Three trends stand out as different organizations responded differently to the changed political context. The most remarked-upon one is the intensified process of NGOization. It was also accompanied by the development of more issue-based and advocacy networks, as well as the emergence of short-term conjunctural alliances. The dilemmas and complexities of engaging with the state and political parties also brought a re-evaluation of strategies and the autonomy versus integration debates of the early 1980s re-emerged but in new forms.

The professionalization and formalization of feminist organizations into NGOs with paid staff, often supported by foreign funding, continued in the period after the return to competitive electoral politics. Nikki Craske (2000) argues that in Latin America it reflected the continuing internationalization and institutionalization of feminist movements. Most NGOs were still involved in empowerment, education, and the provision of services for women that they had traditionally undertaken, but they took up a role in policy advocacy for example with states and international organizations (Alvarez 1999). Many feminist NGOs participated in various international and regional conferences and the preparatory activities surrounding them in the first half of the 1990s (Alvarez 1998). 'Advocating feminism', by which Sonia Alvarez (1999) means advancing a gender policy agenda, became an increasingly important part of many NGOs' activities. Their links to a wider women's movement enabled them to do this as their dual positioning gave them a kind of political hybridity (Alvarez 1999). However it did bring with it a number of interlinked problems.

NGOs are often seen as proxies for civil society and other political actors. It is often assumed that they can represent civil society without the need to directly involve grass-roots organizations. However, their increasing institutionalization and technocratization means that they can easily become divorced from the grass-roots women's organizations that they are assumed to represent. In a changed domestic and international climate, many newly elected governments made some effort to fulfill their gender commitments for example with regard to CEDAW. Many states turned to feminist NGOs as 'gender experts' to supply the research and consultancy services that they could not provide for themselves. As we see again in Part IV, Veronica Schild (2002) details how, in the Chilean case, the restructuring of state welfare provision meant that NGOs were also increasingly subcontracted to implement the welfare programmes introduced by the Concertación government. She believes that these changes have negative implications for the NGOs' relationships both with the state (that become increasingly clientelistic) and with the poor women's organizations that they work with. The poor women's organizations cannot get the contracts from the state on their own account as they are deemed to be insufficiently trained and professional to provide these services. Schild (1998) argues that the NGOs have to forego many of their more feminist aims in order to implement the government's programmes to turn poor women into 'market citizens'.

The development of larger and more effective issue networks also occurred alongside the increasing NGOization of feminist organizations. In El Salvador although the historic closeness of many women's organizations and feminist organizations to the left continued, some single issue organizations that could appeal across political boundaries were also formed. For example the Association of Mothers Seeking Child Support played a role in campaigns around maintenance arrears and child support payments from absent fathers (Ready 2001; Shayne 2004). Networks around domestic violence and reproductive rights have been particularly important on a national, regional, and international basis. In South Africa for example, the Reproductive Rights Alliance (RRA) was formed in 1995 as a focused sectoral alliance of women's organizations to provide a united front in support of a pro-choice position. It took advantage of the relatively favourable international context created in the early 1990s and used the language of the Cairo Population Conference and the Beijing Women's Conference to lobby key ANC figures and increase support for a pro-choice position in civil society. It also participated in an ad hoc parliamentary committee established to consider changing the existing law on abortion that dated from the apartheid era (Albertyn et al. 1999). Spurred by impetus provided by organizing around regional and international conferences, regional networks on women's health, women's rights, and domestic and sexual violence were among the most important of those active in Latin America in the 1990s.

Short-term conjunctural coalitions also emerged to campaign around certain issues at particular moments. A broad spectrum of organizations that might not be able to work together on a longer-term basis can come together for a limited period and then the coalition fades away subsequently. The quota law passed in Argentina in 1991 was supported by an alliance of different women's organizations that cooperated with women in political parties and the legislature in a campaign to help to get the quota law passed. And as we see in Part IV, another short-term coalition organized to prevent a pro-life clause from being inserted into the new Argentine constitution (Htun 2003: 163).

Competitive electoral politics therefore provided new opportunities for advocacy and for organized women to influence the more open political processes. A number of feminist NGOs have specialized in providing training for women to enable them to enter politics on a local and national level and to exploit these new opportunities more effectively. In South Africa a number of women's NGOs joined to monitor and improve women's descriptive representation. For the 1999 elections they produced an election bulletin and ran workshops to highlight gender issues. In the first half of the 1990s activists could capitalize on the desire of newly elected governments to appear open and democratic—thereby helping their reintegration into international society—to press gender claims citing new international norms (Friedman 2006). Large-scale international events such as the Beijing Women's conference held in 1995 and the preparations that surrounded it also acted as a spur to reinvigorate women's organizing and raise the profile of gender issues on a national and regional basis (Alvarez et al. 2003).

The new political context also opens up debates about the wisdom, utility, and effectiveness of engaging with the state and political institutions. As we have seen many feminist organizations believed that engaging with the state was worthwhile and legitimate and that it was possible to construct a state that could respond to women's needs. However, not all feminists shared this belief. The opposing views were expressed through the reworking of the old 'autonomy versus integration' debate that had taken place in parts of Latin America in the early 1980s in the form of the *autónomas* versus the *institucionalizadas* (Alvarez 2000). In the 1990s, *autónomas* (autonomous feminists) emerged as a significant symbolic, if not numerically important, force particularly in Chile. Although not an internally coherent group, they certainly had an impact on wider feminist debates. At stake was the issue of how far to engage with national and international political institutions. At their most extreme, *autónomas* argued that engaging with the state was tantamount to collusion with neo-liberal patriarchy and that the NGOs that did so were corrupt, undemocratic and had sold out by implementing a neo-liberal agenda that could be of no benefit to women (Alvarez et al. 2002). The divisions between the different strands of feminism came to a head at the 1996 regional Encuentro held in Cartagena in Chile. However, by the late 1990s they had faded once more as some *institucionalizadas* had accepted the legitimacy of a number of the *autónomas* criticisms of the possibilities offered by engagement with the state and the *autónomas* themselves had become more fragmented (Alvarez et al. 2003: 562).

The impact of engagement with the state on the feminist movements themselves has also to be considered. As we have seen, many feminist NGOs accepted state contracts and it is claimed that, as a result, they had to moderate their activities and curb some of their more radical aims. A number of commentators have discussed this broader question of how far close links with the state and international donors compromise the autonomy and control that feminist NGOs have over their own agendas as they become dependent on those institutions for funding and contracts. Sonia Alvarez (1999) concludes that NGOization is a strategic response to democratization. It has brought benefits as some feminist NGOs, together with the global feminist lobby, have successfully pressured newly democratic Latin American governments for gender reforms. But at the same time their ability to advocate has been undermined by some of the other consequences of NGOization such as their increasing distance from grass-roots organizations.

It has also been argued that the effectiveness of feminist movements was sometimes compromised as key activists went into various different state institutions such as the legislature, the government, and the bureaucracy, particularly if a new women's ministry was established, and the new government was relatively sympathetic to feminism. This migration can have negative consequences for the organizational capacity of women's movements. Some feminists claimed that the Chilean movement was 'beheaded' by the influx of feminists into different parts of the state such as SERNAM, the state women's machinery, set up by the incoming Concertación government (Schild 1994). But this view is not universally accepted. Franceschet (2003) for example argues that SERNAM has provided women's movements with new opportunities and resources. In El Salvador some feminist organizations such as Las Melidas (MAM) maintained their ties to the FMLN and the electoral arena in the post-transition period. As a result MAM had a limited but explicit presence in the legislature and according to Shayne (2004: 58) became the institutional anchor of the El Salvadorean feminist movement.

We can assess these arguments by looking at the fate of some of the groups that organized to put gender issues on the agenda of the transition prior to the founding elections. Both the women's Concertación in Chile and the WNC in South Africa had been set up to influence the later stages of the transition and the first elections and it was not envisaged that they would continue to exist afterwards. Both contained a large number of key women active within political parties as well as women's organizations and who subsequently entered the new government, SERNAM, or the legislature. Three of the seven women elected to the Chilean legislature had been prominent members of the women's Concertación.

The women's Concertación faded away and although an attempt was made to organize around the 1993 legislative elections, it was not very effective.

Following the success of the WNC in South Africa, many activists assumed that it would continue as the basis of a national women's movement even though its original brief had been more limited. A debate about the WNC's future ensued at the conference to ratify the Women's Charter for Effective Equality (Kemp et al. 1995: 153–4). A number of women's organizations wanted it to continue as an autonomous structure with a lobbying role to ensure that the formal commitments to gender equality were translated into action. After some heated debate, it was decided that no woman who represented a political party could have a leadership role in the WNC. Inevitably, given the numbers of activist women who were moving into parliament and government, the WNC lost a tier of experienced leaders with an immediate effect on its capacity. This decision has been seen as a tactical error by many feminists.[13] But others argue that the virtual withdrawal of the ANCWL from the organization also reduced its ability to function effectively (Hassim 2002b: 727). Therefore although the WNC continued to exist, it was only a shadow of its former self and could no longer command the support of most women's organizations. A key question is therefore not only how far different movements interacted with the state and the electoral system but the ways in which the nature of the polity affects women's movements interaction with it.

❖ CONCLUSIONS

We have seen huge variations in the levels and kinds of women's mobilization during the different stages of various kinds of transition. It was very hard for autonomous women's organizations of any sort to emerge under state socialism. It was also difficult for women's movements to emerge in the post-transition period where they had not already existed. There has subsequently been relatively low levels of women's organizing in the ex state socialist polities compared to many ex-authoritarian ones. However, levels do vary between the cases, with Poland exhibiting the highest levels of activity, in part a result of the longer traditions of civil society organizing and of the spur provided by the serious immediate threats to existing gender rights. NGOs, often supported by external donors keen to foster the development of a vibrant civil society, have been the primary form of organization with groups sometimes forming conjunctural alliances around particular issues. But these organizations have not had much apparent success at articulating gender issues.

In contrast, a range of women's movements emerged under different authoritarian regimes. Many played an important role in the opposition to dictatorship and some also articulated gender issues effectively. But there are few examples of women's organizations, led by feminist activists sometimes with strong links to political parties, coming together to influence the transition and even then their efforts had varying degrees of success. In the post-transition period many pre-existing women's organizations that played an important role prior to the new era of electoral politics, moved away from their previous *movimientista* approach of mass rallies and demonstrations. In part they could no longer mobilize the numbers and in part their activities now took different forms (Craske 2000). How far this constitutes a demobilization is contested but undoubtedly activity levels declined as activists either withdrew or changed their focus.

It is therefore difficult to draw overall conclusions about women's organizing in the post transition period. The implications of the NGOization of civil society, the new emphasis on service delivery and role of donor funding were different for different organizations. The international context also changed over the post-transition period. The high point of international women's organizing and international norm change reached by the mid-1990s was already accompanied by a backlash that led to a climate of retrenchment. Different movements responded differently to these changing conditions. The interaction between some women's organizations and the new polities increased. Some, often feminist, organizations chose integration while others—often human rights and popular movements—remained outside and became more marginal. But where governments were hostile to gender concerns or the polities were characterized by clientelism, corruption, personalism, or other characteristics associated with delegative democracy, many women's organizations were wary of too close a relationship.

It is also hard to judge the effectiveness of different women's organizations' efforts to influence the political process and improve women's descriptive and substantive representation at this point in the book. Organizations varied in the ways in which they framed gender issues and the extent to which they could articulate those issues and get them on the policy agenda. We cannot understand why some movements were more effective than others just by looking at movements and their activities in isolation. In these new conditions movements lose activists but they can also gain allies and sympathetic 'insiders' within the legislature, government, and parts of the bureaucracy such as SWMs. We also have to consider whether these new insiders can form alliances with movements outside the state and how far they maintain ties with movements that they have come from. It is therefore important to look at the roles that a range of actors—not just those in women's organizations—play in translating the articulation of gender issues and their positioning on policy agendas into positive gender outcomes, as women's movements on their own are unlikely to achieve change in the post-transition context. Particularly in the later stages of processes of transition we have to examine the electoral, state, and the constitutional/bureaucratic arenas before we can fully understand what happened to different women's organizations, their influence, and eventual policy outcomes. It is to the electoral arena that we now turn.

❖ NOTES

1 At the same time, writers on social movements have often said very little about democratization. This is, in part, because until recently many were primarily concerned with the first world and established liberal democracies.

2 Which also corresponds to Foley and Edwards's (1996) category of civil society one and Fine and Rai's (1997) category of civil society as concept.

3 FSAW was made up of the ethnically based bodies of the Congress Alliance. It therefore multiracial rather than non-racial (Walker 1982: 172).

4 Interview with Jirina Siklova, founder member of Charter 77. Interview Prague, November 2005.

5 The rapid, but also pacted, transition in the GDR stands out as a partial exception to this pattern as women did come together as women between the collapse of the old regime and the founding election. The range of women's groups that had emerged prior to demonstrations that provoked the collapse of the regime included the influential Women for Peace as well as some feminist organizations. A critical mass of women's organizations, which included feminists influenced by international feminism, existed prior to the regime's collapse. Key actors were then in a position to organize to influence the transition with the support of other women's organizations. These groups came together to influence the short-lived transition before the GDR was absorbed into West Germany (the parliament lasted from March to September 1990). When the Berlin Wall fell, some prominent feminists circulated a public letter demanding that women should participate in the transition process and just one month later 1,200 women from more than 60 women's organizations met in Berlin (Einhorn 1993, 2003). They formed the UFV, the Independent Women's Association. The UFV programme, produced in 1990, contained demands around reproductive rights, domestic violence and equal rights. One of its aims was also to get representation for women on the roundtable then being established. Despite resistance, they did gain some seats to represent women's issues but even then found it difficult to get heard (Schaeffer-Hegel 1992).

6 Interview with Maria Elena Valenzuela an academic, feminist activist, and later part of SERNAM, January 1996.

7 Interview with Jirina Siklova, Prague, November 2005.

8 Interview with Maria Adamik, one of the founder members, Budapest, September 2005.

9 Interviews with Hebe Bonafini, Presidenta of the Madres, Buenos Aires, June 1996; and Rosa Rosanblit, member of the Abuelas, Buenos Aires, June 1996.

10 Interview with Sola Sierra, Presidenta AFDD, Santiago, January 1996.

11 *The Guardian*, Monday, 15 November 2004.

12 Interview with Maruja Barrig, Lima, August 1996.

13 Interviews with Mavivi Manzini, Johannesburg, July 2003 and Pethu Serote, Cape Town, July 2003.

Part III ❖ The Electoral Arena

If the analysis of women's organizing is only the starting point of any gendered understanding of transitions to democracy and their outcomes, we must broaden our analysis to include formal institutional arenas. Using the discussion of the gendered nature of institutions like political parties and the state in Part I as a starting point, Part III will concentrate on the electoral arena. To determine the extent of women's participation in the electoral arena and its significance during transitions to democracy, we will analyse three major themes: the level of women's descriptive representation in the post-transition period which is often seen as the key indicator of women's overall role in electoral politics; the roles that women have played in the conventional political arena during various stages of transition; and the contribution that women active in conventional political arena have made to any improvements to women's descriptive and substantive representation. The purpose of this part of the book is therefore twofold: to explore the range of factors that influence levels of women's descriptive representation and the roles played by different women actors in the electoral arena. We saw in our discussion of the democratization and the gender and politics literatures that political parties and electoral systems are central to any analysis of the conventional political arena and our analysis will therefore focus on both.

Patterns of descriptive representation exhibit some marked differences in a range of post-transition contexts. The overall trend after the (re)establishment of competitive electoral politics was for the election of relatively few women initially, with slightly more in East Central Europe than Latin America and for levels to then increase gradually (see Table III.1). These figures mirror international trends. At the beginning of 2006 a global average of 16.3% of all members of parliament (MPs) were women, up from 9% in 1987 (IPU). Female representation in the parliaments of East Central Europe declined sharply after the collapse of state socialism. In crude numerical terms the founding elections brought a reduction from an average of about 33% female representation to only 8.8% in national legislatures in East Central Europe. The average figure for women's representation increased over the second and third post-communist elections to 10.7% and then to 13.7% of the total (Saxonberg 2000: 155). But this overall trend disguises some marked

Table III.1. Percentage of parliamentary seats in single or lower chamber occupied by women

	1990	1995	2000	2005
Argentina	6.7	25.2	26.5	36.2
Brazil	5.3	6.6	5.7	8.6
Chile	5.8	7.5	10.8	15.0
Czech Republic	10.0 (25.4)	10.0	15.0	17.0
El Salvador	— (12.0)	10.7	9.5	10.7
Hungary	7.3 (20.2)	11.4	8.3	9.1
Peru	6	10.8	20.0	18.3
Poland	13*	13.0	13.0	20.4
Russian Federation	— (33.0)	10.2	7.7	9.8
South Africa	— (3.6)	25.0	29.8	32.8

Sources: Inter-Parliamentary Union, United Nations Demographic, and Social Statistics, Millard 2004.

( ) figure in brackets is level prior to founding election.

*Only 35% of seats were contested (women formed 9.6% of those elected at the first fully competitive elections held in 1991).

variations not only between different countries but from election to election within countries. At the beginning of 2006 women's representation in the lower house in Poland had reached a post-transition peak of 20.4% and in the Czech republic it was 17.0%. However, in both Russia and Hungary it had declined to 9.8% in the former and 9.1% in the latter (down from 10.2% and 11.4%, respectively in 1997).

In Latin America very few women were elected to the representative bodies on the (re)establishment of competitive electoral politics. In 1987 women constituted only 5.3% of the parliament in Brazil and 5.6% in Peru. In 1991 women were only 5% of elected representatives in Chile and 6.7 % in Argentina and in 1994 only 9% in El Salvador. Again overall levels have increased over time. By the late 1990s women formed an average of 14% of the elected representatives in the region. But these figures also disguise wide variations. By early 2006 36.2% of representatives in the Argentine lower house were women (up from 27.6% in 1997), the equivalent figure was 18.3% in Peru (up from 10.8% in 1997), 15.0% in Chile (up from 7.5% in 1997), 10.7% in El Salvador (down from 15.5% in 1997) and 8.6% in Brazil (up from 6.6% in 1997). However, South Africa provides a contrast to this predominant pattern of representation. After the first non-racial election in 1994 women occupied 27% of all seats in the National Assembly a figure which had risen to 32.8% in 2006. Therefore women's representation reached the critical mass of 25% (as defined in Part I) in only two of our case study countries in the post-transition period.[1] In South Africa this figure was surpassed at the first election and has subsequently been maintained and in Argentina it was only reached in 1997. Most of our case study countries had low levels (10% or less) of women's representation at the founding election and these rose subsequently to lie somewhere within the moderate category (10–25%). But levels in three cases: Hungary, Russia, and Brazil were still at (or had returned to) low levels in early 2006.

What are the explanations for these patterns? Why are there significant variations? Do these patterns resemble competitive electoral politics in the established democracies or do transitions to democracy present different circumstances and opportunities? How far do different transition paths and the resulting institutional set-ups impact on the nature and levels of women's descriptive representation? In particular do transitions from state socialism and authoritarianism exhibit different trends? As we saw in Part I analyses of women's participation in conventional electoral politics have tended to focus on cultural, structural, and institutional factors in their search for explanations. Much of the literature on women's participation in established liberal democracies highlights the impact of different electoral rules and systems and the key role played by political parties in facilitating or blocking women's participation in all levels of conventional politics, arguing that the mechanisms of party politics reflect unequal gender relations. The choice of electoral system, political parties, and parties systems is also seen as important in determining the political outcomes of transitions to democracy in much of the democratization literature. Therefore, our starting point must be the role of electoral systems and political parties in the gender politics of transition.

There is not, as yet, a large body of gendered institutional research that focuses on outcomes in the electoral arena after transitions from authoritarianism or state socialism. Therefore data remain scarce. However, although still at an early stage, a gendered debate about electoral systems and political parties in transitions to democracy is beginning to emerge. Some feminist scholars have argued that the development of institutionalized party systems after transitions has negative consequences for women's representation and political activities. They claimed that party activity may impede the subsequent development of civil society and particularly women's groups, as democracies become consolidated (Nelson and Chowdhury 1994). Friedman (2000), for example, argues that over the course of Venezuela's two democratic transitions, institutions of interest representation such as political parties and state structures incorporated certain sectors on the basis of class interests, but that the same interests marginalized women. Centralized party structures act to marginalize women and highly institutionalized party systems that rely on political parties established prior to the authoritarian period tend to have the most demobilizing effects (Friedman 2000: 20).

However, there is no unanimity on this view of political parties. The recent work on East Central Europe takes a different focus. In a context where there was less women's organizing prior to the transition, it builds on the analyses of established democracies, particularly in Western Europe, and has begun to explore how far different types of parties and party systems are better or worse for women's representation (Matland and Montgomery 2003). Some analysts have argued that in post-transition East Central Europe institutionalized parties offer women some advantages in contrast to less institutionalized parties (Saxonberg 2000). And as we saw in Part I, many mainstream writers see the development of institutionalized party systems as key in the consolidation of electoral democracies. To assess the impact of institutionalized parties and parties systems on women's representation, we must disaggregate the various factors involved. We must consider not just the relationship between parties, women activists, and the numbers of women elected but also the impact of different party systems on women's organizing. We will then be in a better position to analyse the impact of different women actors in the conventional political arena on women's substantive representation and gender outcomes.

We will not look at non-democratic regimes in any great detail in this part of the book. Electoral arenas were either limited or curtailed completely and, apart from communist parties under state socialism, political parties rarely played significant roles and any meaningful political activity was often located in the kinds of oppositional movements that we have looked at in Part II. Therefore, after a brief discussion of regime breakdown and transition taken together in one section, we will focus primarily on the post-transition phase in the rest of Part III. But we do need to assess the significance of developments prior to the founding election as modes of transition vary. The speed at which political parties form or reform can also depend on how far the transition is gradual and pacted. In many cases negotiations over the nature of the institutional set-up take place as the transition develops and the women friendliness of those outcomes varies considerably. The type of the transition and the accompanying institutional legacies of non-democratic rule will therefore be an important component of any analysis of the role of institutions during the post-transition phase.

In this part of the book we also focus on those women actors who, once transitions were underway, chose integration with formal institutions such as political parties, examining their relationship with the institutions they were involved in. After a brief discussion of women's roles in the conventional political arena in non-democratic regimes, our analysis of the transition and post-transition phases will ask two questions. First, what roles do women activists play within the electoral arena, particularly in political parties as the main institutions that channel participation? Second—an issue which comes to the fore in the post-transition phase—what are the implications of institutional choices, such as the nature of the electoral system—for women activists and for levels of women's representation overall? We can then draw some conclusions about the implications of different kinds of party systems and electoral systems for women's representation and the extent to which the activities of key women actors, particularly feminists, can make a difference with regard to measures to increase women's descriptive and substantive representation in the post-transition phase.

❖ NON-DEMOCRATIC REGIMES

In keeping with their largely traditional notions about women's roles, most authoritarian regimes did not have meaningful participation by women in political institutions whether in governments or, if they existed in any form, legislatures. Many military regimes attempted to abolish 'politics', closing down congresses and banning or severely restricting the activities of political parties, often blaming civilian politicians for the problems that had led them to intervene. Although military regimes varied in the degree to which power was institutionalized, most military governments consisted of both military personnel and civilian technocrats. The senior-most levels of military establishments unsurprisingly contained no women and there were few women among the ranks of the civilian technocrats. In Chile, women were excluded from membership of the legislative council as this was reserved for commanders-in-chief of the armed forces; during the 16 years that the Pinochet regime was in power, only two women became ministers of state (Valenzuela 1991: 163). However, Pinochet did appoint a substantial number of women as mayors at the local level as part of the reorganization of local government. A similar pattern predominated under the apartheid regime in South Africa. From 1948 the racially exclusive white parliament was controlled by the National Party after all other groups had been disenfranchised. White women had been granted the vote in 1930 but very few ever became MPs. In the last whites-only election in 1989 the proportion of women MPs reached 3.6% (up from only 2.4% in 1987) (Ballington 1998). There was very little opposition to the apartheid government within parliament. However, one of the best-known figures was Helen Suzman, a long-standing Johannesburg MP who used her position in parliament to raise questions about detentions and other abuses.

In contrast, state socialist regimes professed a commitment to women's equality in the public sphere. They also had far more institutional trappings than the majority of authoritarian regimes. In addition to mobilizing women in separate women's organizations controlled by the ruling communist parties, efforts were made to ensure that 'representative' bodies also contained women as their composition was supposed to mirror wider society. Loose quotas, in the form of guidelines on composition, were employed and as we have seen on the eve of the collapse of state socialism women made up an average of 33% of the representatives. These figures varied across states. In 1984 women comprised 32.8% of deputies in the Supreme Soviet and 49.5% of the deputies in the parliaments of the union republics and the autonomous republics of the USSR after the 1980 elections. In Eastern Europe the figures were somewhat lower—21% and 20.2% in Poland and Hungary in 1985 and 25.4% in Czechoslovakia (Millard and Popescu 2001).

THE ELECTORAL ARENA ❖

However, the claims of equality and quota systems that gave women considerable numerical representation under state socialism were often important for symbolic purposes only. Such women were known as 'milkmaid' politicians and had different backgrounds and educational levels to the male politicians. They participated in bodies that played a predominantly ceremonial role 'rubberstamping' legislation initiated by the party-state leadership. Indeed Matynia (2003) citing Malgorzata Fuszara, claims that in Poland there is evidence of a drop in women's representation during times of political thaw when parliament gained a greater degree of power. In October 1956 the percentage of female parliamentarians dropped from 17 to only 4%. Wolchik (1998: 156) also argues that despite the obligation on all to be politically active, in Czechoslovakia a lower level of participation was tolerated from women than from men in comparable positions. Frances Millard (2004) offers a less dismissive analysis, arguing that participation in these bodies should not be considered entirely worthless because, however ritualistic the formal sessions, they did give women some experience in the public domain and because, given the high official status accorded to women's participation, the symbolic dimension also had some importance.

Although women had quite high levels of representation in the legislatures, power and decision-making lay elsewhere in the upper echelons of the communist parties. There were few women in the top party decision-making ranks of the party. In Czechoslovakia, only 10.7% of members of the Central Committee were women in the mid 1970s and they were rarely members of the politburo or the presidium (cabinet) (Wolchik 1979). While women made up 35% of ordinary members of the Sozialistische Einheitspartei Deutschlands (SED) in the GDR, women comprised only 13% of the central committee members in 1986 and no woman had ever entered the politbuto (Einhorn 1992). Those women who did enter high office were often segregated into the 'less important and gender stereotyped fields of healthcare, education or culture' (Fodor 2004). Therefore, despite the claims of equality, few women were in the political elites at the time of the breakdown of state socialism. Nor were there many women in positions of power within the regimes in any of our cases studies of authoritarian rule.

❖ THE BREAKDOWN AND TRANSITION

We will examine the breakdown and transition in one section as it is often hard to separate the key events in the (re)creation of the conventional political arena occurring during the breakdown from those occurring during the transition. It is also not possible to generalize about the degree to which the initiative lay within the conventional political arena during the breakdown of non-democratic regimes and any subsequent transition processes. It depended on the type of transition and also on the nature of the arena itself. In rapid transitions—both from

❖ THE ELECTORAL ARENA

authoritarianism and state socialism—the breakdown of the non-democratic regime and the transition happened in quick succession or even simultaneously. As a result there was little time for political parties to (re)form and play a significant role in the ongoing processes. In contrast during longer drawn-out transitions, a gradual liberalization facilitated the (re)emergence of some political actors as important players during the transition itself or even prior to it. Political parties had more time to (re)constitute themselves and play a potentially significant role in any negotiations that might take place as part of a pacted transition. We also need to differentiate between those transitions in which conventional political parties were involved and those in which actors from organizations outside the conventional political arena—such as broad opposition fronts like Solidarity in Poland and Civic Forum in Czechoslovakia or revolutionary organizations like the ANC or FMLN—were important players. These groupings were often in the process of transforming themselves into political parties. All these configurations exhibit differences in terms of the interaction between women actors and political institutions.

Prior to the transitions from state socialism virtually no organizations had been allowed to exist that were not sanctioned by or linked to the ruling party. However there were signs of pluralism within some communist parties. Party factionalism and a reformist wing were evident in both Poland and Hungary by the late 1980s (Lewis 2000: 8). But there was no formal political opposition; alternative parties were not permitted and did not even function clandestinely. Therefore fully formed pluralist political parties could not play a key role within the first phase of the transitions from state socialism. As we have seen, despite the attempts of the communist parties to minimize dissent, opposition to the regimes did emerge. Some of these opposition groups and movements became important actors in the transitions, participating in any negotiations to determine the new institutional structures and forming the nucleus of a number of the political parties that contested the founding elections.

Relatively drawn-out pacted transitions took place first in Poland and then in Hungary, before the more rapid transition in Czechoslovakia. In Poland negotiations between the regime and Solidarity began after the regime had lost a referendum in 1987 and Solidarity had launched a wave of strikes in 1988. The process set in motion a domino effect that contributed to the collapse of state socialism in other parts of East Central Europe (Elster et al. 1998: 65). There is some evidence that after the liberalization of 1987 women did not enter into prominent leadership positions as Solidarity became more formalized, if not actually legal. Women formed only 1% of round-table negotiators—only one sat at the round-table (on the Solidarity side) and only five women took part in the separate sub-tables (four of these were on the Solidarity side) (Matynia 2003).[2] And no women were present at the informal negotiations in which all the final decisions were taken. Little space for raising gender issues existed and the few actors who wanted to do so

THE ELECTORAL ARENA ❖

did not have the capability. As a result of these negotiations in which Solidarity had underestimated its strength, transitional power-sharing elections were agreed upon in which only 35% of seats would be contested. Women's representation dropped from 20 to 13% in the elections of June 1989 as Solidarity won all the contested seats (Matynia 2001). Solidarity continued to dominate the political scene until the first fully free elections that mark the end of the transition were held in the autumn of 1991.

The Hungarian transition that followed swiftly afterwards emerged from its pattern of evolutionary change. Lewis (2000) claims that the reformist Hungarian communist party put it in motion before it was forced into it. Opposition groupings were already active. Indeed the Hungarian Democratic Forum (HDF), established in 1987 included some representatives of the reformist wing of the ruling party as well as alternative opposition groups and was characterized by Linz and Stepan (1996: 302) as 'populist and somewhat rural and traditional and nationalist intellectuals'. The League of Young Democrats (FIDESZ), a more formally organized political group, emerged the next year. Women did play a significant role in founding this movement of young liberal minded intellectuals and five women were part of its Presidium (a ruling body) during this period (Montgomery and Ilonski 2003: 115). But according to Montgomery and Ilonski (2003: 118) its transformation into a political party changed its goals and leadership. As a result the 'café-intellectual wing' that included important several women was eventually expunged, as it moved to the right. A loose alliance of urban and socially liberal organizations such as the greens, independent worker, and student organizations also coalesced into the Alliance of Free Democrats (AFD).

The roundtable talks, containing genuine negotiation, began in March 1989 and resulted in multiparty elections in March 1990 (Elster et al. 1998). Seven opposition groupings participated in the talks—four of which were 'historic' parties that pre-dated state socialism and had reformed, such as the Independent Smallholders party, together with the three new ones—the HDF, FIDESZ, and AFD. As few women actors played an important role in the major Hungarian opposition groups particularly the HDF, few women participated (and not as feminists) in the roundtable negotiations that began in 1989 and gender issues certainly did not figure in them.[3] The subsequent elections were contested by parties that had grown out of these pre-existing political organizations. They were won by the HDF that gained 25% of the vote and 43% of the seats. Women's representation fell to 7% as the parties had nominated few women candidates.

The very rapid transition in Czechoslovakia was not negotiated (Linz and Stepan 1996). As we saw in Part II, the hardline regime collapsed very quickly after ten days of demonstrations and the roundtable negotiations that followed were, according to Elster et al. (1998: 65), the unilateral imposition of terms by a victorious opposition that could have got more but for the fact that they overestimated the strength of the party regime and its level of support. The elections held in June 1990 were won by Civic Forum, the broad opposition front that had participated in the negotiations, with 46% of the vote. But, unlike Solidarity, Civic Forum had only been founded in November 1989 and had little chance to build up grass-roots support or an organizational structure (Lewis 2000). Women were active in Civic Forum but as Wolchik (1998: 159) notes, they had predominantly secondary service rather than policymaking roles. The women involved were also unlikely to see themselves as feminists. Siklova (1993: 77) claims that many women dissidents did not want to go on to play prominent roles in the newly reconstituted conventional political arena but instead wanted to return to their previous lives from which they had been excluded for political reasons. As a result the constitutional outcome of transition was decided without the input of women organized as women and women formed only 10% of those elected.

Therefore there were few women in high positions in either the communist party elites or in any existing opposition movements in any of our case study countries at the time of the collapse of state socialism. Women's presence in the often anti-feminist opposition continued as the transitions progressed, whether they were rapid or slower and pacted. But few women dissidents made the transition to high-level participation in the newly constituted political parties. And those women who were active in the newly formed political parties rarely wanted to press gender issues or raise the question of ensuring women's political representation as 'women's claims to equal rights were associated with the communist past and therefore suspect' (Jaquette and Wolchik 1998a: 7). The opposition groupings themselves did not feel that they had to appeal to women voters on the basis of a progressive gender agenda.

In contrast, the reconstitution of the conventional political arena often began during, or even prior to, transitions from authoritarianism, even if the political initiative lay outside a largely inoperative conventional political arena. But the speed of these events and the degree to which the process was controlled by the non-democratic regime varied from case to case. We will look first at our three Latin American military regimes. In Brazil and Chile political institutions and parties began to reform as part of process that was tightly controlled by the authoritarian governments that restricted which parties could operate and in what ways. Left-wing and working-class parties frequently experienced continuing restrictions, while parties of the centre and right were allowed the greatest freedom of action. This period of transition was marked by the decision of some political parties, often those representing the middle classes and centre of the political spectrum, to form pacts with the military and initiate a negotiated transition.

In Chile, the political parties of the centre and 'renovated' left decided that the Pinochet regime would not be removed through popular mobilization but

THE ELECTORAL ARENA ❖

through reaching agreements with the military (Petras and Leiva 1988). Those groups and parties (primarily on the far left) who opted for 'ruptura', namely a more violent overthrow of the regime based on social mobilization, rather than *negociación*, found themselves increasingly outside the process of negotiated transition. In the more rapid 'crisis' transition in Argentina the military withdrew in the midst of economic crisis and military defeat. An exit under these circumstances constrained the influence of the armed forces over the terms of transition. As a result the Argentine transition has been characterized as an unpacted and 'free' transition. The political parties could refuse the overtures of the military and in which as a consequence, few restrictions were placed on the political system.

In the face of these new conditions of transition, some women activists decided to move into conventional structures like political parties to change them from within (Sternbach et al. 1992). This participation in institutional politics was particularly apparent in the more drawn-out negotiated transitions in Brazil and Chile. Feminists largely concentrated their efforts in the parties of the left and centre. During this period, women already active within the opposition political parties, the *'políticas'*—political activists, primarily left wing who did not see themselves as feminists—were joined by feminists who now believed that the way forward could not lie simply in maintaining autonomous feminist movements as these alone were not enough in the changed circumstances (Fisher 1993). The old antagonism between *feministas* and *políticas* was somewhat reduced in this period, and indeed the distinctions between the two became increasingly blurred as *políticas* became more sympathetic to ideas associated with feminism (Serrano 1990).

In Chile, following their strategic decision to enter the unfolding political process in the mid 1980s—for example by participating in the Asamblea de la Civilidad in 1986—many feminists worked in the political parties of the centre and left, campaigning for increased influence for women within the party structures (Molina and Serrano 1988, Valenzuela 1990). Women in one sector of the Partido Socialista (PS) organized a women's section: the Federación de Mujeres Socialistas (FMS). In 1981–2 many Brazilian feminists saw the newly formed Workers Party (PT) as the potential expression of social movements and became active inside the party (Alvarez 1990a). Formed in 1979, the PT had emerged not just from the 'new unionism', but also from the social movements, including women's movements, active in and around Sao Paulo (Keck 1992). Therefore it was heralded as one way in which the popular sectors could have some representation in institutional politics overcoming the dilemmas of autonomy versus integration and it was also expected to have higher levels of women's representation. In the 1980s, women—particularly those feminists who believed that electoral politics was the way to achieve gains for women—also played an active role in the Brazilian opposition party Partido do Movimento Democrático (PMBD) (Alvarez 1994). This migration resulted in the establishment of overtly feminist women's organizations such

❖ THE ELECTORAL ARENA

as the PMDB's Grupo de Estudos da Mulher and the PT's Comissao de Mulheres that struggled with male party leaderships to get them to endorse gender issues that had been politicized by women's movements over the previous decade (Alvarez 1990*a*).

There is some evidence that in the more fluid conditions of the transition (compared to more 'normal' periods of competitive electoral politics) women activists were able to capitalize on the relatively high profile achieved by women's organizing during the breakdown of authoritarianism. Many political parties, particularly those that had been in opposition to military rule, were keen to show support for women's anti-authoritarian activities and appear 'modern'. As a consequence of the activities of FMS, in the aftermath of the 1988 plebiscite the Chilean umbrella left grouping Partido por la Democracia (PPD) and the PS introduced quotas for internal party bodies of 20% in the PPD and 25% in the PS. But these did not extend to candidate selection for the upcoming elections. In Brazil, in both the PMDB and the PT, feminists had some success in raising a number of gender demands (but not the decriminalization of abortion). Although some self-avowed feminists were candidates in the elections of 1982, it was the PDS, the government party that fielded the largest number of women candidates of any party overall (Alvarez 1990*a*).

Women activists within parties also experienced many of the problems common to more normal periods of political activity. During the 1980s women activists found it hard to exert any influence within the PT and the party continued to be male dominated with few women in positions of power. In her analysis of PT activities at the neighbourhood level, Caldeira (1986) found that the core organizers were men and women were reluctant to get involved as they felt that the party was inhospitable to them. And despite the gains they had achieved, Chilean women activists were disappointed with women's continued lack of influence on the unfolding political process and the selection of very few women candidates for the forthcoming elections. As a result, we saw in Part II that women active in the parties of the centre–left coalition, the Concertación, together with independent feminists, formed the Concertación de Mujeres por la Democracia to try to advance women's interests.

In the somewhat different cases of El Salvador and South Africa, neither of the main opposition groupings that took part in the negotiated settlements that resulted from the insurgent transitions was a conventional political party at the time. Women in both the ANC and the FMLN played an active role and attempted to impact on the unfolding processes but with differing results. The FMLN had been formed in 1980 in El Salvador when the five existing left-wing revolutionary groups came together in the face of the escalating conflict and repression from the civilian–military alliance that ruled in the 1970s. After its declaration of war, the FMLN launched a rather premature and unsuccessful 'final offensive' in 1981 and civil war continued for another decade until the Peace Accords were signed in January 1992. A high number of women participated as combatants, forming between 27 and 34% of the five different armies and 36.6% of the polit-ical cadres within the different organizations that made up the FMLN (Shayne 2004: 35). Luciak (2001) cites the relatively large proportion of women among the military leadership (22%). But other commentators point to the glass ceiling that only predominantly middle-class educated women could break through, and even then not as feminists (Shayne 2004: 42). As we saw in Part II, the different groups that comprised the FMLN established a second generation of auxiliary women's organizations after the earlier party-linked women's organizations had been repressed, but for primarily pragmatic and instrumental reasons rather than from a great commitment to feminism.

As a result women's rights were not a central part of the peace negotiations or written into the Accords even though three high-ranking women commanders—Nidia Díaz, Lorena Peña, and Ana Guadalupe Martínez—took part in them (Luciak 1999). None of them was an advocate for women's rights at that time and one, Lorena Peña subsequently confirmed to Ilija Luciak (2004) that women's issues did not come up in the negotiations. Indeed the limited initiatives that did exist were ignored by the FMLN negotiators. An executive director of AMS claimed that the negotiators did not even read a document submitted by the women's groups within the FMLN that argued for example that women should benefit from land distribution. As we saw in Part II, as a consequence Mujeres 94 was formed to try to influence the political parties in the run-up to the elections of 1994.

At the same time as many women within the women's organizations tied to the FMLN became increasingly feminist and autonomous, some of the women who remained within the FMLN after it became a political party in 1992 also challenged the leadership for the first time after the Accords were signed. And in the face of some opposition from within the FMLN a national women's secretariat was formed in 1993. However, in contrast to its previous position as a revolu-tionary organization when it made very few references to women's emancipation, the programme of the new party did contain a statement about women's rights (Luciak 1999: 55). But the FMLN hierarchy remained somewhat hostile to separate women's activities and projects and was reluctant to give them any funding. There-fore, although FMLN leaders were forced to pay more attention to a gender agenda during the transition period and particularly during the election campaign, many women activists still felt that they had to form an autonomous movement.

South African women organizing within the ANC had more success. After being forced into exile as a consequence of the increased repression in the 1960s, the ANC had created an armed wing, Umkhonto we Sizwe (MK) and women formed 20% of its cadres. It had also adopted the more radical rhetoric of national liberation, adding another strand to its charterist rights-based doctrine that was dominant in the 1950s. As a national liberation movement the ANC also had

highly organized structures outside South Africa with complex rules and procedures. Women activists had always played important roles within the ANC and
MK.

At the beginning of the 1980s the newly formed ANC women's section had
declared that the struggle against apartheid was their primary objective amid a
belief that feminism was a white women's concern (Geisler 2000: 605). However,
by the end of the decade, resistance to feminism within the ANC Women's Section
had broken down. ANC women activists in exile, often influenced by women's
organizing within South Africa, international feminism and the disappointing
experience of other national liberation movements, had begun to agitate for
different understanding of gender issues within the ANC (Hassim 2002a: 223).
ANC women activists managed to reconcile the more 'motherist' agenda of older
women activists with the new concerns of younger women (Geisler 2004). At
conferences and workshops, ANC women activists raised the issues of women's
low representation (only 3 of the 35 members of the National Executive Council
(NEC) were women in the late 1980s) and the need for new understandings
of the relationship between national liberation and women's liberation, openly
questioning the assumption that the first would automatically lead to the second
(Albertyn 1994: 47).

By 1990 the ANC itself had started to take gender issues seriously as a result of
these campaigns and the actions of women in the wider struggle against apartheid.
In 1989 the ANC's constitutional guidelines included gender equality although
they did disappoint a number of feminists (Geisler 2000: 611). And ANC women
realized that on their own they did not have sufficient power or influence to
achieve their goals. As we saw in Part II, ANC women activists in exile came
together with internal activists at the Malibongwe conference in January 1990
that was convened by the ANC women's section. It discussed how to achieve gender equality in the final constitution, women's political representation, national
women's machineries, as well as the need for a national women's movement. It
recognized that national liberation did not necessarily guarantee the liberation of
women. The conference also envisaged that ANC women activists would play a
key role in the formation of a national women's movement within South Africa
(Meintjes 1998).

The South African transition from white minority rule to black majority rule
began just two weeks after the Malibongwe Conference with the unbanning of the
ANC and other prescribed organizations in February 1990. The ANC, which until
then had been a liberation movement, now had to begin to reconstitute itself as
the major opposition political party. The nature of the ANC as a left-wing party
committed to equality on the basis of citizenship for all made it easier for feminists
within it to get issues incorporated into ANC policy and get ANC support with
the MPNP negotiations. Feminists continued to be active within the ANC itself.
The Malibongwe resolutions were taken to the ANC executive which issued a

THE ELECTORAL ARENA ❖

policy statement on the emancipation of women in South Africa in May 1990 that acknowledged that women's emancipation had to be addressed in its own right (Cock 1997: 77). The leadership had therefore publicly accepted the legitimacy of a 'gender agenda' that included positive action to increase the number of women in important positions within the ANC, the recreation of the ANCWL (defunct since the 1960s), a mass women's movement, and a campaign for a charter of women's rights that 'will elaborate and reinforce our new constitution'.[4]

Despite their low levels of representation within the ANC power structures, many women activists saw a strong women's section as a vehicle to build on some of the gains of the 1980s. As part of the ANC's transformation into a political party, ANCWL was relaunched in August 1990 as an autonomous organization. It absorbed women activists within South Africa as well as many returning women exiles who were keen to ensure that it would maintain some independence and not become like other women's leagues (Geisler 2004). It could also bridge the differences between older activists and younger feminists and was able to have a significant impact. However, its position within the ANC was also somewhat uncertain. Some feminist commentators at the time pointed to a lack of support and resources (Meintjes 1990). Its first attempt to get the ANC to adopt quotas (30% women in the NEC) ended in defeat at the 48th ANC congress held in July 1991 (Meintjes 1998: 78). This defeat was seen as a strategic failure by key women activists and further evidence that on its own, the ANCWL could not successfully pressure the ANC. They were determined not to let it happen again. It reinforced the conviction of many ANC activists of the need for a strong organized presence for women outside the ANC as well as for allies in key places within the ANC hierarchy. A 33% quota did go through in 1993 at the behest of the NEC in the run-up to the 1994 elections and was used for candidate selection. The ANCWL activists were also instrumental in arguing that gender issues should be integrated into all ANC policy including the Reconstruction and Development Programme (RDP) that served as its election manifesto (Albertyn et al. 1999: 14).

As we saw in Part II, women activists within the ANC played a central role in efforts to ensure that women were not excluded from the two rounds of formal multiparty negotiations about the future of South Africa that formed the core of the transition. From early on ANC women as well as other women activists had felt that an independent women's voice was needed to ensure that women's issues were addressed in the negotiations process (Meintjes 1998: 78). But initially women were excluded from the negotiating teams and only 23 of the 400 delegates to the CODESA were women. After an outcry, women activists achieved a (largely symbolic) victory in 1992 after the ANCWL pressured the ANC to support the proposal for the establishment of a multiparty Gender Advisory Committee (GAC) (Geisler 2004). It was set up to monitor the negotiations and make recommendations just as CODESA collapsed amid political violence.

❖ THE ELECTORAL ARENA

Fear of exclusion from the transition was also a catalyst for the formation of the broadly based multiracial WNC (discussed in Part II) and set up on the initiative of the ANCWL. It included party women's sections and many ANC activists among its diverse range of constituent organizations. However even though it had close ties with the ANCWL, it was not controlled by it; the ANCWL could not be hegemonic within the WNC or the wider women's movement because of its weak links to internal women's organizations. In 1993, the second round of the MPNP negotiations commenced and, after pressure from the WNC and women activists in the political parties, there was one women's delegate on each political delegation and technical committee. ANC women also participated in the cross-party women's caucus that existed among women delegates from the different political parties and devised ways in alliance with women (legal) academics and activists to make strategic interventions into the negotiations that none could have made on their own. As a result a number of important gains in the legal and constitutional arenas were consolidated in the post-transition period.

South Africa and El Salvador therefore exhibit some important differences from each other. In El Salvador as women activists became increasingly feminist in orientation, they felt that they had to detach themselves from the FMLN and create an autonomous movement. But women organized as women pressing gender demands were unable to exert much influence over the transition processes or the FMLN itself. In South Africa some feminist organizations already existed outside the ANC by the time the transition began and increasingly feminist ANC women could work together with them both inside and outside the ANC without feeling that they had to detach themselves from it. As a result they had more impact over those processes of transition.

A range of patterns—both in terms of the extent to which political parties and other formal political institutions were involved in transitions and the extent to which women were active within any of these parties or institutions—emerged during the breakdown and transition phases. On the whole, organized political parties did not play a significant role in transitions from state socialism and women organized as women pressing gender claims did not influence any of the important opposition groupings. Nor did groups contesting the founding elections feel that they had to appeal to women voters with a progressive gender agenda. In some transitions from authoritarianism, particularly in some of the more drawn-out and pacted transitions, political parties played an important part. Women, organized as women, often as feminists, and sometimes from within women's sections, were active in some parties, particularly in those of the centre and centre left. Often they could capitalize on women's oppositional roles under authoritarianism with parties who were keen to woo women voters and to demonstrate how modern and democratic they were. But although organized women attempted to influence some of the political parties that were important political players during the transition, on the whole they did not influence any negotiations that took place between the outgoing non-democratic regime and the opposition. The only instance where women, organized as women, influenced not only the dominant opposition groupings from within but also the actual negotiations was in South Africa.

We can now see that the patterns of female representation that resulted from the founding elections were to be expected. In South Africa, the ANC won a landslide victory, gaining 252 of the 400 seats in the national assembly. Largely as a result of their quota, 27.7% of those new MPs were women. In contrast, the unofficial communist quotas that had existed for women disappeared in the aftermath of the transitions from state socialism in East Central Europe. The first fully competitive multiparty elections were also won by opposition groupings—Solidarity in Poland, Civic Forum in Czechoslovakia, and a conservative coalition led by the HDF in Hungary. None felt the need to field large numbers of women candidates and as a result only 9.6% of Polish, 7.3% of Hungarian, and 10.0% of Czechoslovakian legislators were women. Parties opposed to the non-democratic regime were elected in Argentina (the Unión Civica Radical (UCR)) and Chile (Concertación) and, despite the actions of organized women in Chile and the keenness of political parties like the UCR to attract women voters, very few women candidates were fielded or elected. As a result levels of women's representation were low. In Chile fewer women were elected in 1989 than under the Allende government in power prior to the military coup in 1973. In El Salvador the right wing ARENA party defeated the FMLN and as a result only 9 (10.7%) of the 84 legislators elected were women. It now remains for us to trace what happened to women's participation in the conventional political arena in the period after the founding elections and to consider the most convincing explanations for the patterns that we see.

❖ POST-TRANSITION

Levels of women's representation vary considerably in the post-transition period and these variations do not straightforwardly correspond to transitions from either authoritarianism or state socialism or the outcomes of those transitions whether electoral democracy or the 'grey zone'. In 2004 both Brazil and Hungary had low levels of women's representation at the same time as Poland and Argentina had much higher levels. In 2005 all of our eight case study countries were considered to be free by Freedom House and had improved their standing in terms of political rights and civil liberties over the previous decade (see Table III.2).[5] Of our two comparator cases, Peru had also improved its rating by 2005, moving from the 'grey zone' of a Partly Free rating to a Free rating in 2001. Russia, however, had moved out of the 'grey zone' to be classified as 'Not Free' in 2004 for the first time since its transition. There is no obvious correlation between

Table III.2. Freedom house ratings

Countries electoral system (2003)		Political rights (1994)	Civil rights (1994)	Overall freedom rating (1994)	Political rights (1999)	Civil rights (1999)	Overall freedom rating (1999)	Political rights (2005)	Civil rights (2005)	Overall freedom rating (2005)
Argentina	Pres/Parl Democ Fed	2	3	Free	2	3	Free	2	2	Free
Brazil	Pres/Parl Democ Fed	2	4	Partly free	3	4	Partly free	2	3	Free
Chile	Pres/Parl Democ	2	2	Free	2	2	Free	1	1	Free
Czech	Republic Parl Democ	1	2	Free	1	2	Free	1	1	Free
El Salvador	Pres/Parl Democ	3	3	Partly free	2	3	Free	2	3	Free
Hungary	Parl Democ	1	2	Free	1	2	Free	1	1	Free
Peru	Pres/Parl Democ	5	4	Partly free	5	4	Partly free	2	3	Free
Poland	Pres/Parl Democ	2	2	Free	1	2	Free	1	1	Free
Russia	Pres/Parl Democ	3	4	Partly free	4	5	Partly free	6	5	Not free
South Africa	Pres/Parl Democ	2	3	Free	1	2	Free	1	2	Free

Source: Freedom House (www.freedomhouse.com).

Key:

Pres/Parl Democ Presidential/Parliamentary Democracy
Parl Democ Parliamentary Democracy
Fed Federal System

Freedom House ratings and levels of women's representation. Russia and Hungary, countries at opposite ends of the freedom ratings both had similarly low levels of women's representation at the same time as Chile and South Africa—countries with similar freedom ratings—had significantly different levels of women's representation. Without any obvious correlations between the nature of the previous non-democratic regime or the overall outcome of the transition and levels of women's representation, we need to examine all our case studies together, looking in turn at the different factors that might give us more convincing explanations for the variations in our range of cases.

Some political scientists have argued that cultural and structural factors are key in the analysis of representation in polities other than advanced industrial democracies. Matland's study (1998: 119) of 16 less developed country (LDC) democracies (including Argentina, Peru, Brazil and El Salvador) and 24 advanced industrial democracies concluded that none of the conditions affecting women's representation in the developed world appear to have a significant effect on the LDC democracies as particular idiosyncratic conditions within each country are more important. He (1998) argued that a certain level of development is necessary for the institutional variables that are important in advanced industrialized democracies to take effect. A number of political scientists working on non-first world areas have taken issue with this argument that low levels of women's representation outside the 'advanced industrial democracies' are due to low levels of development or 'traditional' attitudes such as 'machismo' in Latin America—citing for example the low levels of female representation in the United States that cannot be attributed to a lack of women in professional employment.

Both Mala Htun (2001) and Frances Millard (2004) discussing post-transition polities in Latin America and East Central Europe respectively, argue that analyses need to be more sophisticated as notions of 'culture' and 'development' are often too crude and imprecise to be explanatory variables. It is necessary to understand how 'culture' is mediated, as in Latin America opinion surveys show positive attitudes to women's leadership; and if Argentina is omitted, there is no obvious relationship between economic development and women's representation. Institutional factors therefore need to be accorded more significance. Indeed Htun (2001) argues that institutional and party variables are the most important factors in Latin America. There is no clear correlation between level of development as evidenced by GDP per capita and women's representation in our case study countries. Of all our case study countries, South Africa has one of the highest levels of representation and one of the lowest levels of GDP per capita at the same time as Hungary has a relatively high level of per capita GDP but a low level of representation. Therefore, to explain the patterns of women's representation in post-transition polities described on page 94, we will utilize some of the hypotheses that have been developed for the analysis of long-standing democracies and structure our discussion around institutional factors dividing them into two main components: electoral rules and structures and political parties.

❖ Electoral Rules

How far can these variations in levels of women's representation be accounted for by differing electoral rules? Much of the existing work on women's representation in post-transition contexts has sought to test the received wisdom derived from the experience of the developed world where it is proposed that, in the absence of effective and appropriate electoral quotas, systems organized around proportional representation (PR) with high district magnitude, high electoral thresholds, and closed party lists facilitate higher levels of female representation. In a single member district (SMD)/first past the post system (FPTP) where only one candidate can win, selectors will play safe in their choice of candidate and this will work against women. In contrast in a context where a large number of candidates are elected from any constituency (high district magnitude), selectors are more likely to engage in 'ticket balancing'. They will put forward a range of candidates (e.g. varying in gender, race, and age) in order to appeal to the largest number of voters. Higher electoral thresholds are also favourable to women, as a system which allows a large number of parties (high party fragmentation) to each get a very small number of seats, will result in the bulk of those representatives being men as they are more likely to be at the top of party lists. Finally, closed party lists are seen as helping women candidates as they enhance the control of party machines over candidate selection and every candidate's position on the list is determined by the list selectors. In contrast an open list system can allow the electorate to exercise a bias against female candidates by voting preferentially for men, enabling their election whatever their position on the list (Htun and Jones 2002).

Where these propositions have been tested in post-transition polities, the results are mixed rather than unambiguous. Overall they back most of the propositions outlined above but there are some other factors to be considered. Leaving the analysis of the impact of electoral quotas to a separate section, we see that higher levels of women are elected in most of the PR than in the SMD/FPTP systems. However, none of our case study counties use an entirely SMD/FPTP system. Parts of East Central Europe use a mixture of PR and FPTP systems and South Africa and our Latin American case study countries have PR systems. The data from East Central Europe show us that women fare better in pure PR systems than in ones that have a mixture of the two. And in mixed systems women tend to do better in the PR part (Millard 2004). In the vast majority of cases where the electoral system was changed away from FPTP in favour of a more proportional one, more women were subsequently elected (Matland 2003: 331). However, the effect is not strong. In our case study countries we see that the Czech Republic and Poland, with relatively high levels of women's representation and a substantial increase in those levels over time, had purely PR systems and Hungary and Russia had lower levels overall in their mixed systems. Montgomery and Ilonski (2003) argue that part of the explanation for Hungary's low level of female representation lies in the negative impact of the majoritarian element of its very complex mixed system. However Russia provides a contrasting case because, unlike Hungary, more women have been elected under the FPTP part of the electoral system than in the PR part. Moser (2003) argues that much of the explanation for this phenomenon lies with factors external to the electoral rules particularly the nature of the political parties and party system.

There is less evidence about the impact of district magnitude and electoral thresholds. What there is seems to back up the prevailing wisdom for long-standing liberal democracies. Siemienska (2003: 226) for example argues that the high level of Polish party fragmentation that resulted from the very permissive proportionality embodied in the electoral rules used for the 1991 elections (29 different parties and groupings were represented) had negative consequences for women. Heinen and Portet (2002: 160) argue that Polish women have difficulties getting on lists in winnable positions because 'for the most part parties are grouped in large coalitions and the creation of individual slates must first of all represent each of the organizations in a given coalition. Since the (male) leaders of this collection of small parties must be given places on the slates, the opportunities for women are minimal'.

More consideration has been given to the question of open versus closed lists. But the evidence does not necessarily concur with the proposition that women will do better with closed lists. First, there are a number of examples in both Latin America and East Central Europe where open list systems seem to bring no disadvantage for women and some evidence that women have benefited from an open list system where voters can demonstrate their preferences. In Poland preference voting has consistently resulted in more women being elected than if the results had been determined entirely by list order (Saxonberg 2000; Siemienska 2003: 228; Millard 2004). In Peru, during the 1995 congressional elections, a number of women candidates benefited significantly from the open lists and were moved by voters nearer to the top of their lists (Waylen 1996). However, there was significant discontent with the political and party system in the 1990s in Peru and it has been suggested that women were favoured by some voters as new and less corrupt than the old stalwarts (Waylen 1996; Htun 2001). Second, closed lists will only increase levels of women's representation if women are placed in winning positions on party lists. Sperling (1999: 117) claims that most Russian parties placed women candidates' names at the bottom of party lists in 1993, excluding them from the top third, ensuring that few women were elected.

Htun (2001) and Millard (2004) both argue that closed lists are most effective when combined with a placement mandate. And the most common form of placement mandate is some form of quota whether it is a party or legislative one. Htun's analysis of our Latin American case studies demonstrates that closed list systems only result in high levels of women's representation if they operate concurrently with a nationally binding quota law that includes an effective place-ment mandate. Effective quotas are the one form of electoral rule that can make a big difference not only to the numbers of women selected but also to their positions on party lists. Quota laws therefore have such a potentially significant impact on levels of female representation that we will discuss them separately after looking at all the other institutional factors.

Electoral rules therefore can affect the numbers of women elected to repre-sentative bodies in post-transition contexts but they cannot provide the whole explanation. Except in relatively rare cases, it is political parties that select can-didates and they play a key role in the process of determining who gets elected. Electoral rules are one important factor that shape the decisions and recruitment strategies of those party gatekeepers. But individual parties vary greatly in terms of the number of women candidates they put forward. In the absence of effective quotas, electoral rules are only one of a large number of factors that determine the number of women that parties select as candidates and their position on party lists. No discussion of women's representation in the post-transition context can be complete without a detailed consideration of political parties.

❖ *Political Parties*

Women often find it hard to become candidates and, if selected, are placed in seats or positions on party lists that makes their election unlikely. How do different parties and party structures influence the numbers of women who get elected? As we saw in Part I, in many post-transition polities, parties and party systems have not established themselves as viable and sustainable institutions, raising concerns about their capacity to train political leaders and channel and represent interests. In the least institutionalized party systems without formal rules, procedures and developed party structures (sometimes described as inchoate) political behaviour is less structured and parties are often not the key political actors. Systems are more susceptible to personalism and patrimonialism. Uninstitutionalized parties are volatile and unstable, lack legitimacy and often produce unpredictable out-comes (Mainwaring and Scully 1995; Lipset 2000).

To date, there have been few systematic analyses of the impact of weakly insti-tutionalized parties on women's representation in post-transition polities. But by examining the research that has been undertaken on political parties in first the developing and then the developed world, we can determine the factors that might have an impact on post-transition political parties. In one of the only discus-sions of the topic, Goetz and Hassim (2002: 308) argue that, in the developing world:

parties may be too weakly institutionalized to provide the democratic internal rules which can give women sufficient purchase to exert leverage and make demands for inclusion. In many developing country contexts, particularly in authoritarian states, parties may be such blatantly hollow vehicles for kleptocratic families or ethnic groups, lacking any but the flimsiest organizational structures, decision-making processes, and ideologies, that there is simply nothing there for women to engage with. There may be no discernible party platform, if politics is a matter of appealing to ascriptive loyalties, rather than broad ideas and programs. Party systems and the ruling party, may be insufficiently institutionalized for women to begin to start challenging rules which exclude women—simply because there are no firm rules and rights, only patronage systems and favours.

Although Goetz and Hassim (2002) are describing a more extreme situation than in most post-transition polities, some weakly institutionalized parties in new democracies share a number of these characteristics. Entrenched (and longstanding) party cultures that include informal structures of power, clientelism, and factionalism within parties (both formal and informal factions are frequently characteristic of less institutionalized parties) have a negative impact on levels of women's representation (Goetz and Hassim 2002).

There are more analyses of the party characteristics that influence women's representation in long-standing liberal democracies that examine many of the factors that we need to consider. In her study of twelve 'advanced industrial democracies', Miki Caul (1999) looked at four key party characteristics—organizational structure (including degree of centralization, institutionalization, and level of candidate nomination); ideology; the proportion of women party activists; and the presence of gender-related representation rules—that have been hypothesized to affect the numbers of women MPs. In her bivariate analysis, high levels of institutionalization are a predictor of women MPs (but neither centralization nor newness of party appear very significant) and candidate nomination at lower levels is also associated with a higher number of women MPs. Ideology is also significant. It appears that parties on the left generally have more women MPs than parties on the right, and ultra-right parties have virtually none. However, on average conservative and rural parties tend to have more women MPs than socialist parties, but 'new left' parties are better than 'old left' parties in terms of numbers of women representatives. Caul (1999) also finds a moderately strong and statistically significant relationship between the numbers of women in party national executives and the number of women MPs, with a lagged effect between increased numbers of women in national executives and higher levels of women MPs (this relationship also works in lagged terms for middle and lower level activists). Unsurprisingly the presence of candidate rules also has a lagged effect in increasing the numbers of women MPs.

Caul (1999) also carried out a multivariate analysis of the data. She discovered that numbers of women MPs are related to the nature of the electoral system and to the presence of women activists, particularly at high levels. The level of women activists, particularly on the national executive, is also the most significant predictor of candidate rules. Parties with high numbers of women in the national executive and low levels of institutionalization have a higher incidence of candidate rules. Candidate rules, if implemented, have a significant impact on the levels of women's representation. Her hypothesis is that low levels of institutionalization can make it easier for women on the national executive to get candidate rules passed but the key factor is the presence of women activists. However activism also interacts with ideology. A new left ideology is the best predictor of high levels of women activists. Caul (1999) has therefore confirmed what others have already suggested that party structures, party ideology, and role of women activists, are significant factors in determining levels of women's representation in advanced industrial democracies. Candidate rules are a dependent variable because they often come about as a result of interaction between one or more of the first three other factors. Caul's later work (2006) reinforces and develops many of these findings—particularly the key role played by women's mobilization and women activists in positions of power within parties, who can effectively highlight the value of women's votes and select the right allies within party hierarchies.

Combining the insights of both Caul (1999, 2001, 2006) and Goetz and Hassim (2002), we will use Caul's first three categories (structures, ideology, and activists) and see how they relate to different post-transition outcomes. But we will place much greater emphasis on party institutionalization and consider other factors—like centralization and level of candidate selection—in the light of this.

❖ *Party Structures and Institutionalization*

To date few scholars have theorized the overall impact of levels of institutionalization on women's representation in post-transition polities. Although Matland and Montgomery (2003) and Millard (2004) shy away from drawing any conclusions about the post-socialist states in East Europe because of scarce data, Htun (2001, 2005) has begun to think about the relationship between the degree to which a party system is institutionalized and women's representation in post-authoritarian Latin America. She (2001, 2005) argues that there is no clear relationship between the degree to which a party system is institutionalized and women's representation. In her 2001 study of twelve countries, average levels of women's representation are similar in all her three categories of institutionalized, medium, and inchoate party systems (14, 15, and 13%, respectively). Even though the evidence is drawn from a small number of cases, if we disaggregate it we can see that there is a large degree of variation within the inchoate category ranging from Brazil at 6% to Peru at 18%. But the range was much smaller in the institutionalized category from Costa Rica at 19% to Chile at 11% (but by 2005, it had grown after Costa Rica implemented a quota law and women's representation reached 34% at the same time as it had only grown to 15% in Chile). There is therefore some evidence to support the proposition that uninstitutionalized or inchoate systems can have lower levels of representation for women, but that this will not necessarily be the case. Indeed Russia's uninstitutionalized and inchoate party system has similarly low levels of women's representation as Hungary which has one of the more institutionalized systems.

If we look at the uninstitutionalized parties and party systems among our case studies, there is evidence of greater variation and volatility in the numbers of women than in the institutionalized parties and party systems. Using Kitschelt's typology (cited in Matland 2003: 326) to divide post-transition political parties into one of three ideal types: charismatic, clientelistic, and programmatic, we can see that charismatic and clientelistic parties are likely to predominate in uninstitutionalized systems. Indeed non- or anti-party candidates such as Fujimori in Peru and Putin in Russia, who are often populists, can often command support in uninstitutionalized or inchoate party systems. Charismatic parties, based around an individual leader and clientelistic parties rooted in patronage networks, are themselves unlikely to be institutionalized and will lack clear and transparent rules for the nomination of candidates. They are often centralized under the control of one or more party leaders (Matland 2003: 326). In the absence of formal rules, candidate nominations are often decided in secret with no accountability to party members. In these conditions women are only nominated if party leaders wish to do so.

Under some circumstances, these low levels of institutionalization can provide opportunities for certain women. There is evidence from Peru in the 1990s that in a discredited and collapsed party system (namely virtually a no-party situation) more women were elected as they were seen to be above party politics and less corrupt than male politicians. The 10.8% (compared to 5.6% in 1985) of those elected to congress in 1995 were women, many of whom were part of loose new groupings such as Cambio 90/Nuevo Mayoria rather than members of long-standing political parties. Macaulay (1996) claims that women's representation increased dramatically in Brazil in 1980s during a period of maximum fragmentation of political parties. But women candidates were often selected for particularistic reasons. At least half of the elections were consistent with the features of an under-institutionalized system. Women were elected as individuals or because of their family name not as the representatives of a political party as such. It has even been suggested that some Argentine women deputies elected after the implementation of the quota laws in 1991 were chosen because they were the partners/relatives of male politicians or party hacks thought to be manipulable by party hierarchies now searching for malleable women candidates.[6] Therefore although the dominance of elites, patrimonialism, and clientelism, characteristic of an uninstitutionalized party system may favour some individual women, it does not necessarily facilitate a long-term increase in the total number of women active in conventional politics.

Russia provides more evidence that extremely under-institutionalized or inchoate party systems can also work against women. Russia is often described as having a non-party party system and Millard (2004) claims that in 1999 that an astonishing 51.3% of candidates in the single member seats were independents without any party affiliation of whom 9.6% were women. Independents won 105 (46.67%) of the 225 seats. But women comprised only 3% of the total number of independents (3 seats). It has been suggested that women are disadvantaged as candidates, not only as independents but also within the loose and patronage-based parties, by their lack of private economic resources to promote their candidacies and ensure their election (Matland 2003: 324).

As we saw in Part I, less institutionalized party systems often produce volatile and unpredictable outcomes from election to election. This variability can also have an impact on women's representation. Although the average percentage of women MPs in the three post-communist elections in fourteen countries in East Central Europe increased from 8.8% in the first election to an average of 10.7% in the second election to 13.7% in the third election, these figures conceal large variations. Five countries (Estonia, Latvia, Russia, Slovakia, and Slovenia) saw a decline in the proportion of women between the first and second elections. One of the major reasons for the variation in levels of women from election to election in East Central Europe is the volatility in support for different parties. In Poland the percentage of women elected in 1993 increased from 9 to 13 in the lower house and 8 to 13 in the upper house. This increase was due to the victory of the left and centre–left parties and the almost total defeat of the right wing parties (Siemienska 1998: 137). But a similar pattern can also be discerned in the relatively more institutionalized Hungary. In 1994 women's representation increased from 7% to 11% but declined to 8% in 1998. This variation was due primarily to the defeat of a moderate conservative coalition government led by the HDF by a social democratic coalition led by the Hungarian Socialist Party (HSP) in 1994. A centre–right coalition led by FIDESZ then won in 1998.

This volatility can be so severe that parties appear and disappear very quickly. Many new parties have been unable to secure a stable place in the new parliamentary system in post-transition Eastern Europe. Alliances shift and parties change their names frequently. Many do not appear to be very durable between one election and the next due to shifting electoral preferences, weakly developed structures, and shallow social roots. Some could not really be called political parties. Although women's parties are not generally typical of small parties, Women of Russia (WOR) does provide one illustration of this phenomenon. The WOR bloc was hurriedly organized in the two months before the Federal assembly elections held in December 1993 and rather surprisingly won 8% of the total vote. Of the 11.4% of the total seats won by women (13% in the lower house and 5% in the upper house), mainly from single member districts, approximately 33% of those in the lower house (the Duma) were won by women who were part of WOR. It had been formed by a group of women, mainly from the women's sector of Soviet public activity (many from the Soviet Women's Committee) with some from independent women's organizations such as an entrepreneurs association, who, while not overtly feminist, were dismayed at the lack of attention paid to women's issues by the main parties (Sperling 1999: 119). However, in the December 1995 elections despite having three deputies from single member districts, WOR failed to jump over the 5% hurdle necessary to get representation in parliament and disappeared as a political bloc. As a result the percentage of women in parliament declined to 10% (Buckley 1997; Sperling 1999: 115–29). These more unpredictable outcomes in less institutionalized party systems need to be assessed on a case-by-case basis.

However, on their own institutionalized parties, often falling into Kitschelt's third category of programmatic parties based on an ideological vision of a good society, are not enough to ensure high levels of women representatives. Indeed many institutionalized parties in new democracies also have low levels of women's representation. Among our case study countries we have the contrasting examples of South Africa where the ANC, the dominant institutionalized party, has high levels of women's representation and Chile and Hungary where a number of institutionalized parties have low levels. Institutionalized parties have formalized rules and procedures for candidate selection, but these vary considerably, for example in the extent to which they are transparent and democratic. Some electoral rules enable party leaders to maintain control of candidate nomination. Closed lists give nominators both the control over who becomes a candidate and over the likelihood that they will get elected through control over their position on the list. The extent to which procedures are centralized or decentralized also impacts on the control exercised by party leaders. If parties and party leaders want to prevent the selection of women candidates, these kinds of rules will enable them to do this. However, if they are in favour of selecting women candidates, all the formal rules will generally allow this too. As a result, in some cases centralized procedures seem to benefit women and in other cases decentralized procedures appear preferable.

Matland (2003) argues that in Eastern Europe there is some evidence that some programmatic parties, particularly communist successor parties, have locally based procedures that can favour women. The communist party in the Czech Republic selects candidates at the local level (where women form 50% of district nominating committees) and has the highest number of women representatives of all the Czech parties (Saxonberg 2003: 256). But there is evidence from El Salvador that in FMLN candidate selection procedures for the 1994 and 1997 elections, women did better in at the national level because the lists were voted on by the National Council rather than local parties (Luciak 2001: 204).

❖ THE ELECTORAL ARENA

Much therefore hinges on the extent to which party rules and procedures concentrate power in the hands of unaccountable party leaders or make parties democratic, transparent bodies that represent their members' views and are responsive to pressure. Factionalized parties with relatively weakly institutionalized structures are difficult to pressure for change in their internal organization and even if changes to party rules are made, it can be difficult to ensure that they are implemented. In more institutionalized parties, a combination of formal rules and procedures with high levels of internal democracy can ensure that rules that facilitate the election of women, for example making selection procedures more transparent or even adopting quotas, are introduced and implemented. But there is some evidence from Latin America of the pragmatic instrumentalism of some parties that adopt quotas to ward off pressures for greater internal democracy (Htun 2005).

Many post-transition parties have been under pressure to adopt more accountable and transparent decision-making processes, particularly with regard to candidate nomination as a way of improving the quality of democracy. The introduction of primary elections to decentralize the nomination process is one option. But in some cases where party leaders are reluctant to cede power, they prefer to defuse pressures for party democratization by adopting gender quotas. A quota system allows them to maintain control over the nomination process that would be reduced in a move to a primary system (Baldez 2004*a*, 2004*b*). There are therefore no clear links between the levels of institutionalization of parties and parties systems and levels of women's representation in post-transition polities. On its own the institutionalization of parties and parties systems is not enough to ensure the selection of women candidates. In the face of rather inconclusive evidence about the impact of institutionalization, we also need to consider the significance of our other two factors: ideological orientation and women activists.

❖ Ideology

A variety of parties, spanning a broad ideological spectrum, operate in post-transition polities. They can be classified on a left/right continuum, according to their support or opposition to non-democratic rule and the mode of any opposition. They range from parties that supported the non-democratic regime and the once hegemonic communist successor parties that are still influential in parts of East Central Europe, to parties such as the ANC and FMLN that had participated in guerrilla struggles against authoritarian regimes before becoming more orthodox political parties and contesting elections. These parties coexist with the more typical Christian Democrat, socialist, right-wing, nationalist, and rural parties. Some predate the non-democratic regime, while others have been newly created. Many parties also display populist/charismatic tendencies. Some populist parties, such as the Peronist PJ in Argentina, have long histories, but others that have emerged more recently in East Central Europe and Latin America are often no more than a vehicle for a charismatic leader. If some of the variation in levels of female representation is because certain parties field more women candidates than others, how far can these variations be attributed to party ideology?

Our starting point is to consider Caul's proposition (1999, 2006) about parties on the left in the post-transition context. Do parties on the left have more women candidates than right-wing parties and what happens in populist parties?[7] We need to be aware of the large range of left wing parties in the post-transition polities. For our purposes it is useful to divide them into three main types: (*a*) (centre) left parties that are closest to new left and include 'renovated left' and social democratic parties such as the PPD in Chile and the Social Democratic Party in the Czech Republic; (*b*) (ex) communist parties such the Hungarian Socialist party and the Communists in the Czech Republic and in parts of Latin America such as Chile; and (*c*) ex-revolutionary parties such as the FMLN and ANC.

In post-socialist polities, the levels of women's representation vary considerably between different types of parties. Left-wing parties do tend to have more female candidates and more elected female representatives than right-wing parties. In the Polish legislative elections held in 1997 the percentage of women candidates varied between 25% for the left-leaning Union for Labour and 11% for the more right wing Electoral Solidarity Alliance (Heinen and Portet 2002). Many of these left-wing parties have their roots in the old communist parties. Indeed the Czech communist party still exists and in 1990 had the highest proportion of women MPs of any party. Communist and communist successor parties also often have more established structures and selection procedures as well as deeper roots in society than some of the newer parties that can sometimes favour women. Left-wing parties are more likely to have high levels of women's representation if they are communist successor parties, but also if they have modelled themselves on their European social democratic sister parties as some of the parties in EU accession countries have done (Matland 2003). Some of these parties, for example the SLD-UP in Poland and the HSP in Hungary, have even introduced quotas which has further boosted their level of female representation (Millard 2004).

In post-authoritarian Latin America, major left-wing parties also tend to have more women representatives than those on the right (Htun 2001). But again the picture is not altogether straightforward. In Chile the renovated left parties of the PPD and the PS have far higher proportions of women representatives than their coalition partners, the Christian Democrats (CD) (Waylen 2000). Women made up 19% of PPD deputies, 18% of PS deputies, but only 5% of CD deputies in 2000. The centre–left parties like the PS and PPD in Chile are also more likely to adopt candidate quotas in the absence of national laws. However, in Brazil uniformly low levels of representation are common to all the major parties. In 2001 even the largest left-wing PT that had been expected to have higher levels of women's representation, had only 9% women among its deputies, 1% behind the centrist PMDB (Macaulay 2003).

There is evidence from our case study countries that, once they engage in the competitive electoral process, ex-revolutionary parties also have higher than average proportions of women among their elected representatives. As part of their different party histories to other left-wing parties, women had often formed a substantial proportion of the guerrilla fighters. Since its participation in the non-racial elections, the ANC, a party with a left-wing ideology, a commitment to social justice and a history as a national liberation movement, has had high numbers of women among its elected representatives (far higher than other South African parties). In 1994, 32% of those on the ANC list and 35.7% of ANC MPs subsequently elected were women (Ballington 1998). In El Salvador the FMLN gained 21 of the 85 seats in the 1994 elections and women were 24% of the FMLN total (5 of the 21 legislators). Even though they only held 25% of the total seats, more than half the women elected (5 of 9 and 11% overall) came from the FMLN. After the next election in 1997, 33% of FMLN deputies were women (there was a 35% quota on party electoral lists). The only other party to elect any women deputies was the right-wing party ARENA and only 14% of their deputies were women (Luciak 1999).

However, there is also significant women's representation in some of the parties of the Right in many post-transition polities. But right-wing parties, too, are not a homogeneous group and divide into nationalist, populist, liberal, religious, extreme right-wing parties—as well as the renovated modern right that has emerged in countries such as Chile. Matland (2003: 338) claims that centre–right parties that are coherent and contain significant numbers of intellectuals often provide a favourable environment for women candidates in East Central Europe. Some of the populist, nationalist, and right-wing parties also have higher levels of women as their candidates than might be expected (Millard 2004). Indeed Saxonberg (2000: 151) argues that it is surprising that populist parties 'send nearly as high a percentage of women to parliament as leftist parties do'. However, there are great variations between populist parties. A number of left-leaning populist parties have high levels of female representation. But in some cases right-wing populist parties, such as the Republicans in the Czech Republic in 1996 had the highest percentage of female MPs at that time.

On the other hand, other right-wing populist parties have very low levels of female representation. Populist parties also display great volatility in the number of women representatives that each of them has over time. Many right wing traditionalist parties also have few women elected representatives. In Poland the Fatherland party and Centre–Polish Alliance Agreement, both with close ties to the Catholic Church, sent no women representatives to parliament in 1993 (Fuszara 2000: 280) and women have also fared badly in the agrarian parties in

Poland and the Russian regions. At the same time another traditional right-wing and Eurosceptic party, the League of Polish Families, has had high levels of female representation (Millard 2004). Matland (2003) argues that right-wing parties that lose their intellectual wings often become more hostile to women in East Central Europe. In Hungary FIDESZ turned to the right, becoming for example anti-abortion, after its liberal intellectual strand that included a significant number of women left the party (Montgomery and Ilonski 2003: 118). There were also differences between the successor strands to Solidarity in Poland. Women fared worse in the right-wing anti-abortion AWS (Solidarity Election Alliance) than in the smaller more liberal breakaway Democratic Union (later Freedom Union) (Matland 2003).

In our post-authoritarian case studies, some right-wing parties also have quite high levels of female representation. In Chile 13% of the deputies from Renovación Nacional (RN), a renovated and modern party of the right, were women in 2000. Evidence is again mixed for populist and corporatist parties. Although they have frequently focused on women as a sector, for example attempting to mobilize support from women in women's sections, they have not always promoted women representatives or put women in positions of power. In Chile, UDI, a right-wing party with populist tendencies and a history of support for Pinochet, had no women representatives in 2000, at the same time as it made successful efforts to mobilize large numbers of poor women at the grass roots (Waylen 2000). In Argentina the long-standing populist Peronist party Partido Justicialista (PJ) has a long history of women's participation. During the first Peronist government in which Eva Peron (Evita) played a significant role, women were organized into the Partido Peronista Femenino (PPF). It has been claimed that unofficial quotas also existed within the PJ and as a result the number of women in Congress reached nearly 25% in the 1950s helping to normalize high numbers of women in Congress. In the late 1990s both the PJ and FREPASO (a centre–left party) exceeded the national quota but UCR, the centre party fell below it by 2% (Waylen 2000). There are therefore no unambiguous findings and, as we see when we discuss quotas, there is also some evidence to support Matland and Studlar's contention (1996) that right-wing parties will sometimes adopt more women candidates if left-wing parties have done so.

Left-wing parties of all types therefore do consistently appear to have higher levels of women elected representatives than most right-wing parties in the post-transition polities in this study. However, there is some evidence that parties that wish to be seen as modern and democratic, whether on the left or the right, are also likely to have more female representatives. Populist parties (whether of the left or right) also have wide variations in the levels of women's representation making it more difficult to make a general predictive statement. Why do left-wing parties tend to have more women representatives? One part of the explanation is that left-wing parties have more egalitarian ideologies and are therefore more likely to be open to arguments favouring justice for excluded groups. As a result left-wing parties are more likely to adopt candidate rules to ensure that all groups have the opportunity to be represented. Goetz and Hassim (2002) for example claim that ANC's discourse of equal citizenship rights for all regardless of race meant that they were open to a more feminist conception of democracy and the attendant ideas of quotas. But what is it that prompts some parties to adopt and implement quotas and not others? This brings us to the final part of our explanation: the impact of women party activists on levels of women's representation.

❖ Women Activists

Analysts of first-world democracies have argued that women activists are central to improvements in women's representation (Lovenduski and Norris 1993; Caul 2001, 2006). The evidence from our post-transition cases both supports this view and confirms some of the trends we observed in the earlier phases of transition. Even those scholars who focus primarily on the impact of institutional and electoral features recognize the part played by women activists. Matland (2003: 334), reviewing data from eleven case studies from post-socialist East Europe, concludes that the presence of women in party forums where decisions are made is 'truly crucial'. Htun's study (2001: 24) of post-authoritarian Latin America confirms 'the theoretical point that a strong cadre of women activists in the party is a key factor in women's electoral success'.

The extent of women's activism in different post-transition political parties appears fairly similar to that found in long-standing democracies in the first world. Women form a much higher proportion of party members, affiliates, and grass-roots activists than they do of party governing bodies, decision-making structures, or elected representatives. In post-authoritarian Latin America in the late 1990s women were on average 40–50% of members and affiliates but only 20% of governing bodies, (although this figure did range from a low of 3% to a high of 50%). In Argentina women were 47.7% of affiliates in all parties but only 7.2% of party directorates in 1993 (Informe Nacional 1995). This difference occurred in all sorts of parties except those with effective internal quotas. Although women made up 48% of all PT affiliates in Brazil, they formed only 20% of the delegates to the PT conference in 1988 and only 6.1% of the national directorate in 1991. However by 1998, 30.2% of the PT directorate were women after a 30% internal quota had been introduced in 1991. But women's electoral fortunes have been mixed. They made up 14.3% of PT deputies in 1990. This figure rose to 21.2% in 1994 but had fallen back sharply to only 9% in 2001 (Macaulay 2003).

In Chile it has been estimated that women made up 40% of grass-roots levels activists in the Concertación (the centre–left governing coalition) and 50–60% of activists on the right in the mid-1990s.[8] Fewer women were found in the higher echelons of these political parties. In 1997 there were no women in the political commissions of the right-wing parties. But in the Concertación parties in 1997, women formed 33% of the PS political commission (up from 20% in 1994); 27% of the PPD political commission (up from 21% in 1994), but only 17% of the Christian Democrat (PDC) Consejo Nacional (up from 10% in 1995). The numbers of women in internal party positions increased because the PPD and PS quotas for internal party positions reached 40% after the return to competitive electoral politics (and subsequently the PDC, after pressure from PDC women, adopted quotas of 20% for some internal party positions) (Waylen 2000). In El Salvador only 14% of the FMLN National Directorate were women in 1994 even though women formed about one-third of the membership and 25% of the candidates for the 1994 elections but by 2001 women formed 40% of the leadership structures (Luciak 2004).

The data from post-socialist Eastern Europe also concur with the more general picture that although women often form a relatively high proportion of party members, they form a much smaller percentage of candidates and elected representatives. But scholarly attention has focused primarily on candidate selection rather than on the role of women activists because party membership figures are either nonexistent or notoriously unreliable (Millard 2004). Fodor (1998: 158) estimates that in 1992 women made up 40.4% of FIDESZ party members, 8.7% of its elected representatives, and 7.7% of its executive body; 34.4% of Hungarian socialist party members, 9.1% of its elected representatives and 15.4% of its executive body; and 25% of HDF party members, 3.0% of its elected members and 4.8% of its executive body. In the 1990s women formed an average of around 30% of party members in the Czech republic, ranging from 52% of the KDU-CSL (Christian Democrats) to 43% of the KSCM (Communists) but only 25% of the CSSD (Social Democrats) (Saxonberg 2003: 251). But women formed only 15% of the KDU-CSL elected representatives, 15% of CSSD representatives and 25% of KSCM representatives in 1998. Our data therefore show that overall female party membership figures cannot always provide an accurate guide to levels of female candidates or elected representatives from that party and that high levels of women in party leadership positions are usually the result of quotas.

In order to understand the circumstances in which women activists can be effective in increasing women's representation in post-transition polities, we need to look at who the activists are and how they organize, the kinds of parties they are active within and the strategies that they adopt. We will focus our attention on women activists organizing as women around gender issues both within party women's organizations as well as more generally. Not all parties have women's sections and, where they exist, these organizations do not all undertake the same kinds of activities or organize around gender issues. As we saw under state socialism, the women's sections of the ruling communist parties were usually nothing more than a vehicle to organize women in support of the party. During the 1990s, only two Czech political parties—the Social Democrats and Communists—had women's organizations that were actively involved in politics, and even then the influence of the Social Democratic women declined over the decade. Women's organizations connected to other political parties played a more traditional role such as fundraising (Saxonberg 2000). This is a common pattern. In South Africa, with the exception of the ANC, the role of women's sections in all the parties that had them, such as the National party, was a mainly traditional one of fundraising and tea-making (Ballington 2002). A basic condition therefore for the effectiveness of any women's section in increasing women's representation is that it is politicized, women are organized within it around gender issues and it has a certain degree of autonomy in its activities.

Whether organizing within women's sections or outside of them, women activists appear to be most effective if a significant number of them are feminists committed to enhancing gender equality within their parties. In the post-transition period, feminists continued to be active in the ANC, the FMLN, the PT and the PS, PPD, and PCD in Chile. Women activists find it easier if they are organizing in parties of the left that are relatively sympathetic to gender issues. Politicized women's organizations that contain feminists are more likely to exist within left-wing parties. As we have seen feminists have often had a close, if not frequently antagonistic relationship, with political parties on the left and often made strategic decisions to become active within a party or became increasingly feminist in orientation while they maintained their activities within the party. They often felt that establishing autonomous women's organizations was a necessary and strategic move to give women activists a base from which to campaign to further gender issues within their own party. In many cases women activists also appear to have their greatest success in increasing women's representation by advocating gender quotas. They often can get parties to adopt gender quotas for internal party positions before they will adopt gender quotas for candidate selection.

There is also some evidence that parties with relatively well-institutionalized structures can be more amenable for women activists. Weakly institutionalized party structures can provide obstacles to women's organizations trying to promote meaningful change in internal party organization and structures. In Argentina, a women's section of the PJ was formed in the early 1980s and following pressure from women in the Federal Capital, the party charters were amended in 1988 to introduce some positive action measures (Bonder and Nari 1995). But implementation of these measures was not easy. By 1998 the PJ had introduced a national quota of 30% for internal party positions but women still formed only 6.1% of the party's governing body in that year (a decline from 9.8% in 1994) (ECLAC 2000).

Indeed the cases in which women activists had an impact in the period immediately after the transition are those in which women were already organizing as

THE ELECTORAL ARENA ❖

women within political parties prior to the founding elections. In El Salvador, for example, feminists continued to organize within the FMLN. Building on the networks and contacts established during the war and the transition, FMLN female militants subsequently had some success around issues of gender equality (Hipsher 2001: 62). Following the failure to achieve a 30% quota for candidates in the 1994 election, the newly created Women's Secretariat continued to fight for gender equality but often with few resources and in the face of resistance from the party. But in 1995 a quota based on levels of female party members was acted upon and as a result women formed 33% of those elected to the National Council (Luciak 2001: 159). The National Council then voted for five women to join the fifteen person Political Commission and also voted for a national list of candidates for the 1997 containing 45% women (Luciak 2001: 206). Women formed 30% of all candidates but women activists had greater success at the national level and in urban areas particularly in the capital San Salvador.

In some post-socialist polities, women activists have had a positive impact on some political parties but not until some time after the collapse of state socialism. Again these cases confirm the general trends we have already noticed. In Hungary the communist successor party, the Hungarian Socialist Party, has maintained the greatest formal ideological and historical commitment to women's equality of any major party. (Montgomery and Ilonski 2003: 122). It also has an active women's caucus with 1,000 members that meets regularly and sponsors large-scale events. The party first accepted a 20% quota for party leadership positions and in 2002 implemented a candidate quota, despite resistance to affirmative action from party members and local party organs. As a result women formed 24% of the HSP candidates up from 9% in 1998 (Millard 2004).

In Poland, much of the substantial increase of women's representation to 20.2% in 2001 is attributed to the improved organization and mobilization of women arguing for greater representation (Siemienska 2003: 239). Until the 2001 campaign only those women's organizations directly connected to political parties like the Democratic Union of Women of the SLD and the Women's League of the Labour Union had fought around women's representation, but they were joined by almost fifty other women's organizations in a Pre-electoral Coalition created a few months before the elections. One of their slogans was 'I've had enough of this. I support the election of women' (Siemienska 2003: 232). Women already in parliament also supported the actions of the Pre-Election Coalition. Siemienska claims that, although it was not associated with any particular party, the most visible evidence of the success of this coalition was the decision of the winner of the election, the left-wing SLD-UP (Democratic Left Alliance-Labour Union) coalition to adopt a candidate quota, rejecting party lists that did not contain 30% women. As a result 36% of their candidates were women.

In the post-transition period women activists within political parties also continued to experience problems. The impact of women's sections can be affected by party factionalization and personalism as well as by changes in the balance of power within the party. The ANCWL that had been so active during the transition became a shadow of its former self after Winnie Mandela became its head in December 1993 (Geisler 2004). As a result a number of feminists left in frustration in 1995 preferring to put their energies into the mainstream of the ANC and were followed by a mass resignation of eleven members of the ANCWL executive in 1997 (Goetz and Hassim 2002, Geisler 2004: 86). The ANCWL subsequently stopped playing an important role campaigning around gender equality issues within the party and became effectively moribund. The Women's Secretariat of the FMLN found that its influence within the party was reduced when the reforming wing dominated between 1997–9, taking over from the orthodox faction that had been more sympathetic to gender equality claims (Luciak 2001: 155).

Indeed some feminists within political parties began to doubt the wisdom of separate women's sections arguing that they can lead to marginalization. In Chile feminists continued to be active within the parties of the centre–left, using a number of strategies and tactics to increase women's influence in the post-transition period. Many feminists changed their views as to the most effective way to organize in political parties after the return to competitive electoral politics. At the instigation of women activists in the PS, a vice-president for women was created in 1992 to ensure that gender concerns would be mainstreamed in the party. This occurred after the growing recognition that, despite raising awareness of gender issues, the FMS the party women's section, had very little power and capacity to pressurize party institutions and had become ghettoized, doing little to advance the position of women within the PS.[9] In an extension of this argument, the existence of women's parties has been seen as a sign of the weakness of women activists and women's movements, rather than as a sign of strength. Indeed Moser (2003: 163) has argued that in Russia the three groups that came together to found WOR initially wanted to support women-friendly parties, but unable to get a positive response, they were forced to form their own electoral bloc.

Therefore women activists and women's sections find it hard to achieve their aims if they are without sympathetic allies in positions of power within political parties that are open to claims of gender equality, but also if they are without allies in women's movements outside of the conventional political arena. Many feminists active within political parties such as the ANC and PT have also had ties to and been active in women's movements outside of the conventional political sphere both during the transition and post-transition phases. Indeed Caul (2001) has claimed that in Western Europe, political parties that are open to movements outside of the party are more likely to be open to women's claims for greater representation. Women activists and women's sections therefore need to be active politically within a favourable opportunity structure in order to achieve increases in the representation of women. And they also need an avowedly feminist component. All the women's sections that achieved a high profile and had some success in raising gender issues within their parties included significant numbers of feminists committed to reducing gender inequality. They were also able to forge alliances with sympathetic senior figures within the party. The adoption of gender quotas for internal party positions can be one step in this process. Indeed quotas have been the predominant measure that women activists have fought for to increase women's representation both internally and electorally. It is therefore worth considering the effectiveness of quotas as a method of increasing women's representation in a separate section.

❖ Quotas

Quotas—both for internal party positions and for candidate selection in national and local elections—have been the major strategy advocated by women party activists, and feminists in particular, to increase women's representation within conventional politics. Despite some fears, expressed for example by feminists in the PS and PPD in Chile in the mid 1990s, that quotas could become ceilings if they were not large enough to provide critical mass,[10] many activists have campaigned for their introduction. These campaigns were helped by external factors such as the regional preparations for the 1995 Beijing Women's Conference, growing international support for quotas in the aftermath of the conference as well as the example of quotas implemented elsewhere. Two of our post-authoritarian case study countries—Argentina and Brazil—introduced electoral quotas through legislation in the post-transition period. In Argentina the electoral quota was also enshrined in the constitution. Electoral quotas were also introduced by one or more political parties, primarily on the left, in all of our other case study countries, except Russia, and even more have introduced quotas for internal party positions (see Table III.3). This reflects more general experience as adoption of quotas has become widespread globally (Dahlerup 2006). Beginning in Argentina, between 1991 and 2000, eleven Latin American countries adopted national quota laws that obliged political parties to include a minimum number of women (typically between 20 and 40%) as candidates for legislative elections (Inter-American Dialogue 2001). As a result, selection procedures, so often problematic for potential women candidates, are not to be determined entirely by political parties but also by law in those countries that adopted legislative quotas (Htun and Jones 2002).

Many quotas would not have been adopted without the campaigns of feminists within political parties, particularly on the left, and outside. These campaigns have taken different forms depending on the prevailing opportunity structure. In the pioneering case of Argentina, the campaign for quotas succeeded for a number of diverse reasons. The precedent for quotas had already been set by the PJ in the

Table III.3. Electoral and party quotas in 2006

Country	Constitutional quota	Electoral law*	Sanctions	Party	Quotas (%)	
Argentina	Yes	1991 30%	Yes	PJ	35	
Brazil	No	1997 25%	Ineffective	PT	30	
Chile	No	No	N/A	PS	20 1998	i
					30 1997	
					40 1999	we
				PPD	20 1988	i
					40	we
				CD	20 1988	we
Czech Republic	No	No	N/A	CSSD (social democrats)	25	
El Salvador	No	No	N/A	FMLN	35	
Hungary	No	No	N/A	HSP (Hungarian socialists)	20	
Peru	No	1997 25% 2001 30%	Ineffective			
Poland	No	No	N/A	SLD	30	
				UP labour	30	
				UW	30	
Russia	No	No	N/A			
South Africa	No	No	N/A	ANC	30	

Source: International IDEA website (www.idea.int, www.quotaproject.org).

we = weakly enforced; i = internal.

* Year passed + % age quota.

1950s. Although the quota law was put forward by a UCR (Radical) politician, it was supported by an alliance of women both from the political parties and a range of NGOs. The government women's body, the Consejo Nacional de la Mujer, also participated in the campaign. Feminists involved argued that a deliberate part of the strategy was to stress that quotas would help to make Argentina a modern and fully democratic society and as such they were attempting to use the opportunities afforded by the post-transition context.[11] Finally, President Menem supported the legislation because at that time he was sympathetic to women's issues and wanted to be seen as a modern president.

Attempts to introduce national quotas have not always been successful in post-authoritarian polities. In Chile in 1997 a bill 'to promote the right of women to participate in national public life' by altering the electoral system through the introduction of national quotas was introduced into congress by ten parliamentarians from the Concertación (including prominent women deputies such as Fanny Pollarolo and Mariana Aylwin). It proposed that neither sex should form

THE ELECTORAL ARENA ❖

more than 60% of internal party positions or candidates for municipal or national elections.[12] However, it was killed off in committee. The institutional legacy of the political system designed by the Pinochet regime means that change of this kind is hard to achieve without executive support (Franceschet 2001). The executive control over legislation, combined with the lack of women on important congressional committees means that it is difficult, even with cross-party support, for women deputies to get laws passed without strong backing from the government.[13] Another attempt was made in 2003. But neither attempt had widespread support either from deputies inside the legislature or from women's organizations outside of it, contributing to their lack of success (Franceschet 2005: 100). Indeed many activists within parties that have quotas like the PS, PDC, and PPD have mixed feelings about their value and desirability.

An effort to introduce quotas also failed in El Salvador in 2000. A number of female legislators from both the political Left and Right introduced a law proposing a minimum quota of 30% for either sex for all public office and party leadership positions. It only obtained forty-one of the forty-three votes that were needed. According to Luciak (2004), one of the initiative's supporters argued that the sponsors of the measure had not got the support of the women's movement. She believed that if they had worked together, female legislators and women's organizations could have exerted enough pressure to get the law passed.

In contrast to our post-authoritarian case studies, for the first ten years after the collapse of state socialism, quotas were not a major campaigning issue for women activists in East Central Europe. Although there was less resistance to quotas for internal positions in some parties, quotas, particularly for national elections, were too heavily associated with the discredited communist period. As a result they were initially regarded, even by those who could be considered to be potential supporters, as a tool of oppression of those groups they were designed to support (Siklova 1993: 79). But in 1995 although the Czech communist party did not have quotas, the Central Operative Electoral Staff did suggest that 'nearly 50% of candidates should be women, especially in "leading positions" ' (Saxonberg 2000: 155).

Opposition to quotas has declined over time (Einhorn 2006). By 2002 candidate quotas had also been implemented by some parties—often communist successor parties and those parties with the most organized women party activists—in Poland, Hungary, and the Czech Republic. In 2001 in Poland, the electorally unsuccessful UW, the Freedom Union, with UD, the Democratic Union, an evolution from the intellectual wing of Solidarity, as its dominant partner, also adopted a 30% quota and as a result women filled 31% of its list positions. The adoption of a quota is not so surprising as both UW and UD had a history of women's involvement and fielding relatively high numbers of women candidates. The winning SLD–UP alliance also applied quotas to their own electoral lists after the failure of their effort to get quotas enacted into electoral law (Millard 2004). In Hungary only the Hungarian Socialist Party had introduced candidate quotas for national and regional lists. And in the Czech Republic only the Social Democrats, the CSSD, had some form of quota and women were 25.1% of its candidates for the elections held that year. Although the feeling among many Czech feminists is that the quotas have not been very effective.[14] Therefore quotas, that had been unthinkable in the immediate post-transition period, had been adopted by a few left leaning parties within ten years. But national quotas were still unthinkable. In Russia an attempt in 2002 to add an amendment to the voting rights law that introduced a 30% quota was short-lived, gaining only 167 of the 226 votes needed (Sundstrom 2005: 441).

Once enshrined in legislation, how far do electoral quotas work as a strategy to increase the number of women representatives? Htun and Jones (2002) argue that, where they have been adopted in Latin America, quotas have increased the proportion of female representatives by an average of 5%. But this figure conceals a huge variation. In Argentina the proportion of women representatives in the Chambers of Deputies initially increased to 28% while in Brazil it fell from 7 to 6% after quotas were introduced. Several characteristics of the Argentine electoral system and its institutions make quotas effective. Party lists are closed, the rank ordering is determined by the party and voters simply choose a list rather than a candidate. Unlike some quota laws where parties can comply with the law by simply putting women in unelectable positions at the bottom of party lists, the Argentine *Ley de Cupos* (quota law) stipulates that women have to be placed in winnable positions, in at least every third position on the list. Argentina has an intermediate district magnitude electing five legislators from the average district (Htun and Jones 2002). Compliance by parties also increased over time.[15] Initially poor, with some parties and regions complying less than others, continued campaigning by women activists increased the effectiveness of the law. Initially only individual women who had felt badly treated could challenge a list, risking the wrath of their party (Jones 1996). After changes instituted in the 1994 constitution, the Consejo Nacional dela Mujer (CNM) and others could mount challenges and party electoral lists could be rejected if they did not have sufficient women in appropriate positions.

However, in contrast to the Argentine case, the Brazilian electoral and quota laws function in such a way that their introduction has made little difference. The open list system, the 'birthright candidate' laws that mean that incumbents have the automatic right to run for re-election and loopholes in the quota laws which enable parties to leave list slots vacant rather than nominate women, combine to make the existence of a national quota an irrelevance (Htun 2001). The Brazilian case therefore provides further evidence that quotas have to be well designed and appropriate to that electoral system in order to 'fast track' increases in women's representation.

The imposition of quotas can also have a 'contagion' effect. A national quota brings increased pressure to bear on other institutions and organizations, such as trade unions, to institute similar measures. By 1998 laws replicating the national quota had also been enacted for provincial elections in twenty out of Argentina's twenty-four provinces (Jones 1998: 21). Reinforcing Matland and Studlar's arguments (1996), a quota adopted by one party can also encourage others to nominate more women for fear that they will lose women's votes. In 1994 the traditionally all-white parties in South Africa fielded more women candidates than they ever had previously after the ANC implemented its quota (Ballington 2002; Britton 2006). A women's party can also have a similar impact. A mild contagion effect was observed in Russia in 1995 when the total number of women candidates increased and the number of female MPs outside of WOR rose from thirty-seven in 1993 to forty-six (Saxonberg 2000: 151). Women had increased visibility on a number of parties' lists and were ranked slightly higher than they had been in 1993 (Buckley 1997: 163). But conversely, Moser (2003: 164) claims that after WOR failed to cross the 5% electoral threshold in 1995, other parties felt less pressure to nominate women candidates as they believed that its failure showed that gender equality did not appeal to voters.

However, there is also some evidence about party behaviour that reinforces some of scepticism about quotas as they can be adopted for instrumentalist reasons. In addition to the evidence from Latin America that some parties have adopted quotas to ward off pressures for greater party democracy thereby actually reinforcing existing centralized and undemocratic candidate selection procedures (Baldez 2006), Barbara Einhorn (2006) claims that some social democratic parties in East Central Europe adopted quotas to facilitate their entry into the Socialist International but subsequently ignored them.

❖ *What Do Women Do When They Are Elected?*

One central argument that is often used to justify the imposition of quotas is that women legislators will behave differently to men—for example that they will change the dominant political culture—or that they will act for women namely in the interests of women in general thereby improving women's substantive as well as descriptive representation, particularly once a 'critical mass' of women legislators is reached. Therefore one final question to consider is whether there is any evidence that larger numbers of women representatives make a difference in post-transition legislatures. Htun and Jones (2002) compare the Argentine legislature with others with fewer women. However, despite some evidence of more activity around family issues, they find few differences in terms of the voting and legislation initiation patterns of women representatives. Party loyalty is often more important than gender considerations and women elected to legislatures are not necessarily interested in gender issues. It is useful to bear in mind Friedman's caveat (2000) about the narrowness of this approach that equates achieving more seats for women candidates at various levels with the representation of 'women's interests' (whatever they may be considered to be). It is not enough to only consider the gender of the actors without being concerned with who the women are, for example the nature of their beliefs, how they organize within legislatures if at all, and the gendered nature of the structures they have to work within. Indeed Hannah Britton (2002, 2005) argues that the example of women MPs in South Africa casts doubt on the critical mass thesis as other factors apart from gender are central, particularly as the increasingly professionalized 'second generation' women MPs elected in 1999 had lost touch with women's organizations outside parliament.

One important facet of this question of how far women will act for women is the extent to which women organize around women's issues across party lines once they are elected and how far women legislators remain tied to ideological positions of their parties. Do the nature of the transition path and the resulting institutional set-up have any impact on the activities of women representatives? Are there more possibilities for cross-party organizing among women deputies in less institutionalized contexts where party discipline is less rigidly enforced?

The evidence is mixed. Some significant cross-party organizing was possible in Poland through the Women's Parliamentary Group (WPG) founded in 1991 (Siemienska 1998: 139–42). Women of the Democratic Left Alliance (SLD) (which included reformed communists) and the more right-wing Democratic Union were the most active within it. The WPG campaigned around issues of family welfare, divorce, and abortion law reform within parliament as well as trying to set up links with wider networks of women outside of parliament. However, Siemienska (1998: 142) reports that when the WPG developed a joint position on an issue, problems with agreeing strategy and tactics often followed. Over time, WPG became increasingly dominated by women from the SLD as disputes between the different parties increased but as we have seen it did play a significant role in the broad-based pre-electoral coalition of women (Siemienska 2003: 232). As we see in Part IV, despite the relatively high party discipline in Argentina, there was some significant cross-party organizing among women around gender issues in the Constituent Assembly of 1993 established to design a new constitution.[16] The so-called 'lipstick lobby' has also organized within the Brazilian legislature to press gender demands.

Relatively strong discipline within the party system can mitigate against cross-party alliances. In Chile women legislators of the Concertación had some limited contact with some sympathetic women politicians in RN on issues relating to the welfare of women, children, and families. Although the impetus for the 1994 Abandonment and Family Support Bill (which stipulated the level of support for a deserted partner and children) came from women representatives from both the Concertación and RN, the potential for cross-party alliances was further limited by the extreme politicization of gender issues such as divorce and reproductive rights (Franceschet 2005). But the numbers of women legislators has been relatively low with few feminists among their numbers. The feminists were also concentrated in the PS and PPD, not the CDs, the dominant party within the Concertación during the 1990s. As a result discussion of anything that threatened the gender status quo was extremely limited during this period in Chile.[17]

The impact of relatively strong party discipline can also be discerned in South Africa. Racial, class and ideological divisions have been seen as far more salient than any unity gained through shared gender interests (Geisler 2000: 622). Women MPs are under pressure to vote in ways that are consistent with their party's position on an issue. The ANC expected MPs to vote according to its pro-choice position on abortion while National Party and Inkatha Freedom Party women were expected to vote according to their parties' anti-abortion stance (Geisler 2000: 622). Attempts were made to establish a multiparty women's caucus WPG early on but cross-party organizing was not very successful (Walsh 2006). It did not have the support of the minority parties—the leadership of the National Party was opposed to it and it was seen as an ANC-front (Geisler 2000: 622). It could not provide 'either a support structure or a lobbying point for women MPs' (Goetz and Hassim 2002: 318). In El Salvador some cross-party organizing has been possible, despite the ideological differences between the parties, but only on some issues. Women could unite across party lines around quotas, maintenance, and domestic violence but not around abortion or economic rights (Hipsher 2001: 150–5). A number of factors therefore play an important role in determining whether cross-party organizing can take place among women representatives. Any divisions between women MPs, in terms of differing party ideologies and the extent to which they see themselves as representing 'women's interests', as well as the nature of the issue under consideration, are central.

Are single party women's caucuses more effective in organizing around gender issues than cross-party organizations in parliaments? Only a limited number of political parties have them. In South Africa only the ANC has a women's caucus, founded after only two women were appointed as ministers in 1994. Geisler (2000: 621) highlights the divisions that exist even among ANC women MPs arguing that the caucus represents younger black professional women and not older activists. However Goetz and Hassim (2002: 318) argue that the caucus 'acted as a key pressure point within parliament, along with the Joint Standing Committee on the Improvement of the Quality of Life and Status of Women (JSCIQLSW)' which began as an ad hoc committee to oversee the implementation of CEDAW but after skilful lobbying by ANC feminists was upgraded to a proper standing committee. As we see in Part IV the actions of a number of overtly feminist ANC MPs such as Pregs Govender played a key role in ensuring the Joint Standing Committee, and the ANC women's caucus could identify legislative priorities and lobby for policy changes particularly in the first parliament (Albertyn, Hassim, and Meintjes 2002).

The other major example of a women's grouping in a legislature was the short-lived WOR bloc in the Russian parliament. Because it had its origins in the Soviet Women's Committee, it could not be identified as feminist and although women were mentioned in the WOR election campaign there was more emphasis on the need to preserve social protection (Buckley 1997: 64). Overtly feminist organizations initially kept their distance from it, refusing any links in the 1993 elections. Indeed a number of feminists from the Independent Women's Forum ran without success for the Yabloko liberal political party (Sperling 1999: 117). But despite having only twenty-three seats for such a short period, WOR did play a significant role in the Duma. WOR deputies were instrumental in the establishment of the Committee on the Affairs of Women, the Family and Youth, and influenced several pieces of legislation that had implications for women such as the bill revising the Family and Marriage Code (Sperling 1999: 125). Overtime WOR rhetoric drew closer to that of the independent women's movement and even though it remained unwilling to be identified as feminist, it did forge more links with women's organizations outside the Duma.

The experience of women organizing within legislatures underlines some important themes that have emerged in the analysis of the factors that determine the levels of women's representation. Despite arguments about 'critical mass', it is not necessarily the overall number of women legislators that is the key factor in translating descriptive representation into women 'acting for' women. The importance of a feminist presence among female legislators, the necessity of links to women's movements outside the legislature, and the importance of party ideologies that are open to women's claims for equality are all central. Without the presence of these factors, there is no reason why women legislators will take on a gender agenda simply because they are women. In keeping with the conclusions that Weldon (2002) draws from her study of thirty-four democracies, the election of large numbers of women will not necessarily result in dramatic changes or improvements in women's substantive representation.

❖ CONCLUSIONS

We are now in a position to draw some comparative conclusions about the factors that have influenced the varying levels of women's descriptive representation in the post-transition period and the importance of the roles played by different women actors in the electoral arena. There is no significant correlation between the nature of the non-democratic regime, whether state socialist or authoritarian, and subsequent overall levels of women's representation. Our other findings broadly concur with the conclusions that have been drawn from the analysis of the long-standing democracies. The nature of electoral rules and parties and party systems do make a difference. Parties on the left in both post-state socialist and post-authoritarian polities do tend to field more women candidates and therefore if they are electorally successful, levels of women's descriptive representation can be relatively high. Left-wing parties are also more likely to be open to gender claims and to introduce both candidate and internal quotas. Although different electoral systems do exhibit differences in their levels of female representation, an effective and appropriate electoral quota is the rule most likely to 'fast track' an increase in female representation. In an international context where overall levels of female representation are rising and support for quotas has increased, there has been less resistance to electoral quotas in our post-authoritarian polities. In post-state-socialist polities no national quotas have been instituted but a few parties on the left have introduced quotas after the political legacy of state socialism became more distant and resistance to quotas has declined.

Some trends do appear more exaggerated in post-transition polities than in long-standing democracies. The lack of institutionalization of some parties and parties systems leads to greater electoral volatility and with it, significant fluctuations in levels of descriptive representation. But there is also evidence that overall levels of women's representation can sometimes benefit from inchoate party systems but these are also more unpredictable. It is therefore hard to draw overall conclusions about the impact of institutionalized parties and party systems on women's representation in new democracies.

However, our understanding of many of these trends cannot be completed without an analysis of the role of women actors, and more particularly feminists, within the electoral arena. Feminists are more likely to be active within parties of the left, particularly in authoritarian and post-authoritarian contexts, and there are numerous examples where they played a key role in the introduction of quotas at both party and electoral levels. We can only begin to speculate whether, in some cases such as Brazil which has a low level of women's representation in spite of an electoral quota, feminist activists chose not to focus their energies on other arenas seen as more open and rewarding than electoral politics. We will need to consider not only the impact that might have on levels of representation but also on gender outcomes. Indeed we must be nuanced in our understanding of the roles played by women legislators and the significance of raising levels of female representation. In line with the scepticism that many analysts display for the concept of 'critical mass', 'sheer numbers' of women do not necessarily make a difference. A whole host of other factors come into play as a comparison of Argentina and South Africa can demonstrate.

The vexed question of the relationship between women's descriptive and substantive representation will be considered again in Part IV where we examine a range of different gender policy outcomes and how they come about. From the analysis in this part of the book, there is little evidence that, on its own, high levels of women's descriptive representation will necessarily result in either the articulation of gender issues, particularly of a strategic kind, or the placing of those gender issues on the policy agenda. We can now move on to examine the factors affecting women's substantive representation in the constitutional/bureaucratic arenas before finally considering gender-policy outcomes.

❖ NOTES

1 In early 2006 twenty-eight countries reached or surpassed this figure of 25%. Argentina was ranked 7th and South Africa was ranked 14th by the IPU.

2 Elzbieta Matynia (2001) describes the Polish roundtable talks in some detail. Of the 452 negotiators, only 5 of those at the three main tables were women. The constitutional lawyer Janina Zakrewska was one of the leading actors on the political team for Solidarity. Zofia Czaja sat on the political table for the government. Helena Govalska, Grazna Staniszewska, and Irena Wocjicka sat on the economy table for Solidarity. The negotiations lasted for 59 days and the first plenary session was broadcast on television.

3 Interview with Maria Adamik, founder member of the Feminist Network, Budapest, September 2005.

4 Interview with Mavivi Manzini, July 2003, Johannesburg; Statement of the National Executive Committee of the ANC of the Emancipation of Women in South Africa, 2 May 1990.

5 Freedom House is a US-based NGO founded over 60 years ago to support democracy and freedom. It produces annual 'league tables' of democracy and freedom that are widely cited.

6 Interview with Sylvia Chejter, feminist activist, Buenos Aires, June 1996.

7 Populist parties are hard to characterize on a left–right continuum as they can have ideologies that have left and right-wing elements.

8 This information comes from Riet Delsing who undertook research on positive action measures for women within the Chilean political parties for SERNAM in 1995 (interview, Santiago, January 1996).

9 Fanny Pollarolo, a PS deputada and PS vice-president for women was hopeful that the creation of this position would enable women activists to have more influence on the mainstream of the party (interview, Santiago, January 1996).

10 Mária Antonieta Saa, the PPD deputada, ex-mayor of Conchali and women's representative in the Asamblea in 1986, stressed this in an interview (Santiago, January 1996).

11 Interview with Gloria Bonder, Director of CEM and ex-member of Menem's women's cabinet, Buenos Aires, May 1996.

12 The deputies who introduced the bill realized that it would not succeed but wanted to raise the issue of quotas. For a discussion of the difficulties of 'feminist policy making' see Liesl Haas, 'Legislating Equality: Influences on Feminist Policymaking in Chile', Paper presented at XXI LASA Congress, Chicago, 1998.

13 Liesl Haas, 'Legislating Equality: Influences on Feminist Policymaking in Chile', Paper presented at XXI LASA Congress, Chicago, 1998.

14 Hana Havelkova, Jirina Siklova, and Alena Krizkova all made this point independently in interviews, Prague, November 2005.

15 Caul argues that there is generally a time lag between the imposition of quota and a noticeable increase in the number of women elected as party compliance tends to increase over time.

16 Interview with Maria del Carmen Feijoó, member of constituent assembly Buenos Aires, May 1996.

17 Fanny Pollarolo, the feminist, PS deputy for District Three (Calama), and PS vice-president for Women, stressed this in an interview with the author (Santiago, January 1996).

Part IV ❖ The State and Policy Outcomes

The final part of this book deals with the relationship between transitions to democracy, women's substantive representation and policy outcomes. One of the major tasks of this last section is to complete our analysis of the circumstances under which a transition to democracy can alter different women's access to policymaking and with what results. Do some transitions to democracy offer greater opportunities for gender policy reform than others and why? How far do the differing starting points and transitions paths contribute to different gender outcomes? Indeed do some transitions offer more opportunities than periods of more normal politics? Are some gender reforms easier to achieve than others? To answer these questions, any analysis of the outcomes of transitions must consider not only descriptive representation and substantive representation in the conventional political arena but also women's substantive representation in policy formation. This can take two forms: the ability to participate in policymaking processes and to impact on policy content—characterized by Stetson and Mazur (1995) as 'access and influence'. We have already considered the ways in which gender issues can be articulated and placed on the policy agendas of some transitions. We will now look at the conditions under which this articulation can be translated into positive gender outcomes (defined in Part I as an improvement on the previous situation), before considering the impact of social and economic restructuring on those outcomes.

The various factors that contribute to policy development in different issue areas have long been the subject of debate. If we characterize the policymaking process as a conflict over competing policy frames with policy development explained as an interaction between interests, ideas, and institutions, we must examine the behaviour of different actors both inside and outside the state in their attempts to influence the policymaking process as well as different institutions (Mazey 2000). We have already looked at some actors within the conventional political arena. In Part III, for example, we saw how the openness of political parties to a gender agenda is dependent on a range of factors such as ideology and the role of female party activists. We saw in Part II that women's movements were the most important actor outside the state to articulate certain gender issues, particularly in the breakdown and early stages of a number of transitions, and that some movements then attempted to get these issues on to the policy agenda of transitions. But the roles played by other non-state actors, such as religious organizations that may have very different ideas about gender relations, can also be important. We must also divide the institutional context into its domestic and international components, as well as looking at the different decision-making venues in both the electoral and bureaucratic arenas. We need to consider the influence of international conferences and their follow-up mechanisms, the development of international norms and rights regimes and the international women's movement on policymaking and legal reform processes in different areas. And the ways in which the desire of many post-socialist polities to join the European Union (EU) has impacted on gender policy.

Therefore, in order to understand the processes whereby different gender reforms can come about, we need to breakdown our analysis into a number of components. We must examine the situation prior to the transition, looking at the gender regime and the key actors involved. We can then look at the institutional context that emerges during and after the transition. Having explored these factors, it is possible to establish the impact of these different actors and institutional configurations. We will examine the state and bureaucratic arenas, examining state women's machineries (SWMs) as the key mechanism that has been used to improve women's substantive representation in the policymaking process. We will then look at post-transition policy outcomes. Beginning with outcomes in the constitutional/legal arena, we will focus on the ways in which constitutions create frameworks that embody certain conceptions of gender rights. We will then look at three gender rights issues—marriage and divorce; reproductive rights and abortion; and domestic violence. Because rights in each area can be framed in different ways and have different national and international regimes overseeing them, attempts to reform policy in each area vary considerably.

However, as narrow legal frameworks and policies that grant rights are a necessary but not sufficient condition for those rights to be effective, it is also important to examine not only constitutional and legal frameworks but also the wider social and economic conditions that affect women's ability to enjoy and operationalize these rights. The social and economic policies that have been introduced alongside transitions to democracy are hugely significant. The final part looks how the supposedly 'gender neutral' policies of economic and social restructuring, that have so often been associated with transitions to democracy, are gendered. It concentrates on two key areas: market reforms and welfare restructuring. Both have been central to reform programmes and both have a differential impact, not only on men and women, but also on different groups of women, that affects efforts to increase women's descriptive and substantive representation.

❖ THE STATE AND POLICY OUTCOMES

❖ NON-DEMOCRATIC REGIMES

❖ *State Socialism*

As we saw in Part II, state socialist regimes were officially committed to equality between the sexes. Influenced by the socialist analysis of the 'woman question', they had an explicit commitment to improve the position of women and implement policies to achieve this. They also attempted to bring about a comparatively rapid transformation and modernization of the pre-existing order by dismantling and reforming social relations, ideologies, legal, political, and religious systems (Molyneux 1981). They implemented similar kinds of economic policies, with a leading role for the state, nationalization of the commanding heights of the economy, collectivization of agriculture, and an increase in the welfarist role of the state. Within this framework women were to be emancipated through the removal of class relations and through entry into paid employment. As a result of this understanding of women's oppression and the measures needed to combat it, relations between men and women were not seen as antagonistic or contradictory (Molyneux 1981).

Most socialist states implemented policies based on this formulation of the 'woman question'. However, Molyneux (1985) argues that, on the whole, the commitment of socialist states to women's emancipation was subject to three qualifications. First, sex equality was not a priority, the main concerns were economic development and social stability. Equality was realized only in so far as it contributed to or at least did not detract from other priorities. Indeed Fodor (2004*b*: 4) argues that in the post-Second World War context of 'rapid and intensive industrialization, women's labour was needed to replace men who left clerical work to take up better paid blue-collar positions in the new steel factories' in East Central Europe. Second, the concept of sex equality was based on the notion of male and female roles being symmetrical and complementary rather than undifferentiated. Third, 'emancipation' was often seen primarily as emancipation from the constraints of a traditional social order (Molyneux 1985*b*: 51).

In legal terms, most socialist states introduced sweeping changes to the pre-existing order to give women equal rights and status to men in civil law. These were implemented after the revolution of 1917 in the Soviet Union and in the late 1940s in the countries of East Central Europe. Marriage laws were reformed and divorce was legalized and made available to women on the same terms as men. Women were granted equal property rights within marriage (Molyneux 1985*b*). The secular socialist states, although decrying religious belief, saw the heterosexual monogamous nuclear family created through civil marriage as the basic unit of society, with a conventional division of labour between men and women within it. At the same time women were also drawn into the labour market in large numbers. By 1980 women made up about 50% of the workforce in East/Central

Europe facilitated by the state provision of childcare. But there was some variation between different countries in terms of both women's economic activity rates and maternity and childcare provision. By the end of the 1980s, 84% of Hungarian, but only 74% of Polish women were considered economically active (Fodor 2004b: 5).[1] Following the lead of the Soviet Union, abortion laws were liberalized in much of East Central Europe in the 1950s giving most women some access to abortion (Zielinska 2000). However, as a result of fears about the declining birth rate, pronatalist policies—including incentives such as generous leave schemes and allowances for women with small children—were widely introduced in the 1970s (Wolchik 2000).

'Emancipation from above' inspired by the state socialist analysis of the woman question meant that, often at much earlier dates than first world societies, women had been granted an impressive raft of legal rights on paper. The state undertook to provide social welfare in the form of education, health care, and provision for children and the elderly. Many countries had also become signatories to a number of international conventions and treaties during the state socialist era. Poland ratified not only CEDAW in 1981, but also various ILO labour conventions pertaining to the equality of men and women in the labour market (Heinen and Portet 2002). But Einhorn (1991) has argued that because the rights that women enjoyed in these societies were 'given' rather than won through struggle, they were often taken for granted.

In practice the reality was also sometimes rather different. Some of the laws contradicted each other. For example there was a discrepancy between the equal rights granted to women in the 1952 Polish Constitution and the ninety occupations that they were excluded from in the Labour Code (Heinen and Portet 2002). Because the Polish labour code, was not altered, along with other civil codes, to take account of the international conventions, their effect was also minimal. Women often experienced the 'right to work' as more of a duty than an opportunity and they were concentrated in low-paid, low-status, and gender-segregated occupations. On average women earned about 70% of male wages (Galligan and Sloat 2003: 3). However, women did make inroads into gender-atypical occupations. According to Pollert (2003: 334), 'women's exclusion from the high pay and status of heavy industry also led to the unintended consequence of their high-educational attainment, which drew them into certain professions'. In Poland women moved into medicine, business and economics, and some legal areas. In Czechoslovakia women formed 60% of medical students and 40% of doctors (Pollert 2003).

At the same time, the policy implications of the economistic analysis of women's subordination meant that nothing was done to change men's roles in either the productive or reproductive spheres. Family and gender relations within the private sphere were left untouched and women retained responsibility for the domestic sphere. Apart from the provision of childcare, attempts to socialize domestic labour, for example through the provision of laundries and canteens, did not amount to much. The generous maternity and childcare leave provision introduced in the 1970s only applied to mothers, not fathers. Women were seen primarily as mothers who were also workers but who still retained almost sole responsibility for the domestic sphere. Men and women accordingly had different patterns of work. There was little childcare available for children under three. It was therefore common for women to take time out of the labour market to look after very young children and then return to full-time work as there were very few opportunities for part-time work (Fodor 2004*b*).

The dominance of these ideas about men and women's roles also resulted in very little discussion of sexuality, sexual violence, or relations between men and women since there was little notion that women's oppression might stem from men as a group or patriarchy. Effective contraception was frequently not available and in the Soviet Union abortion was used almost routinely in the absence of other less invasive methods of fertility control. In other countries, pronatalism affected women's ability to control reproduction. At one extreme, fears about the declining birth rate in Romania led to severe restrictions on the availability of contraception and abortion introduced by the pronatalist Ceaucescu regime from 1966 (Baban 2000). Women therefore faced a double (if not triple, if one counts attending meetings and being active in the public sphere) productive and reproductive burden in societies that did not prioritize the provision of labour saving, consumer goods (Waylen 1994: 345).

Under state socialism the policymaking process was closed. Few actors outside of the state and the communist party were involved to any significant degree in the design of policy and there were few women within the policymaking elites (Fodor et al. 2002: 480). As autonomous women's movements were not allowed, they could not influence policymaking either. Even the Catholic Church, although it played an oppositional role in Poland and the GDR, could have little direct influence over policymaking as state socialism was avowedly secular. However, in Poland the communist government was mindful of the stance of the Catholic Church towards issues such as abortion (Zielinska 2000).

As a result, the changes in civil codes and laws implemented from above have been labelled 'patriarchal-paternalistic policies' (Dolling 1991). Indeed Gal (1997: 41) has claimed that under state socialism, the state took on a directly patriarchal role through its paternalistic intervention into the private sphere. And rather than seeing their involvement in the labour market as emancipation, many women felt that the extensive intrusion of the state into their lives and bodies was a problem. The fall in the birth rate (often called the 'birthrate strike') experienced in much of East Central Europe in 1970s and 1980s has been seen as direct response to the huge demands that state socialism placed upon women.

A mixed legacy was therefore inherited at transition—women's rights were enshrined in legal frameworks that were unsurpassed almost anywhere else in world, but these rights had been granted from above not won through struggle at the grass roots. Women had also achieved high-educational levels and made inroads into many professions. But pay differentials and gender segregation remained whilst women endured a double if not triple burden since relationships in the private sphere were unaltered and the provision of welfare and consumer services was inadequate. At the same time, notions of women's emancipation had become associated with discredited old order. There was a widespread desire to sweep away many things associated with state socialism and, even in the negotiated transitions, many of the old communist elites could only retain influence if they could be seen to have transformed themselves.

❖ *Authoritarianism*

The umbrella term authoritarianism can encompass a much greater variety of non-democratic governments than state socialism. As authoritarian regimes do not share a common overarching ideology there is less homogeneity both in their general policies and their policies towards women. But although they are less likely to have explicit set of policies about women, many authoritarian regimes are on the right of the political spectrum and, as part of that, hold traditional notions about women's roles, sometimes invoking religious beliefs as a justification. Under the authoritarian regimes we are looking at, gender regimes were predominantly conservative with limited provision, not only of gender rights, but social and economic rights as well. On taking power, most authoritarian regimes did not sweep away the existing legal frameworks in the same way as state socialist regimes did, but maintained them alongside existing social and economic structures. They also remained relatively isolated from changing international norms around gender rights.

In South Africa, the predominantly Afrikaner National Party presided over the extension of existing racially discriminatory systems after it took power in 1948. The roots of the racially based social and economic segregation that characterized apartheid lay in the colonial period, developing after the creation of South Africa in 1910. Apartheid became more restrictive and tightly enforced. The black majority were only allowed to live in certain areas—the 'tribal homelands' which later became Bantustans, and were therefore deemed to be migrant labourers elsewhere in South Africa. They were subject to strict influx controls enforced through legislation which, after a great deal of resistance, was extended to women. Coloureds and Indians were subject to restrictions through the 'Group Areas Act'. Apartheid policies were justified by a right-wing white supremacist ideology that emphasized the necessity of separate development for different races. Within it, was a conservative vision of gender relations that saw white women primarily as mothers within traditional families (but divided black families) (Gaitskell and Unterhalter 1989).

❖ THE STATE AND POLICY OUTCOMES

Apartheid therefore did not have the same impact on all women since women of different races were subject to different legal frameworks, leading Bozzoli (cited in Albertyn et al. 1999: 3) to talk about a 'patchwork quilt of patriarchies in South Africa'. As well as South African law, black women were subject to customary law that technically denied them adult status so that they could not own or inherit property or gain credit. Rights over children also remained with men (Meintjes 1998: 65). Black men and women were also subject to different regimes under the migratory labour system and movement restrictions imposed on the non-white majority. White women were subject only to South African law that gave them significant rights and legal benefits over other women, such as the right to vote, but discriminated against them in comparison to white men for example in property and tax laws. In addition access to abortion was restricted and there were no effective laws against domestic violence (Seidman 1993: 296).

Military regimes in Latin America often maintained legal codes that included *patria potestad* (male control over children) discriminatory marriage and property laws, severe restrictions on divorce and reproductive rights particularly abortion, and were unlikely to include any equal rights clauses or effective laws to combat domestic violence. Indeed, in contrast to the more direct 'public patriarchy' of state socialism, authoritarian regimes inherited a system whereby the state only indirectly upheld the patriarchal rights of individual men through family and property laws. However, some authoritarian regimes did institute some limited gender reforms, for example by improving women's property rights or legalizing divorce, at the same time as others consolidated and deepened existing conservative gender regimes.

Mala Htun (2003) has explored why the Brazilian military regime was more reformist than the Chilean and Argentine regimes and on some issues not others. The regimes displayed different ideological positions on gender, ranging from extreme social conservatism in Chile, moderate conservatism in Argentina in the 1970s to a more socially neutral position in Brazil at the other end of the spectrum (Htun 2003). And attitudes towards gender were not always constant between different military regimes in the same country. For example in Argentina the bureaucratic authoritarian regime of the 1960s was less socially conservative than the neo-liberal regime in power in the 1970s. Indeed the 'bureaucratic authoritarian' regimes in Brazil and Argentina in the 1960s saw themselves as technocratic and modernizing. This mixture of the 'traditional' and 'modern' often resulted in beliefs and outcomes that had a contradictory impact on women.

The military came to power in Brazil in 1964 professing to uphold traditional Christian values of God, the family, and the elevation of motherhood at the same time as implementing technocratic and modernizing policies that increased educational and employment opportunities, particularly for middle class professional women (Alvarez 1990a). The military government also created a special commission on the status of women in 1975 and introduced several legal changes

THE STATE AND POLICY OUTCOMES ❖

that advanced women's rights in the 1970s and 1980s. The Chilean military regime mobilized women according to its very conservative discourse of motherhood at the same time as this conflicted with the consequences of its neo-liberal economic policies (Waylen 1992b). The roles played by non-state actors, such as the church and elite issue networks also varied. Brazilian women's movements had more opportunities for access to the state under the liberalizing military regime of the 1980s than their counterparts in Chile or Argentina. Much of the Church played an active oppositional role in Brazil and Chile but the more conservative Argentine church did not challenge the military regime.

As a result of all these factors, changes in gender policy varied between states. In all three countries, military regimes wanted to modernize the civil codes that included marriage and property laws. In Argentina and Brazil, the decision-making on this 'technical issue' was left to elite expert networks of lawyers who favoured 'modern' liberal law and sat on the modernizing technocratic commissions set up to design the reforms. The revised codes were adopted with little debate and few objections from actors outside those networks. Marriage and property regimes were reformed in Argentina in 1968 and in Brazil in 1977 giving women equal property rights. But in Chile, social conservatives within the regime, that included the First Lady and representatives from the network of Mother's Centres (CEMA-Chile), objected to the reforms proposed in 1979 and they were shelved. Even the purely symbolic reform that was finally adopted in 1989 faced further protests.

The Brazilian military government went further and as a consequence of elite network lobbying of congress, backed up by public support, supported efforts to introduce divorce which became legal in 1977. Conflict between the regime and a radicalized church, critical of abuse and injustice under the military regime, meant that the regime had little incentive to placate the church by suppressing a divorce law. In contrast in Argentina reformist coalitions lacked a congress to lobby and the tacit alliance between the church and the socially conservative military regime meant that the introduction of divorce was impossible. In Chile, because of the extreme social conservatism of the Pinochet regime, the legalization of divorce was unthinkable despite its conflict with parts of the church (Htun 2003).

Similar patterns are seen with regard to reproductive rights. In all countries abortion remained illegal under most circumstances. However, the Brazilian military government liberalized regulations on contraception in 1979 and in 1983 the regime organized a national women's health programme designed with advice from feminist women's health practitioners (Htun 2000: 13). At the other end of the spectrum the Chilean military regime attempted to restrict the access to birth control that had been sanctioned by the Christian Democrats in the 1960s and extended under Popular Unity (Waylen 1992a: 157). As one of its last acts before it left power in 1989, the military regime outlawed even therapeutic abortions—the only type that had been allowed under Chile's already very restrictive laws (Valenzuela 1991).

Therefore a limited number of (primarily state) actors were involved in policy-making in non-democratic regimes. Apart from a small number of cases where elite issue networks of lawyers were influential, non-state actors did not play significant roles in bringing about reform. However, at the time of transition gender rights and the gender status quo—regulating for example women's access to employment and education—varied considerably between authoritarian and state socialist states. Under state socialism, women theoretically had a range of rights encompassing divorce and abortion as well as the right to the state provision of social welfare. In contrast, for many women, access to a whole range of rights was very poor under authoritarian regimes. Despite the limited 'modernizing' reforms implemented by some military dictatorships, most authoritarian regimes enforced a range of discriminatory laws and prohibitions on abortion.

❖ POST-TRANSITION OUTCOMES

Post-transition polities do not begin with a blank slate. Both the gender rights status quo in existence at the time of transition and the institutional legacy of the non-democratic regime contribute to the size of the policy window for gender reform open to actors in the post-transition period. The speed and openness of the transition as well as the balance of forces at the point of transition affect the institutional legacy left by the outgoing non-democratic regime.

In the negotiated South African transition, although the legal position of many women was poor despite some last minute liberalizations, the institutional opening for certain legal reforms was relatively large. The ideology of apartheid was fatally discredited and it was recognized, even by its most conservative supporters, that many of the glaring legal and political inequalities that characterized the apartheid regime could not remain in place with the move to majority rule. The existence of a policy window for the introduction of measures to reduce inequality on racial grounds also meant that space existed for the introduction of some measures to reduce gender inequality. A discourse that all races should be incorporated into citizenship on equal terms could be used for gender as well as race. However, there was also an assumption that, although a political transition would take place, many of the underlying economic structures (and therefore the accompanying inequalities) would remain in place and as part of the negotiated transition many of the advantages of the white minority were to be safeguarded. In Chile the negotiated transition resulted in the continuing influence of the extremely socially conservative military and the political Right. As a result the institutional opening was relatively small.

In El Salvador, the negotiated transition and the continuing power of the Right also limited the size of the policy window. Substantive gender reform would therefore be difficult to achieve despite the activities of pro-reform actors. However, in Brazil the relatively gender-neutral attitudes of the Brazilian military meant that, although the drawn-out negotiated transition gave the military some influence over policymaking, it would not use it to block gender reform. As we will see it also meant that the constitutional assembly could be a positive arena for the discussion of gender reform. In Argentina its hurried exit from power meant that the more socially conservative military was not in a very strong position to block gender reform. The association of the Church with the military regime also lessened its ability to stymie reform efforts. As a result the policy window for gender reform was open on certain issues. The desire of many new governments to appear democratic also meant that there were some opportunities to frame gender rights reforms in terms of discourses of human rights and citizenship.

In Eastern Europe, many of the transitions from state socialism were relatively speedy even if they were negotiated. Despite the emphasis of some opposition groups, particularly those dominated by dissident intellectuals, on the need for meaningful citizenship and individual rights (which could potentially include gender rights), there was also a wholesale rejection of 'emancipation from above'. Indeed the rejection of state socialism was often associated with a revival of 'traditional' values of god, family, and nation that had within them a conservative vision of women's roles (Waylen 1994). There was a widespread feeling that as a result of the policies and ideology of the previous regime, women's economic role had become too burdensome at the expense of their roles within the home and family (Wolchik 1994).

Goven (2000: 287), for example, argues that there were three currents visible within Hungary in the 1980s that translated into the subsequent political positions of major political parties on women and gender relations. The 'dissident' opposition (which became the liberal parties) embraced liberalism with an emphasis on individual rights that would coexist with a private sphere that had a traditional gender division of labour. The nationalist or populist opposition (which formed the Christian nationalist parties) argued that women had been turned against motherhood and were destroying the nation. Even groups and individuals associated with the socialist parties attributed various social problems such as the high divorce rate to women's full-time employment and inadequate mothering (Goven 2000: 288).

There were therefore few opportunities to frame gender rights in terms of much broader discourses of human rights and citizenship. As a result, discourses advocating improved women's rights were absent from the discussions surrounding the transitions as were organized women's movements that could make these arguments. The policy window for improving gender rights was small in the aftermath of most transitions from state socialism as, if anything, many favoured a return to more 'conservative' gender policies. The opposition groups that took power in the founding elections were no exception.

Transitions to competitive electoral politics also expand the range of political and civil society actors involved in attempts to change the gender rights status quo through the policymaking process. Within the state, different actors come to the fore in the electoral and bureaucratic arenas in the post-transition period. The openness of political parties to gender reform becomes crucially important after they gain electoral office. We saw in Part III that political parties on the left of the political spectrum are often more open to claims of gender equality and are therefore more likely to be persuaded that policy reform is needed. In some cases, political parties such as the ANC in South Africa and some of the more left-wing parties of the Chilean Concertación were poised to play important roles and women activists had already raised gender issues within them. In other cases, the left was discredited or lacked sufficiently widespread support.

Outside the state, the strength of women's movements and other key actors, such as the church, becomes more significant. We saw in Part II that in South Africa, Brazil, and Chile (and to a lesser extent in El Salvador and Argentina), organized women movements were already keen to take advantage of any opportunities provided by the transition to democracy to effect gender reforms. As a result of their actions, women's organizations were considered part of the broad opposition to non-democratic rule. They had already placed gender issues on the agenda of the transitions both in terms of improving women's representation and introducing gender rights reforms. In contrast in East Central Europe, there were no large-scale organized women's movements that had played a role in the transition and could present programmes for reform.

But in some Eastern European countries other actors—such as the Catholic Church in Poland—that had been excluded from significant influence under the previous regime, could now attempt to have more influence over certain policy areas to retrench some established gender rights. In Brazil, Argentina, and particularly Chile, the Catholic Church retained some influence depending on how far it had been an oppositional actor, and it was determined to use this to prevent certain reforms. However, there were also more opportunities for actors, both within the conventional political arena and state as well as outside it, to use newly constructed international gender rights norms in support of their campaigns as newly elected governments were often more susceptible to pressure to implement measures that would make them appear modern and democratic than their predecessors.

In the post-transition period, the primary locus for organized women's engagement in policymaking and gender mainstreaming in the bureaucratic arena has been the state women's machineries. Before we examine the extent of gender-policy reform and different policy outcomes, we must look at these state women's machineries.

THE STATE AND POLICY OUTCOMES ❖

❖ State Women's Machineries

As we saw in Part I, one of the major ways in which some feminists argue that women's substantive representation can be improved is through the establishment of state women's machineries (SWMs). Both as a result of global pressures such as the setting of international norms (embodied for example in the 1995 Beijing Platform for Action), the UN women's conferences and the activities of women's movements nationally and internationally, a large number of SWMs have been established since 1975 (Rai 2002). In many cases, their creation has coincided with a move from a non-democratic regime to a more competitive electoral system. But despite this overall trend, they were often set up for very different reasons, with different structures, powers, and resources and therefore with different capacities to represent 'women's interests' in the policymaking process. Some therefore had 'insider' and others 'symbolic' roles (Lovenduski 2005). In order to understand the particular role played by SWMs in transitions to democracy and the impact that the context of a transition has on a SWM, it is useful to explore a number of themes that will help us to assess their varying utility and effectiveness as well as their ability to give different groups of women 'policy influence and access'. We will examine how and why they were set up, the resources they have been allocated, and the accountability and participation of groups outside the state as well as the importance of the wider political context within which they have been operating.

The SWMs in our case study countries vary hugely. In three of our case study countries, women's policy machineries were set up directly as a result of the efforts of organized women during the process of transition. The establishment of a state women's machinery had been placed on the agenda of these transitions and accepted by influential political parties. Sympathetic elected governments in Brazil, Chile, and South Africa established a women's machinery relatively early on, largely as a consequence of campaigning by women activists within political parties, legislative bodies, and women's organizations. In Brazil a federal body, the National Council on Women's Rights (CNDM), reporting directly to the President, was established in 1985 as a result of pressure from activists and women legislators and following the establishment of women's councils in some cities such as Sao Paulo (Pitanguy 2002). It was created as the result of a legislative proposal developed by a multipartisan parliamentary women's commission and was composed of women legislators from the PMDB, the PFL, and the PT, 'representatives of civil society' linked to autonomous women's movements and academics specializing in women's studies. It was formally lodged in the Ministry for Justice and charged with promoting policies to eliminate discrimination against women (Alvarez 1990a: 221; Macaulay 2003: 18).

After the campaigning by the Chilean women's Concertación, described in Part II, the establishment of a women's machinery was part of the Concertación's election manifesto. Despite opposition from the Right and the Catholic Church which forced some downgrading of its roles and structures, the Servicio Nacional de la Mujer (SERNAM) was created through legislation in 1990 and partly modelled on similar bodies created in Spain and Brazil in the aftermath of their transitions. Although its head was appointed at Cabinet level, it was located in the ministry of planning. Its brief was to 'collaborate with the executive in the design and coordination of public policies which put an end to the levels of discrimination that affect women in the family, social, economic, political and cultural arenas' (Waylen 2000: 786).

Prior to the transition, women activists in South Africa had also given some thought to the design of a SWM as the main vehicle intended to promote gender equality within the state (Albertyn 1992). After some delays, it was established three years after the first democratic elections and largely in ways that the activists had envisaged. Rather than one women's ministry, it was hoped that the creation of a 'package' of institutions in the form of 'strategic nodes' within government, the legislature, and civil society as well as an independent statutory body, would avoid problems—such as marginalization—that had been experienced elsewhere (Albertyn 1995).

Within the government, the Office of the Status of Women (OSW) was set up in the office of the deputy president with similar mechanisms at provincial level. It was charged with developing and implementing a national gender policy and with mainstreaming gender perspectives in government through gender focal points. Within the legislature, the Joint Standing committee on the Improvement of the Quality of Life and Status of Women (JSCIQLSW) has played a key role. Initially established as an ad hoc committee to monitor the progress of CEDAW, it was upgraded to a standing committee after lobbying by feminists within the ANC. It has acted strategically, often in concert with the ANC women's caucus and women's organizations in civil society to champion some important pieces of legislation such as the domestic violence bill (Meintjes 2003).

The Commission for Gender Equality (CGE) envisaged in the constitution (see below) as simultaneously monitoring and stimulating transformation in South African society was set up in 1997. It has been seen as relatively successful despite what Seidman (2003) has argued is a structural tension within it between representation (of women's voices in the state) and mobilization (in support of a feminist agenda) which has sometimes brought the two goals into conflict. It was also assumed that the women's movement outside the state would play a key role in ensuring the national machinery's effectiveness and accountability.

In contrast, in the aftermath of the transitions from state socialism in East Central Europe, SWMs were established much later and not as a consequence of the actions of organized women (Jezerska 2002). They were more often a result of international pressure to fulfil Beijing commitments after 1995 and, in some countries, part of the efforts to implement EU-equality legislation in preparation to join the EU, therefore often playing primarily symbolic roles (Galligan and

Sloat 2003). For example in Russia, formal mechanisms—such as a government commission on Advancing the Status of Women and a department for Family, Women's, and Children's Affairs within the Ministry of Labour and Social Development—were established. But they were largely declaratory, created primarily to comply with commitments made by the government at Beijing (Sundstrom 2005: 440).

A similar pattern can be seen in the Czech Republic. Although it promised to fulfil the Beijing Action Plan and establish suitable institutions, it did not address the issue until 1997 and only set up institutions in 1998 because of the pressure exerted by its desire to join the EU (Pollert 2003). A rather complicated set-up eventually emerged. A department for the Equality of Men and Women was established in the Ministry of Labour and Social Affairs (Galligan and Sloat 2003: 31). In 2001 a gender equality section was established within the Government Council for Human Rights to monitor CEDAW, and various other bodies, such as a parliamentary Commission for Equal Opportunities within the Committee for Social Policy and Healthcare and a consultative body, the Government Council for Equal Opportunities for Men and Women, were also set up (Haskova and Kriskova 2003). Some sceptics have suggested that this complexity fragments responsibility and influence (Pollert 2003: 348). In addition most of these SWMs have been set up by order of a government or ministers or presidential decree rather than legislation. The majority of bodies in East Central Europe are also low level and based within other ministries. For example in 1998 the conservative FIDESZ government in Hungary established the Secretariat for the Representation of Women within the Ministry of Social Welfare (Eberhardt 2005*b*).

Many analysts have agreed that the majority of SWMs—even those established as a consequence of women's activism—do not have sufficient resources to fulfil their briefs. As well as lacking finance, often personnel do not have the necessary technical training to carry out oversight and mainstreaming functions in areas such as trade, economics, and finance. This is particularly true of bodies established primarily to comply with international commitments. Sundstrom (2005: 440) quotes a member of a Russian women's NGO who claimed that apart from the formal existence of these institutions 'there is not a single kopeck in the (state) budget dedicated to improving women's status. That means that everything looks well resolved on paper, but in reality, there are practically no concrete solutions'. Other bodies established in East Central Europe have few staff. The Division for Equality between Men and Women in the Czech republic, for example, had only three employees and the Department for Equal Opportunities in Slovakia had two (Jezerska 2002).

Even SWMs set up under relatively favourable conditions after pressure from women's movements were not as generously resourced as activists had hoped. Only in Brazil did the CNDM begin with an initial ring-fenced allocation bigger than many of the smaller ministries (Alvarez 1990*a*: 221; Macaulay 2003: 18). And on occasion, the resources provided for SWMs were less than resources allocated to related bodies. In South Africa, the initial budget for the CGE was only one-third of the budget for other commissions such as those on human rights and youth (Goetz 1997) and the budget of approximately R2 million was not enough to cover the salaries of the commissioners which were already lower than those of commissioners on the other bodies. When it was finally established, instead of the planned six executive staff, the OSW had only two (Geisler 2004). Many other OSW staff were appointed at low levels, particularly in the provinces and therefore despite the location at the heart of government, OSW personnel found it difficult to get their superiors in government departments to take account of gender concerns (Hassim 1999).

In Chile SERNAM was also established with a relatively small budget of US$2 m plus US$1.5 m from outside. Almost three quarters of the initial budget for 1990–91 was allocated to pay for the fifty-nine staff and the remaining quarter for goods and services. Outside funding came primarily from foreign governments (Sweden, Norway, Denmark Holland, and Spain) and NGOs and other international organizations such as the EU, IBRD, FAO, and UNICEF. Much of this foreign funding was short-term but some was replaced by state funding. SERNAM initially benefited from the shift of foreign funding after the restoration of democracy from grass-roots NGOs, which had received resources directly from donors during the dictatorship, to the new civilian government (Waylen 1996: 110).

For all SWMs it also makes a vital difference who the personnel are. In addition to their experience in areas such as finance, whether or not they have any knowledge or sympathy for gender issues or would identify themselves as feminists, is also crucial. These inclinations will help to determine how far they further gender equality within the state or can have good relationships with women's organizations outside the state. But at the same time prominent and outspoken women within SWMs can also garner opposition. On her appointment as Head of the Polish SWM after the election of the SLD in 2001, Izabela Jaruga-Nowacka announced that her office would fight to liberalize the abortion laws and was vehemently criticized by the Catholic Church (Matynia 2003).

The extent to which SWMs give open access to societal actors, enabling them to participate in policymaking processes and are accountable to actors outside the state, is seen as crucial in first-world polities (Stetson and Mazur 1995). The relationship of SWMs with women's organizations outside the state has varied enormously in the post-transition context. The role that NGOs and women's groups played in the establishment of the SWM accounts for some of that variation. If it was established from the top down as in parts of post-socialist East Central Europe, its relationship with women's NGOs is likely to be poor or non-existent. Indeed scholars have not even analysed the relationships of top-down SWMs and women's organizations in contexts where women's movements were weak. Because these SWMs were often set up for pragmatic and instrumental reasons in the absence of pressure from domestic women's movements, they have been the subject of fewer expectations about their roles, even though they may have done little to improve gender equality or women's policy access.

However, if the SWM was established in part as a result of campaigning from below, a closer relationship can ensue but expectations of its future role will be high. As a result relationships between SWMs and women's organizations have sometimes been fraught, as well as mutually beneficial. Many SWMs have been accused of not consulting or representing the full spectrum of women's organizations and even of weakening women's movements outside the state. At the same time, the post-transition demobilization of women's movements undermined the legitimacy of many SWMs within the state, as the strength of the outside constituencies that SWMs could claim to represent bolstered their power. But the question of the relationship between women's movements and SWMs remains unresolved. How far can an SWM play an insider role incorporating the goals of feminists outside the state? Does a SWM represent civil society within the state, is it simply another state institution or can it play both roles at once?

In Brazil, Chile, and South Africa, relationships between the SWM and women's organizations disappointed observers with high hopes for the future. For the first few years of its existence the Brazilian CNDM enjoyed enormous legitimacy, support from the women's movement and was staffed by experienced feminists (Macaulay 2003: 18). However, after two years of intense activity around family planning, day care, and violence against women as well as strengthening the autonomous women's movement, disillusionment set in as many of the new institutions were extremely partisan and had fallen prey to clientelist manipulation (Alvarez 1990a: 248). In both South Africa and Chile, feminists claimed that the equal opportunities plan produced by the SWM did not involve sufficient consultation with women's organizations outside the state. Indeed in Chile, Brazil, and South Africa, activists and scholars have argued that the establishment of the SWM beheaded feminist movements as activists move into paid positions within it (Alvarez 1990a: 247; Schild 1998). Specifically with regard to Brazil, Alvarez (1990a: 255) claims that women's organizations did not form their own autonomous lobby around the new Brazilian constitution in the same way as other social movements because the CNDM spearheaded and coordinated the campaign.

The responsibility that the SWM has for distributing funds for research and projects to NGOs and women's organizations that might previously have gone to them directly under the non-democratic regime, can often result in a clientelistic relationship with some groups more likely to benefit than others (Waylen 2000). Indeed it is often claimed that it is the most professionalized organizations which get the funding as they can fill out the forms and know their way around the system more effectively. As a result grass-roots and popular organizations lose out to the more middle class, often feminist, NGOized ones that provide the 'gender-policy assessment, project execution and social services delivery' that the state and within that SWMs want (Alvarez 1999: 182). SERNAM for example has been criticized for only providing policy access to one segment of women's organizations—feminist and professional NGOs—and for excluding other groups, particularly grass-roots women's organizations, from the newly emerging 'gender policy networks' (Franceschet 2003: 23). But at the same time, Franceschet (2003: 14) has argued that although SERNAM has not had the impact that many desired, it has provided women's organizations with resources, such as grants from its civil society fund, as well as policy initiatives and a discourse of women's right's that they can mobilize around, thus helping to stimulate the emergence of new networks and other forms of women's organizing. SWMs therefore can have the potential to shape the development of women's movements.

The foregoing discussion has made it clear that the political context/opportunity structure is significant in determining the activities and effectiveness of any SWM created in the aftermath of a transition to democracy. In addition to the roles played by women's movements, uninstitutionalized political systems, frequent changes of government, and the ideological complexion of the government in power affect the SWM in post-transition polities. Some symbolic SWMs were set up to serve a president's immediate interests (often by presidential decree) rather than with a firm institutional basis in response to the demands of women's movements. The fate of these SWMs can be determined by presidential whim, particularly if policy is determined more by personalism and populism in particularist and presidentialist democracies than by an ideologically based programme.

Feminists in Argentina for example claim that the Peronist President Menem was initially enthusiastic about women's rights because he had been persuaded that supporting them would help both him and Argentina to be seen as fully democratic.[2] But once he felt they were no longer a priority, the consequences for the SWM were negative. On his election in Argentina in 1991, Menem had established a new body, the Consejo Nacíonal de la Mujer, charged with the implementation of CEDAW and ensuring 'the maximum participation of women in all spheres' (Informe Nacional 1995). It was established by decree as part of the presidential office and was therefore part of that government not a permanent part of the state apparatus. Initially while Menem was still sympathetic, the Consejo had quite a large budget that peaked in 1993. It played an important role in the run-up to the Beijing Women's Conference. The Consejo also produced an equal opportunities plan for 1993–4 and established a number of programmes for example to increase women's political participation.

Subsequently, Virginia Franganillo, its feminist-sympathizing head, was forced out after campaigning against the government's attempt to insert the anti-abortion clause into the new constitution. The issue was a source of conflict in Cairo (the 1994 population conference) as well as in Beijing in 1995, where the Argentine position was the most pro-Vatican and conservative in Latin America.[3] Franganillo's removal prompted the resignation of some of the feminist members of Menem's women's cabinet and signalled the end of the cordial relations that the Consejo had enjoyed with some feminist groups outside the state. After a long delay Menem replaced her with a staunch Peronist who was fiercely opposed to reproductive rights.[4] In the immediate aftermath, few feminist NGOs maintained links with the Consejo, and despite the implementation of a $14 m government Inter-American Bank Development Bank funded plan to establish Consejos in every province, there was a widespread feeling that it had been marginalized from any policymaking role.[5] This trend of unpredictable and inconsistent presidential support has also been confirmed in Peru under Fujimori and in Venezuela (Waylen 1996; Friedman 2000*b*).

The frequent changes of government often associated with less institutionalized systems can also increase the vulnerability of SWMs. New governments of a rather different political complexion are likely to change the policies and institutions of a previous government. They have often downgraded or marginalized already existing SWMs. Indeed Menem, on taking office in Argentina, abolished the existing UCR women's machinery, the Subsecretaria de la Mujer established in 1987, that had only recently become more active under a feminist leadership, before replacing it with the Consejo. Many SWMs are therefore vulnerable if they are not established on a securely institutionalized basis within the state structures. In Brazil, after a four and a half year heyday, the CNDM became marginalized at the end of Sarney's government in 1989 (Macaulay 2003: 19). The minister of justice appointed six new conservative councillors to CNDM against the wishes of the other councillors and deprived the CNDM of budgetary and administrative autonomy. The organization also lost leverage because of the general turn to the right at the state and federal levels (Alvarez 1990*a*: 245–6; Pitanguy 2002; Htun 2003). It was effectively de-institutionalized during the Collor/Franco governments retaining only consultative functions having been deprived of staff, resources and executive capacity (Macaulay 2003: 19). However, at the tail end of the subsequent Cardoso administration, it regained its own executive staff and in 2002 was finally replaced by presidential decree by a new Secretariat for Women's Rights (SEDIM) which was then immediately transformed into the Secretariat for Policies on Women by the incoming PT administration of President Lula.

Jezerska (2002) describes a similar pattern in East Central Europe where some women's machineries have experienced frequent reconfigurations in terms of name, size, membership, and location that have impacted on their effectiveness. In 2002 the newly elected left coalition (HSP–SZDSZ) changed the status of the Hungarian secretariat, moving it into the Ministry of Employment and renaming it the directorate for Equal Opportunities (Eberhardt 2005b). In Poland, rather unusually, the office of the Plenipotentiary for the Family and Women had been established as early as 1991 and operated under the vigorous leadership of Anna Popowicz. However, she was removed in 1992 and Hanna Suchocka, the conservative first women prime minister, did not appoint a replacement. Indeed the office

❖ The State and Policy Outcomes

was not re-established until after Beijing in 1995 and did not become active until the successor appointed by the SLD began to form alliances with women's NGOs (Pollert 2003: 349).

But two years later, the more right-wing Solidarity Electoral Alliance closed the existing office, stopped earlier initiatives, and appointed a male Plenipotentiary for the Family (Galligan 2003: 31). As a result the domestic violence programme that had been launched by the previous SLD government was not implemented leading to a loss of UN funding (Bretherton 2001: 66). But at the same time, the abolition of the monthly consultative NGO forum—set up to consider the gender implications of government policies and programmes—together with the government's departure from its predecessor's Beijing commitments—that formed part of the changes introduced by the Solidarity Electoral Alliance—actually sparked the creation of an NGO association to protest against them (Bretherton 2001: 67). Faced with the weakness of the SWM, Polish NGOs, lawyers, and parliamentarians lobbied separately for equality legislation and an independent equality body. Then, on the election of the left-leaning SLD–UP in 2001, an Office of Governmental Plenipotentiary for the Equal Status of Women and Men was established, headed by Izabela Jaruga-Nowacka who was a long-time activist and leader of a women's organization associated with a left-wing party (Matynia 2003). Again it appears that the election of a right-wing government in Poland in 2005 will have negative consequences for the SWM.

The ideological position of the government/party in power therefore plays a key role. SWMs are more likely to be effective if they are part of governments that have some commitment to gender equality, often because they are on the left and more open to the activities of women's organizations. We have seen this in South Africa and in Chile. But even SWMs established by these governments have faced difficulties. For example ideological divisions within the Concertación coalition added to the pressure that circumscribed SERNAM's activities. During the 1990s SERNAM was headed by a Christian Democrat as they held the presidency and dominated the government. This domination set the tone for the organization and sometimes provided problems for the socialist deputy minister (Baldez 2001). SERNAM steered clear of controversial subjects such as reproductive rights and even divorce in favour of projects focusing on income generation and women headed households (Waylen 1996). This changed somewhat after a socialist president was elected in 2000. However, in both South Africa and Chile, the fate of the SWM and their real levels of institutionalization have not been tested by a change of government.

We have therefore seen huge variations in the SWMs that emerged in the aftermath of transitions to democracy and identified a number of factors that can affect their ability to achieve their aims and facilitate women's policy access and influence. SWMs were helped by the increasingly favourable international context. In the 1990s this trend manifested itself in the preparations for the Beijing

THE STATE AND POLICY OUTCOMES ❖

conference and its aftermath, and for countries in East Central Europe by EU accession. But within the state they also need adequate resources, to be staffed by feminists or those sympathetic to feminism and to enjoy a favourable location that is central to government not in an outlying ministry. A favourable national political context is crucial. Governments and political parties that are sympathetic to gender equality are important, otherwise tokenism is a danger—and as a result any body will be underfunded and understaffed—a criticism which has been levelled even at relatively sympathetic governments such as South Africa (Goetz 1997). SWMs also need an institutionalized position that is safe from changes of government or presidential whim. But this vulnerability is more probable in the post transition context with its greater likelihood of presidentialism and/or delegative democracy.

The SWM's inclusiveness and its relationship with women's organizations outside the state is also significant. SWMs have varied in the extent to which they have facilitated women's engagement with policymaking mechanisms for example through consultative fora and mainstreaming strategies. Support from women's movements outside the state can be crucial to the effectiveness of any SWM and its ability to increase women's substantive representation within the state. As we will see when we consider policy outcomes, the formation of insider and outsider alliances can often be central to the success of any attempts to achieve positive gender outcomes. Therefore we can only make a final judgement about the effectiveness of different SWMs after we have examined some different gender policy outcomes and the role that SWMs played in them.

❖ Constitutional/Legal Frameworks and Codes

But, before we consider particular gender policy outcomes, we will examine one further aspect of the institutional set-up of new democracies that can contribute to gender outcomes: the legal frameworks and codes. Constitutions, for example, can provide important constraining or enabling frameworks that can impact on attempts to achieve changes in gender policy. Indeed in many countries, the decision about the legal framework and constitution of a new polity is one of the first institutional choices to be made. Each of the three options chosen by both post-socialist and post-authoritarian polities has differing implications for gender rights.

First, the new polity can maintain the pre-existing civil codes and even the constitution created by the non-democratic regime. In Chile, the continued use of the 1980 'Constitution in Liberty' was a non-negotiable part of the pacted transition in which the non-democratic regime exerted a considerable degree of influence. The constitution had been designed by the military regime and was inspired by the right-wing philosopher Friedrich Hayek (Waylen 1992a). The newly elected government's capacity to alter it was limited by the system's in-built bias to the Right that made change difficult to achieve. In East Central Europe, despite the desire to sweep away state socialism's legacy in the move towards a market economy and the re-ascendance of traditional values of god, family, and nation, most states choose to maintain the basic framework of the pre-existing civil codes and constitutions. Although gender equality clauses were included in state socialist constitutions, there had been few opportunities to exercise some of the gender rights enshrined within them, because they were often contradicted by civil and labour codes. Many countries like Czechoslovakia and Hungary also made important and often comprehensive modifications such as removing the leading role for the party. The second option is for states to revert to the constitutions that pre-dated the non-democratic regime. Argentina, for example, initially returned to its constitution of 1853. Both these choices maintained the existing gender rights status quo in some form.

The final option is to design a new constitution either as part of the negotiations leading up to the founding election or in the period after the inauguration of competitive electoral politics. As we saw in Part I, the incorporation of gender rights into constitutional design recently has been the subject of feminist activism in some parts of the first world. However the extent to which the design of a new constitution offered the opportunity to create an enabling framework for the realization of improved gender rights varied considerably between our case study countries. In Brazil and South Africa the final constitutions, that included a number of women activists' demands, have been heralded as a positive advance for gender rights. In Argentina, although the new constitution of 1994 did not incorporate the demands of activists to the same extent, an alliance of women actors defeated attempts to incorporate a right to life clause supported by the President. In contrast women actors played no part in the design of the Polish constitutions introduced since the transition. We will isolate the key factors that influenced how far Brazilian, Argentine, and South African constitutions could provide a foundation for positive gender outcomes before briefly using the Polish case as a contrast.

In Brazil the design of a new constitution was part of the gradual transition to democracy. After the direct election of a civilian president, Jose Sarney, in 1985, the new Congress to be elected in 1986 was to form a constituent assembly charged with writing the document. According to Jacqueline Pitanguy (2002: 810), the President of the CNDM from 1986–9, 'the feminist movement seized on the occasion as a unique opportunity to enlarge women's citizenship rights and promote gender equality'. The newly formed CNDM played a key role in this process. It acted as an effective de facto women's lobby and coordinator for the women's movement, holding conferences, seminars, and public forums all over Brazil where proposals for the constitution were formulated, culminating in a Letter (*Carta*) from Women to the Constituent Assembly. The *Carta* included a range of proposals such as changes in labour legislation, family law, day care, and

THE STATE AND POLICY OUTCOMES ❖

other improvements in women's rights such as the explicit recognition of equality between men and women (Alvarez 1990a: 251; Htun 2003: 125). It was endorsed by a broad spectrum of women's groups. The CNDM also served as an effective women's lobby at all stages of the drafting of the charter document. It exerted pressure on legislators and liaised between women's movements and twenty-six female legislators in parliament (the lipstick lobby (*la bancada do batom*)) (Guzman 2004: 19) to press for the inclusion of women's demands.

As a result of these activities and alliances, many women's movement demands were included in the final constitution. Indeed Pitanguy (2002: 811) claims that the campaign was a success and that 80% of demands—ranging from the recognition of women's sexual and reproductive rights as well as equal rights both within the family and outside it to 120 days paid maternity leave—were accepted. However, a number of issues were controversial. Reproductive rights were a key battleground. The issue was raised by feminists who campaigned for the decriminalization of abortion, but a counter-movement, the pro-life lobby (comprising the Christian Right of Catholics and Evangelical Christians), also engaged in some active lobbying in favour of a pro-life amendment (Alvarez 1990a: 254). In the end the CNDM, in a strategic move, withdrew its decriminalization amendment on condition that the pro-life amendment was also withdrawn.

Despite the successes, the overall verdict on the constitution is mixed. Alvarez (1990a: 252) claims that it was those issues that seriously threatened to alter existing gender power relations such as abortion rights which were excluded from the final draft. Finally, the constitution itself became a huge and unwieldy document that was very difficult to implement in a context where legal rights on paper did not always correspond to the rights enjoyed in practice. Their exercise frequently required both further legislation and additional government expenditure. So the completion of the family equality agenda required the reform of Brazil's civil code that proved difficult to achieve (Htun 2003: 127). Therefore it has been more difficult to use the constitution as an enabling framework and the basis for further gains in gender rights than many hoped.

The new South African constitution is one of the most successful in gender terms. As a result of the efforts of women activists during and prior to the transition it had gender equality enshrined within it, and, in contrast to the Brazilian example, it subsequently has proved to be relatively effective as an enabling framework subsequently. From early on women activists both in and outside the ANC had recognised the need to ensure that gender equality was part of any future constitution. The 'charterism' of the opposition that emphasized equal rights for all citizens enshrined in law and the negotiated transition made the process of constitution-writing a key area of contestation for women activists. As a result of their activities within the organization, the ANC Constitutional Guidelines issued in 1988 did incorporate ANC women's demands, even if only in very narrow and formal terms (Albertyn 1994: 47). Indeed the failings of the constitutional

❖ THE STATE AND POLICY OUTCOMES

guidelines were subsequently discussed at an in-house ANC workshop on Women and the Constitution held in Lusaka in 1989.[6] Both ANC women in exile and internal women activists had then agreed at the Malibongwe conference on the need for strategic intervention into the transition process to ensure that their concerns were incorporated into the future constitution.

The triple alliance of women activists, academics, and politicians facilitated by the WNC, organized to influence the political processes that included the writing of the constitution. The WNC protested about the exclusion of non-sexism from the first draft of the constitutional principles. The need for an equality clause in the interim constitution was also accepted early on in the negotiations. The resulting interim constitution therefore contained a commitment to gender equality within a framework of rights. In the end women parliamentarians in the constituent assembly won the argument for the inclusion of the principle of non-sexism when the interim constitution was presented in 1994 (Hassim 2003b: 718). The biggest area of contention was customary law and whether it should be subject to the equality clause. Traditional leaders wanted customary law excluded to safeguard forms of inheritance, property, and marriage that maintained their hereditary power. According to Catherine Albertyn (1994: 59), the WNC, and within it the Rural Women's Movement, lobbied and argued vociferously that to exclude customary law would be to exclude the most oppressed and marginalized groups namely rural black women. Unsuccessful attempts were made to broker a compromise between these two opposing positions. It was not until the last minute of the MPNP that the traditional leaders lost and customary law was made subject to the equality clause. Partly as a result of the attempts to negotiate a solution, the creation of two new institutions was envisaged: Council of Traditional Leaders and a commission for gender equality (CGE) that would be mandated to promote gender equality and make recommendations to parliament about any law affecting the status of women (Albertyn et al. 1999: 93).

The final South African constitution was agreed by the first parliament, sitting as a constituent assembly after a widespread process of consultation (Walsh 2006). It has been called one of the most advanced liberal democratic instruments in the world (Southall 2000: 147). It not only contained a commitment to socio-economic rights, but also included gender equality as one of the founding principles of the new state, strong and substantive equality protection, and the provision for an independent constitutional body to promote gender equality (Albertyn 2003: 104). But at the same time as it has acted as an important enabling framework to extend gender rights, it has been subject to the inherent limitations involved in trying to translate formal rights—whether socio-economic or gender-based—into lived rights in a context of mass poverty and inequality.

In Argentina, a new constitution was not introduced until more than ten years after the return to civilian rule. Although the process of constitutional design was not subject to the kinds of strategically focused campaigns organized by key feminist actors that we saw in the South African and Brazilian cases, nonetheless women did organize inside and outside the constituent assembly to form alliances to safeguard gender rights and ensure that gender concerns were included. After a pact between Menem and former President Alfonsín, the 1994 constitution was designed by a constituent assembly elected in 1993 according to the newly introduced quota law. As a result 26.2% of the assembly members were women who did organize across party lines on some issues. For example after pressure from women members, the quota law was strengthened allowing third parties such as the Consejo to make electoral challenges and CEDAW was enshrined in the constitution (Waylen 2000). But despite this short-term success, Blofield (2006) argues that the alliances forged between feminists and women members could only be temporary as few assembly members were legislators (unlike in the South African and Brazilian cases).

Perhaps the biggest challenge was the defensive organizing to prevent the insertion of a 'pro-life' anti-abortion clause initiated by President Menem in contravention of the earlier agreement with Alfonsín (Blofield 2006). Outside the assembly 109 women's organizations came together as 'Mujeres Autoconvocadas por el Derecho a Elegir la Libertad' (MADEL) and campaigned against the clause, organizing demonstrations, and lobbying assembly members (Guzman 2004: 19). The Consejo also made its opposition to the President's pro-life position public, and campaigned against the clause, leading, as we have seen, to the sacking of its feminist-leaning head. Inside the assembly itself, women members, including those from the governing Peronist party, organized together against the clause and as a result of all these activities it was not included in the final constitution.[7]

These three cases demonstrate that lobbying by key feminists, backed up by cohesive women's movements that gave the issues a high priority, was a vital factor in determining the extent to which gender rights were enshrined in new constitutions. Feminists raised gender concerns, and fought for inclusion, and were sometimes participants in the actual process of constitutional design. The openness of the institutional context, the receptivity of other key actors to gender concerns, and the strength of the opposition to improving gender rights, were also central. In all three cases, women could organize together from both insider and outsider positions to form effective strategic alliances.

There are few other transitions where women's organizing in any form has had a significant impact on the shape of a new constitution. In Poland, for example, although some women's NGOs such as the Women's Rights Centre made submissions, organized women did not have a significant impact on the process of constitutional design that led to the constitution of 1997. The final constitution did include clauses guaranteeing the equality of men and women but this is hard to realize or enforce as it is not backed up by specific legislation and civil codes and is even directly contradicted by legislation in other areas such as labour law. In common with other cases, a right to life clause was one of the most controversial areas. The Catholic Church campaigned successfully for a clause that more clearly included protection for the unborn foetus which was subsequently upheld by the constitutional tribunal (Polish Federation for Women and Family Planning www.federa.org.pl).

The *acquis communautaire* (the totality of EU legislation)is the final factor that we must consider with regard to the constitutional/legal frameworks of countries of East Central Europe. Post socialist Poland, Hungary, and the Czech Republic all saw their futures as lying within the EU and from the late 1990s began to make the requisite preparations, including the full implementation of the *acquis communautaire* for accession in 2004. In the short-term perhaps the most potentially far-reaching changes in women's legal rights in these post socialist countries come from the alterations to their legal frameworks that prospective EU entrants made to bring their countries into line with EU laws. All the EU legislation pertaining to gender equality and gender mainstreaming was adopted (Bretherton 2001). But primary emphasis was given to employment and social policy. Poland for example started negotiations in 1998 and planned to incorporate the *acquis communautaire* between 2001 and 2002. Every year the progress of the harmonization process (in economic, social, and judicial arenas) was monitored. In the area of labour legislation Poland had to implement directives on equal treatment, equal pay, parental leave, part-time work, and pensions. Maternity leave for example was increased from sixteen to twenty-six weeks and some maternal benefits were made available to men as well as women. Poland also introduced the notion of 'indirect discrimination'.

However, there is pessimism as a number of factors lessen the potential impact of the *acquis*. Some sceptics argue that on the EU side, the economic chapter had primacy in the negotiations and there was less concern about the implementation of the social dimensions (which include gender equality) (Matynia 2003). For example virtually nothing was done about domestic violence (WIDE 2003). Heinen and Portet (2002) claim that three factors weakened the impact of the integration process in Poland. The first was ideological. Polish information on European integration stressed how little would change. A leaflet on the equal opportunities chapter spelt out that most of the measures were not compulsory and, citing Ireland as a model, argued that Poland would be able to maintain its own values and traditions. Poland has therefore paid only lip service to the integration of many of the European directives, adopting them simply as a formality (Heinen and Portet 2002). Second, Poland did not have an effective institutional system of control and penalties to ensure that the directives can effectively be implemented. A similar situation can be discerned in the Czech Republic. Positive changes, centring around notions of equality and non-discrimination, were made to the Labour Code in January 2001. But up until the end of first half of 2003, no cases had been brought (WIDE 2003). Finally, although the implementation of the equal opportunities policy is based on gender mainstreaming, it relies on

THE STATE AND POLICY OUTCOMES ❖

the presence of other gender equality programmes that did not exist in Poland or other post-socialist polities (Bretherton 2001: 68). But Heinen and Portet (2002) also believe that the process of integration process is having a positive impact. Many feminists, for example, see it as a way to consolidate a more progressive legal framework around notions of equal treatment. EU standards provide an important reference point that can be used by feminists and women's NGOs, giving them both legitimacy and financial support for their activities.[8]

However, as subsequent sections will demonstrate, 'gender-friendly' constitutions (and the rights enshrined in the *acquis communautaire*) can only provide an enabling framework particularly in some of the less institutionalized polities that have emerged from some transitions. The ability to operationalize paper rights depends on a number of other factors. Additional laws are often needed to make policy on specific issues, policies on paper have to be implemented and enforced, and women have to be able to access those rights and take advantage of new policies. We will now consider three different areas of gender rights: divorce and family law, domestic violence, and reproductive rights in turn to see how these factors work in practice.

❖ Gender Policy Outcomes

To consider how different gender policy outcomes come about, we need to take a number of factors into account: the extent to which reform activists can both frame their campaigns in line with the dominant policy discourse in that area and utilize any international gender rights norms; the openness of the policy context and the strength of counter-movements to reform in that issue area. Different actors, interests, and institutional contexts are therefore involved in each area of gender rights and levels of contestation vary.

❖ Divorce and Family Law

With some notable exceptions, divorce and family law has been the least controversial area. In East Central Europe much of the relatively egalitarian legislation on divorce and property rights in marriage was carried over from state socialism with few efforts to alter it. Only in Poland, where initially both the Catholic Church and Solidarity had quite high levels of political capital because of the oppositional role they had played in the 1980s, was there some pressure for change. After Solidarity won the 1989 elections, a policy window opened for some change in line with Catholic precepts. But, rather than seriously restricting it, the government could only make divorce more difficult and time consuming by putting it in a higher court (Siemienska 1998: 140).

In Argentina and Chile, divorce was still prohibited on the return to competitive electoral politics. In Argentina, a strong reformist coalition of lawyers, feminists, and legislators began to campaign for the introduction of legal divorce almost immediately (Htun 2000). This had widespread popular support and was portrayed as part of the package of changes needed to make Argentina a modern democratic country. The Catholic Church was opposed to the move but although its opposition was strong, it was isolated on this issue (Blofield 2006). Its influence was weak as its authority and legitimacy had been diminished because it had not spoken out against the military regime and its human rights abuses. The new Radical government of Alfonsín also had a secular agenda and wanted to reduce the power of the Church and therefore was unwilling to block reform. As a result a divorce law was passed in 1987 (Htun 2003: 102). *Patria Potestad* (the power of fathers over children) was also altered so that the power was shared equally between men and women. In the absence of powerful conservative forces, a modernizing alliance of lawyers, feminists and legislators could bring about some change, together with a sympathetic government and feminists in the Women's National Directorate established in the Ministry of Health and Social affairs by Alfonsín in 1983.

The situation was very different in Chile. Despite the introduction of eighteen separate divorce law bills into Congress by different legislators, including the feminist María Antonieta Saa, and widespread public support for reform, attempts did not succeed until 2004. The Catholic Church was vehemently opposed to divorce and could wield a great deal of power to ensure that its views held sway. It had significant influence over opinion on social issues like divorce and abortion. Right-wing Catholic thinking and organizations like Opus Dei had made significant inroads in certain sectors of the Chilean elite. Dominant elite opinion was therefore highly conservative. The Church's moral authority was high after its opposition to the Pinochet regime and it had become more conservative during the 1980s and 1990s. The dominance of the CDs within the Concertación gave it significant influence over the new government. The more left-wing members of the coalition were under pressure to maintain unity and not endanger the transition by pressing controversial measures. The Concertación government itself was operating within an electoral system that gave the Right and the military considerable influence for example through their domination of the senate. In addition no bills could succeed without the support of the government to steer them through.

As a result, although some feminists among the legislators and in SERNAM, often from the more left-wing parties of the coalition, supported divorce, their influence was minimal. Because SERNAM itself was dominated by Christian Democrats during the 1990s and felt constrained by the conservative climate, it too refrained from campaigning for the legalization of divorce. Because of all these factors, even the conservatively framed bill—couched in terms of strengthening the family rather than enhancing individual rights—that finally passed in the lower house in 1997—subsequently got stuck in the Senate for several years (Blofield and Haas 2005).

THE STATE AND POLICY OUTCOMES ❖

It was not until a socialist, Ricardo Lagos became president in 2000 that the prospects for the legalization of divorce improved. Now under socialist control, the executive and SERNAM began to speak openly in favour of divorce and pushed the measure through the Senate (Blofield and Haas 2005). Therefore although family law was reformed during the 1990s, equalizing *Patria Potestad* and giving legitimate and illegitimate children comparable rights (despite opposition from the Right and the Church who claimed that it would undermine the family), divorce was not introduced until nearly fifteen years after the restoration of electoral politics.

❖ Domestic Violence

Efforts to change laws and policies around domestic violence demonstrate a similarly varied picture. Although reliable figures about the incidence of domestic violence are notoriously difficult to collect, it is recognized that levels are high in all the countries in our study. Under state socialism, domestic violence was not recognized as a problem, but came into the open after its collapse, making it hard to assess how far the incidence has increased or whether there is just more acknowledgement of pre-existing levels. The incidence of domestic violence is high in Latin America and South Africa. The Inter-American development bank has estimated that domestic violence affects between 25 and 50% of women in Latin America.

Primarily as a result of women's organizing at the national, regional, and global level, the international climate towards domestic violence and violence against women more generally has altered considerably since the 1970s. Women's movements' campaigns to get gender-based violence on the international agenda began in the 1970s, and as a result of patient lobbying of national governments and strategizing at international conferences, an opening was created in the 1980s. Women's rights were explicitly recognized as human rights at the Vienna Conference in 1993 and the use of a human rights framework to create a new international consensus expanded the possibilities for debates about domestic violence and the responsibility of the state to try to eliminate it in the 1990s (Friedman 2006). The UN declaration on the Elimination of Violence against Women then followed in 1994. The Beijing Platform for Action also stated that violence against women was an obstacle to equality, development and, peace. As a result of this changed international climate, resources from international organizations, aid agencies, and NGOs went to national NGOs to fund anti-domestic violence initiatives both campaigning and practical ones such as helplines and refuges. Most national legislation was also passed around the time of the Vienna Conference and the Beijing women's conference when the international climate was at its most favourable (Macaulay 2000).

In Latin America, this organizing also took a regional dimension. Feminist networks such as CLADEM (Comité de América Latina y el Caribe por la Defensa de los Derechos de la Mujer), established in 1987, were active around women's rights, and another network organizing specifically around domestic and sexual violence was set up in 1990 and was formally instituted with organizations from twenty-one countries in 1992. As a result the Organization of American States (OAS) adopted the Belem do Para Convention for the Prevention, Punishment, and Eradication of Violence Against Women in 1994. It surpassed the UN convention in terms of its definition of domestic violence and the actions that states should take to prevent it (Macaulay 2000: 147). Feminists in Brazil have also used the Inter-American Commission on Human Rights to press legal claims that national governments have failed to uphold (Friedman 2006).

However, there are marked differences in the extent to which post transition governments adopted anti-domestic violence legislation and implemented policies to prevent and ameliorate the effects of domestic violence. By 2003 five of our case study countries: Argentina, Chile, El Salvador, Peru, and South Africa had adopted specific legislation on domestic violence and Brazil had legislation in the pipeline. But none of our case study countries from East Central Europe had done so. How can we explain this marked difference between East Central Europe and other transition countries? If we look first at our Latin American examples and then consider the South African case, we can see that the context was very different to East Central Europe. Women organizing during the Latin American and South African transitions had formed part of a democratic opposition that campaigned for transitions to democracy that would put an end to state violence and human rights abuses and substitute meaningful citizenship with full civil and political rights for everyone. These actions facilitated making the connection between women's rights and human rights. Using a human rights framework was therefore a powerful tactic allowing feminists to argue that domestic violence could not be separated from human rights abuses and the violence of the military (Friedman 2006).

Outcomes in individual countries have therefore to be seen in this broader context. In Brazil, feminists had been campaigning about domestic violence since 1975 and had played a key role in the international networks that were active around gender rights (Pitanguy 2003: 817). The women's demands incorporated into the 1988 Brazilian constitution included, almost uniquely in Latin America, a provision on domestic violence that 'the state shall guarantee assistance to the family, as represented by each of the persons that makes up the family, by creating mechanisms to deter violence in the framework of the relationships among those family members' (Article 226, para 8, quoted by Macaulay 2000: 151). According to Pitanguy (2002: 818), this made family violence a state responsibility and potentially it could be held accountable for failing to do anything to prevent domestic violence. Around that time a number of other initiatives took place at both the federal and state levels. In 1991 congress established a committee of enquiry on domestic violence. The first women's police stations were set up in Sao Paulo on the initiative of the state women's body and the feminist PT mayor Luisa Erundina established women's shelters and awareness-raising programmes when she was in office between 1989–92 (Macauley 2005).

But the picture is mixed. Developments at the federal level—such as the weakening of CNDM in the early 1990s, the lack of dedicated resources or the necessary complementary legal changes to make domestic violence a crime in its own right—reduced the capacity for significant change. Implementation therefore largely depended on individual states and could vary with changing circumstance. But by the end of the 1990s the Cardoso administration was more sympathetic to gender issues, the CNDM was revitalized and feminists both within and outside congress used the international discourses and instruments to lobby for legal change, and to push the national and some local administrations to take action for example funding more shelters and women's police stations (Macaulay 2003: 24). Gains were achieved, building on the long-standing activities of women's organizations and the CNDM, but they were still vulnerable to budget cuts and changes in the political climate. The incoming PT government vowed also to improve the situation.

Chile is less well known than Brazil for its efforts in the area of domestic violence. However, the passage of the bill on Intra Family Violence that became law in 1994 was significant for a number of reasons. Even though it was not framed in those terms, it was the first successful piece of women's rights legislation and the organizing around it was one of the most significant post transition mobilizations undertaken by women's organizations. It passed as a result of the activities of a sometimes troubled alliance between feminist legislators, women's organizations and SERNAM. Feminist legislators and women's organizations were disappointed by the final outcome as it differed from the initial proposal introduced by two feminist deputies from the Socialist party. But in an institutional context where the executive dominance over the legislative process and the right-wing dominance over the senate were both very strong, successful legislation needed the support of the executive (Baldez 2001). In this case it meant that the support of SERNAM was crucial but because of Christian Democrat domination, it was relatively moderate in its outlook.

The eventual bill was co-sponsored by SERNAM amid feelings that the SWM had unduly and negatively influenced its final shape. The original bill had been reframed as a measure that was protective of the family (Blofield and Haas 2005). Its name had been changed from the Domestic Violence Bill to emphasize that it was about violence between men and women rather than violence against women; and certain clauses, such as the one that would send violent spouses to prison, were removed. Feminist Groups like ISIS international, the network on violence and other NGOs that had lobbied and campaigned for the bill, felt they had been marginalized from the processes that decided the final form of the legislation (Haas 2004). Its implementation was also severely hampered by a lack of resources. State funding was limited to counselling and awareness programmes and there was

❖ THE STATE AND POLICY OUTCOMES

no provision of funding for shelters (Baldez 2001: 21). Haas (2004) has claimed that the passage of the bill marked a low point in the relationship between feminist legislators and SERNAM that subsequently improved. But the reframed bill could pass relatively easily in socially conservative Chile, because the Church and the Right were not as strongly opposed to this gender reform as they were to some others.

Some similar traits can be discerned in the South African case. A number of factors contributed to the passing of new relatively far-reaching legislation on domestic violence in 1998. It contains a broad definition of domestic violence—in contrast to the Chilean case framed as an obstacle to gender equality—and allows for the arrest of suspected perpetrators without a warrant (Albertyn et al. 1999). Women's groups within South Africa, including some not necessarily opposed to the Apartheid regime, had been campaigning around issues of violence against women since the 1970s. During the transition, new political actors on the domestic scene like the WNC, and key feminists within the ANC and newly reformed ANCWL, also took up the issue. The ANC submitted a document on violence against women to the constitutional negotiations. It drew on the new international protocols on the issue, and the Women's Charter for Effective Equality that contained demands for measures to protect women from violence (Meintjes 2003: 149). In 1993 as part of its efforts to liberalize, even the outgoing NP government had passed its own rather limited Prevention of Family Violence Act but without any consultation. In the period after the first non-racial election in 1994, pressure grew from NGOs, lawyer, and political parties for a new and more effective law.

The new ANC government had committed itself to action against domestic violence as part of its activities around the Beijing conference. Two ministers in the Welfare and Justice departments provided significant support for the domestic violence lobby and in 1995 the government entered into a partnership with civil society organizations in the form of the National Network on Violence against Women. At the same time the South African Law Commission was reviewing the existing legislation and drafting a new version aided by submissions from NGOs and the Justice Ministry (Albertyn et al. 1999). The whole process was speeded up by the intervention of the JCISQLW, the Parliamentary Committee on Women that argued that the legislation should go through parliament as a matter of urgency before the end of the government's first term. The ANC women's caucus in parliament supported it and the Justice Minister expedited the progress of the draft bill so that its progress was uncontroversial. However, despite this success, there were later problems with implementation as inadequate resources were dedicated to it and some of the regulations governing it were inadequately thought out (Meintjes 2003).

The successful passage of domestic violence legislation in El Salvador and Peru also demonstrates the role that can be played by coalitions of actors. Regardless of the historical association of feminism with the Left, left-wing and right-wing women in El Salvador came together in Congress to support the ratification of international conventions and pass quite far-reaching legislation to prevent domestic violence and punish offenders (Hipsher 2001: 154). A similar pattern was seen in Peru where all women deputies in congress voted in favour of the Domestic Violence law regardless of party differences, which was passed in 1993 and amended in 1996. They were supported by feminist organizations outside congress (Blondet 2002: 296).

In contrast, most countries in Eastern Europe have relied upon non-specific legislation such as that dealing with assault and efforts to change the legal status quo have had little success (UNIFEM 2004). In Russia a number of women's NGOs were active around domestic violence in the 1990s, often aided by external funding from SOROS, USAID, and the Ford Foundation among other donors. The NGOs, working from a perspective that sees domestic violence as an issue of bodily harm rather than part of a larger problem of women's inequality, had some success in both changing the perceptions of the public and even some prosecutors as well as establishing refuges and training programmes (Sundstrom 2005: 437). But attempts by women's NGOs to get the criminal code altered failed. According to Sundstrom (2005: 441) several dozen versions of a draft law on the prevention of domestic violence did not progress through the Duma. This pattern has been replicated in some other countries in East Central Europe. Indeed in the Czech Republic, changes to the criminal codes introduced in the early 1990s to increase the privacy of the family in the post-socialist era actually reduced the opportunity for police and doctors to intervene in cases of domestic violence. Legislators also opposed the recodification of the criminal codes to include domestic violence as a specific crime, despite a discussion of the issue by lawyers (WIDE 2003). But there are some signs of change. In 2004 an amendment to the civil code was introduced in the Czech Republic making domestic violence a crime. And in Poland the Government Plenipotentiary for the Equal Status of Men and Women ran a campaign to raise awareness of domestic violence in 2005 (www.stopvaw.org).

Domestic violence legislation has therefore been implemented in a range of contexts. The policy environment has often been sufficiently open to allow relatively cohesive alliances of actors, both insiders and outsiders, using international and regional norms and frameworks and sometimes framing legislation in terms of strengthening the family, to achieve reforms.

❖ *Reproductive Rights: Abortion*

Reproductive rights are one of the most contentious areas of gender policy and provide the greatest challenge to those attempting to achieve positive gender outcomes. We will focus on access to abortion as the most controversial aspect of reproductive rights, and the gender right for which there was the most stark variation between different cases at the point of transition. The right to an abortion is seen by many feminists as a fundamental part of a woman's ability to control her own body; by many religions as a crime against the foetus and by pronatalists as something to be restricted if high birth rates are to be maintained. As a result of these conflicting views, abortion has often been a highly contested issue and following the actions of the global anti-abortion lobby the international climate against abortion has hardened recently. It is therefore strategically quite hard to reframe the legal right to an abortion in a way that fits in with conservative discourse and in the last decade reformers have found it increasingly hard to call upon international norms to support their cause.

We have seen that under state socialism contraception and abortion were available to all women at least on paper after the liberalization of the 1950s, but these rights had not been granted as a result of demands for reproductive freedom or the actions of women's movements. There was considerable variation between different countries. Within many state socialist states the ease with which abortions were granted varied over time according to changes in the perceived needs of the labour market and desired levels of population growth. Access to contraceptives was often restricted by a lack of availability, and abortion sometimes became the only form of fertility control (Gal 1994). Women therefore did not always enjoy the reproductive rights that existed on paper. In sharp contrast abortion, almost without exception, was illegal or virtually illegal under most authoritarian regimes, except sometimes under certain circumstances such as rape and foetal abnormality. However, levels of illegal abortion remain extremely high in many parts of Latin America. Therefore at the point of transition women in state socialist East Central Europe (with the exception of Romania) had greater access to legal abortion than in authoritarian Latin America.

The extent to which abortion has been a key post transition issue has varied. As we will see, the insertion of a 'right to life' clause was a contested area in Brazil and Argentina. In only one case—that of South Africa—did access to abortion increase after the transition to democracy. In most cases, access has remained largely unchanged, despite efforts both to restrict and sometimes to extend it; and in a number of cases, access has been restricted. We therefore need to explore the different factors that determine what happens to abortion rights in the context of transitions to democracy. We will first consider those cases where access has been restricted, then where it has stayed largely unchanged, before examining the one case where it has clearly improved.

In post-socialist East Central Europe the most severe restrictions on access to legal abortion were introduced in Poland. Abortion laws had been liberalized in Poland in 1956, effectively granting abortion on demand during the first trimester of pregnancy. As a result, abortion levels, although lower than the USSR, were similar to other countries in East Central Europe such as Hungary (Heinen and Portet 2002). But these changes were contested by both the Catholic Church and pro-life groups espousing nationalist rather than religious beliefs (Githens

1996: 58). According to Githens (1996: 58), because the Church 'had long served as a symbol of Polish national identity, and under Communist rule had become synonymous with resistance to the regime, its stance on abortion took on a distinctly political stance'. There were renewed challenges to Poland's relatively liberal abortion laws as opposition to the regime increased after the emergence of Solidarity with its close links to the Catholic Church. In response to a public anti-abortion campaign, a ministerial directive made access to abortion more complicated in 1981. But debate was submerged after the imposition of marshal law until in 1989 seventy-eight deputies introduced an anti-abortion bill while Poland was still under communist rule. It provoked huge public debate but was shelved by the communist government before the elections of June 1989 (Zielinska 2000: 26).

After the Solidarity victory, the heated public anti-abortion campaign spearheaded by the Catholic Church continued. At the same time as attempts were made to get an anti-abortion bill through the Sejm, small incremental changes were made—through the introduction of new executive regulations and charges by the Minister of Health and new Codes of Medical Ethics adopted by doctors— to make access to abortion more difficult. Despite the public support for abortion, the pro-abortion groups, including a number of women's groups such as the Federation for Women and Family Planning, lacked the capacity and resources available to the anti-abortion forces particularly the Catholic Church (Zielinska 2000). A powerful coalition of other actors, including politicians and political parties primarily from the Christian and nationalist sectors, experts such as lawyers and doctors and pro-life NGOs, including some women's groups, had also joined forces with the Church, under the umbrella of the Federation of Movements for the Defence of Life. And in January 1993 a more restrictive act was finally passed, severely constraining the availability of abortion except in very limited circumstances.

The 1993 act was finally modified in 1996 after the victory of the post-communist and Left parties in the elections of 1993 that has been partly attributed to their stance on church–state relations and their promise to extend the right to abortion (Zielinska 2000). But a vociferous defence was mounted by anti-abortion forces. In 1995 an estimated 30,000 demonstrators marched in Warsaw against liberalization and previous efforts (including those of the WPG) had been blocked by Lech Walesa's presidential veto. But when it was finally ratified the resulting law was not as liberal as the 1956 legislation and was challenged by a Constitutional Tribunal in 1997.

Despite the liberalization of 1996 access to abortion was significantly reduced. By 2000 the numbers of women having officially sanctioned terminations had declined to only 151. However, these figures hide the large number of abortions that are carried out more clandestinely and the large 'abortion tourism' industry that sends women to nearby countries such as Belarus, the Ukraine and Germany. It is estimated that 80,000 to 200,000 abortions are obtained through these methods. It

❖ THE STATE AND POLICY OUTCOMES

is those women without sufficient resources who have had their choices restricted the most (Heinen and Portet 2002). Furthermore, access to contraceptives of any sort has also come under threat. In 1998 subsidies on contraceptives were withdrawn by the SEL government. As we have seen, a statement on the liberalization of abortion by the new head of the SWM in 2001 reaped public opprobrium (Matynia 2003).

Access to abortion also became more restricted in post-authoritarian El Salvador. Although different groups of women could unite over domestic violence, this alliance fell apart over the issue of abortion in 1997. The catalyst was the rewriting of the old penal code that had specified three conditions under which abortion was not punishable—rape, deformity of the foetus, and to save the life of the mother. Article 137 of the new penal code was almost identical but differed slightly because a new condition allowing a grave danger to the physical or mental health of the pregnant woman had been added. The new code was therefore potentially more liberal than the old one (Hipsher 2001: 157). Feminists in organizations such as Las Dignas and left-wing women particularly some FMLN legislators supported Article 137. However, there was a concerted campaign to make abortion punishable under any circumstances. It was led by the Catholic Church—and Opus Dei members in particular—but also included both male and female conservative politicians in ARENA and the Christian Democratic party as well as male and female members of the President's cabinet. Luciak (2004: 19) claims that a number of female FMLN legislators were also deliberately absent on the day of the vote—which did nothing to reduce the continued tensions between some party militants and members of the women's movement. The campaign in favour of Article 137 could not match the opposition in size and organization, and the legislative assembly voted to eliminate Article 137 from the penal code and to impose stiff penalties on anyone carrying out abortions (Hipsher 2001: 158).

In most of the countries in our study, the pre-existing status quo with regard to abortion has remained relatively unchanged since the transitions took place. But the pre-existing situation, how far the issue is on the political agenda and the degree to which change is either possible or likely, and if so in what direction it might occur, differ markedly between cases.

In (what became) the Czech and Slovak republics, abortion has been far less controversial than in Poland and efforts to restrict it have not succeeded in either country. Under state socialism, pronatalism rather than religious pressure prompted some attempts to restrict abortion from the early 1970s. However, these were very unpopular, largely ineffective in reducing rates and were abandoned in 1987 (Wolchik 2000: 66). By 1988 the rate of abortion had reached a peak of 114,000 or 85.4 per 100 live births (Wolchik 2000: 63). Immediately after the 'Velvet Revolution', the Church started lobbying the Federal Assembly and the Minister for Health for an end to abortion. A consultative commission was set up by the government in 1991 and the ministries of health began drafting new legislation.

But in the relatively secular Czech Republic, the Christian parties were only junior partners in the ruling coalition and the sole modification to the law proposed by the health minister was the introduction of charges for abortions carried out for non-medical reasons. Fees were introduced in 1992 in the context of a more widespread revision of charges for health services. In Slovakia, however, Catholic activists held prominent positions in government such as the minister for health and prime minister. In 1992 the health minister proposed a law on the defence of life in the provision of health services that would restrict abortion. But as expected, the government was defeated in the elections held three months later and the law died with it.

Popular opinion has remained much more firmly in favour of abortion than in Poland. In 1995, 63% of those polled in the Czech Republic supported a women's right to have an abortion under any circumstance and a further 25% supported abortion on health or family grounds (Wolchik 2000: 79). Without any credible threat to abortion rights, there has been no need for a widespread mobilization by women in defence of abortion rights. However, the overall number of abortions did decline steeply after 1990. In the Czech Republic, they fell to around 54,000 in 1994, less than half the number in the peak of 1988. Wolchik (2000: 68) attributes the fall, not so much to the imposition of charges, but to the more widespread use of contraception.

In sharp contrast, the status quo with regard to abortion was extremely restrictive in Chile at the time of transition. As one of its last acts, the socially conservative military regime had banned even therapeutic abortions. As a result of Chile's conservative climate, liberalizing access to abortions was not a prominent part of women's organizing or feminist demands during the transition. Indeed the women who came together prior to the elections to form the women's Concertación had agreed to keep contentious issues like abortion and even divorce off their platform for fear of losing support and being divisive. Even though public opinion has been in favour of the re-legalization of therapeutic abortion, the powerful Church and conservative elite remained vehemently opposed to any change in the post transition period. Rates of illegal abortion remain one of the highest in Latin America (Blofield and Haas 2005). Estimates range from 75,000–200,000 to even 400,000 per annum with six abortions for every ten births. The reluctance of many feminists to even raise the issue of abortion and the continuing influence of the military, the Church and the Right have made any liberalization of abortion laws highly unlikely.

Apart from some efforts by the Right to increase the penalties for abortion, there have been few attempts to even reintroduce therapeutic abortion and revert to the pre-1989 status quo. Although a majority of Socialist and PPD legislators supported this, the Christian Democrat domination of the coalition and the government in the 1990s meant that SERNAM did not raise it as an issue (Baldez 2001: 15). Indeed in 1991 an attempt by some socialist deputies led by the feminist

Adriana Muñoz to introduce a bill to re-legalize therapeutic abortion led to an outcry, the bill got nowhere and Muñoz was vilified and lost her seat at the next election (Htun 2003: 169; Blofield and Haas 2005). The socialist Ricardo Lagos made clear in his presidential election campaign in 2000 that he would not consider the legalization of therapeutic abortion. As a result many feminists put their energies into more general campaigning around reproductive rights, focusing on the right to sex education and to contraception. Some feminists have attempted to raise the issue and initiate a campaign more recently. The Feminist Roundtable on Abortion published the names of over 200 women who had had abortions and a declaration in favour freedom of choice and the right to terminate unwanted pregnancies in a national newspaper on 28 September 2003 (Latin American Day for the Decriminalization of Abortion). However, feminist commentators claimed that it had been met with silence.[9] The new government of President Michelle Bachelet has also indicated that it has no plans to decriminalize even therapeutic abortion, so any change looks unlikely in the short term.[10]

In Argentina, therapeutic abortion had been permitted on a few limited grounds from early in the twentieth century, although abortion itself was illegal. The law remained essentially unchanged throughout the revisions of the penal code introduced by various civilian and military regimes including Alfonsín's Radical government in 1983 (Htun 2003: 146–8). However, very few legal abortions were carried out and it is estimated that there were still between 350,000 and 400,000 illegal abortions every year. Although the climate was not as socially conservative as Chile, the further liberalization of the abortion laws was not a major campaigning issue for feminist groups during the Radical government in the 1980s (Feijoó and Gogna 1990). In the 1990s the agenda became more defensive, further limiting the space for reproductive rights campaigners to advocate the liberalization of the abortion laws, after President Menem's very visible opposition to abortion described earlier necessitated defensive organizing to prevent a retrenchment in the form of a right to life clause. In 1998 March 25 was even declared the 'day of the unborn child'.

However, as we have seen, the government's anti-abortion stance prompted the development of an organizational base of women's groups such as MADEL, initially active around the constitutional clause, that could then carry on campaigning around more general issues of reproductive rights and improving women's access to contraception (Htun 2003). But Blofield (2006) claims that after successfully preventing the insertion of the constitutional clause, feminists demobilized and by 1997 few of the 109 organizations that had formed MADEL in 1994 still existed. They had been divided by disagreements over subsequent goals—whether to campaign more generally around reproductive rights—and strategies—whether to lobby for legislative change or policy implementation—in an unfavourable institutional context where feminists had not formed more permanent political ties with legislators.

THE STATE AND POLICY OUTCOMES ❖

Subsequent presidents have not been so overtly anti-abortion as Menem and, mirroring developments in Chile, a number of initiatives to get change in the abortion laws such as the Foro por el Aborto no Punible, have emerged. As a result of the national Encuentro de Mujeres held in 2003 a national campaign for the right to safe, legal, and free abortion (Campaña Nacional por el Derecho al Aborto Legal, Seguro y Gratuito), made up of a number of women's organizations such as Foro por los Derechos Reproductivos, was launched in 2005 (www.derechoalaborto.org.ar/). This was accompanied by a number of legislative initiatives on the decriminalization of abortion. But in the absence of a significant and cohesive movement and sufficient politicians sympathetic to the issue, it had little chance of success.

Abortion (except under certain limited circumstances) was also illegal in Brazil at the point of transition. However in contrast to Chile and Argentina the Catholic Church, although opposed to abortion, was historically more influenced by liberation theology and remained more pluralist and a less conservative influence overall. The Brazilian military regime was the least socially conservative of the three we have looked at and the social climate in post-authoritarian Brazil has been more liberal. As a result it has been possible for abortion to be the subject of public debate. And it has also been a long-standing issue on the agenda of women's organizations. Even before the transition was complete, feminists had been involved in the legal abortion movement, trying to get abortions for victims of violence in public hospitals from the mid-1980s onwards. In the late 1980s the feminist PT mayor Luisa Erundina established such a service in a hospital in Sao Paulo (Htun 2003: 157). In the early 1990s the Brazilian government took a progressive position on reproductive rights at Cairo. It introduced initiatives to combat AIDs and made condoms and the morning after pill available (Macaulay 2003: 23).

No Brazilian president in office since 1985 has been overtly anti-abortion. Indeed Cardoso was known to support decriminalization and his government tried to take a secular public health rights-based approach to the issue. The PT, influenced by feminist activists, has also had a long-standing commitment to greater access to abortion and a PT government has taken steps in this direction. However, as Fiona Macaulay (2003: 23) points out, abortion is still illegal and there is a significant difference between advocating better access to abortions that are already legal and liberalizing abortion laws more generally. Therefore, although there have been some unsuccessful attempts to completely criminalize abortion, a number of bills have been introduced into the legislature to liberalize abortion including under PT President Lula. In sum, it appears that more of the conditions that might contribute to a liberalization of abortion laws are present in Brazil than in any of our other case studies examined thus far.

It is important at this point to look at South Africa—the only case in which abortion laws were liberalized in the aftermath of the transition—so that we can ascertain the decisive factors that facilitated this unusual change. Under apartheid, abortion was virtually illegal. Although some white middle-class women's groups had begun campaigning for greater access to abortion in the 1970s, it was not until 1990 that support for reproductive rights and within that some very limited support for a pro-choice position developed. At the Malibongwe conference, ANC activist Frene Ginwala included reproductive rights as one of the six key gender issues for the future constitution. Specific women's research and advocacy organizations, such as the Women's Health Project, active around health and women's rights, emerged in the early 1990s and several women's conferences took up the issue of reproductive rights. Although abortion was too divisive for a broad coalition like the WNC, the Women's Charter for Effective Equality did include reproductive rights.

The ANC too, contained a range of different views and although it initially had no public policy on abortion, it began to produce broad statements, for example in the Constitutional Principles, in support of reproductive rights. Some key women activists and senior figures in the ANC such as the future minister for health, were firmly pro-choice. As a result of their activities within the party and in the face of some fierce opposition, a pro-choice position was incorporated into the ANC health programme and the RDP. By 1994, although an openly pro-choice position was still relatively unusual, reproductive rights were on the agenda as part of a broad commitment to gender equality embodied within the framework of rights in the interim constitution (Albertyn et al. 1999).

After the 1994 election, the campaign to further reproductive rights centred on two issues: ensuring the inclusion of a reproductive rights clause within the final constitution and the reform of the 1975 Abortion Law. An effective sectoral alliance of women's organizations emerged, culminating in the formation of the Reproductive Rights Alliance (RRA) in 1995 to provide a united front in support of a pro-choice position. It took advantage of the relatively favourable international context and used the language of the Cairo Population conference and the Beijing Women's conference to lobby key ANC figures and increase support in civil society. A clause entrenching reproductive rights was included within the final constitution, primarily due to the support of senior ANC men and women within the Constitutional Commission and the NEC. This provided a critical part of the framework necessary to facilitate more specific pro-choice legislation.

Building on ANC health policy and the RDP, the feminist and pro-choice Minister of Health established an ad hoc parliamentary committee to consider changing the 1975 law. The RRA participated in this process both formally and informally, arguing for relatively free access to first trimester abortions. Many activists utilized their close pre-existing contacts with MPs. After key ANC MPs had ensured a three-line whip for the vote, the Termination of Pregnancy (TOP) Act was passed in 1996. The measures were achieved by a broad coalition of actors, both 'sympathetic insiders' within parliament and the government, and a focused sectoral alliance within civil society. Building on the gains made prior to 1994, they could use the relatively favourable international context, existing ANC policy, and the rights framework embodied in the constitution to their advantage (Albertyn et al. 1999). TOP was, according to Albertyn (2003: 106), the first law passed to address issues of women's subordination and no other law has demonstrated such extensive feminist influence on parliament. Many of the conditions that facilitated the passing of TOP were therefore put in place during the transition and subsequently were built on by a complex alliance of actors.

As a result of a complex combination of factors, positive gender policy out-comes have occurred in some areas of gender rights. Some positive gender out-comes are easier to achieve than others. Change was more likely in issue areas where there was: a history of women's activism; alliances between activists outside and within government and state that used the opportunities of the transition; and a favourable international environment, that could all combine to achieve policy change that was not possible under the previous non-democratic regime. In some cases the policy environment was relatively open, facilitated by an enabling framework such as a constitution as well as institutions such as SWMs. Our findings also reinforce Htun's (2003) arguments that different issues will engender different levels of opposition from counter-movements—particularly from the Catholic Church which itself had varying levels of influence and legitimacy in different post transition polities. Abortion reform therefore proved very divisive whereas changes to property law and even anti-domestic violence legislation were much less so.

Alliances between different women, both insiders and outsiders, were easier to forge on some issues—political rights, divorce and even domestic violence—than on others such as abortion. The cohesiveness of women's movements as well as the priority that they gave also varied considerably between issues. Some issues could be framed in ways that did not conflict too much with dominant discourses. But the extent to which different groups of women are able to access any new rights and benefit from new policies is also crucially important. It is to the socio-economic aspects of transitions that can affect ability to access rights that we now turn.

❖ SOCIAL AND ECONOMIC TRANSITIONS

We have seen that most transitions to democracy have led to some improvements in women's civil and political rights and, on paper at least, some transitions have also resulted in improvements in gender rights policies. However, a number of other factors help to determine how far these 'paper' rights can actually be trans-lated into 'lived' rights. We have already seen that problems with implementation and a lack of designated resources often mean that measures, for example to prevent domestic violence, do not have the impact in practice that their supporters had hoped for. Different women's ability to access their rights is also affected by their socio-economic position and the ways in which the social and economic restructuring that has accompanied many transitions impacts on that position.

In the growing literature on women and transitions, very little attention has been given to the gender politics of these economic reform programmes. At the same time, both feminist scholars and mainstream political scientists increasingly stress the importance of extending meaningful citizenship to all—often conceived more widely than simply political and civil rights—in ensuring that democracies endure (O'Donnell 1996; Jaquette and Wolchik 1998). This has been accompanied by an emphasis on the significance of high levels of inequality in preventing economic growth and destabilizing democracies (Pastor and Wise 1999; Karl 2005). To have a fuller understanding of both the constraints and opportunities available to women to participate as full citizens in new democracies and of the more general effects of inequality on the functioning of democracies, it is also necessary to analyse the ways in which those programmes of social and economic restructuring have gendered outcomes. Patterns of inequality have been altered in ways that affect the ability of some women to participate fully in the new democracies.

As we saw in Part I, similar programmes, often inspired by neo-liberal ideas, were imposed on a range of states. Indeed this kind of social and economic restructuring has been seen as an integral part of the processes of globalization that have influenced the international economy over the last thirty years. While the same general principles underpin the majority of reform programmes, they have, of course, been implemented in countries with different economies and levels of income and industrialization. In East Central Europe, countries have been undergoing far-reaching transitions from state socialist to more market-based systems that are integrated into the global economy. The Czech Republic, Hungary, and Poland are seen as the most 'successful' post-state-socialist economies, with the highest levels of prosperity, smoothest and quickest transition to the EU and fastest and most organized move to liberal democracy (Fodor 2004b: 2). But they have implemented market reforms with varying degrees of speed and thoroughness. Poland for example adopted quicker shock therapy. Russia has had a less complete transition, troubled by high levels of poverty, instability, and corruption.

Our other case-study countries were all nominally capitalist market economies and have implemented economic reform programmes with varying levels of coherence and consistency. At one extreme, the Pinochet regime in Chile was well-known for its drastic imposition of market reform during the period of military rule. Different governments in Brazil, Argentina, El Salvador, and Peru all implemented market reform programmes with varying degrees of diligence and success. And at the other end of the spectrum, even those governments identified with the left and centre–left felt obliged to either continue or introduce market-based policies. Although the Concertación governments in Chile increased social spending to ameliorate the high levels of poverty they did not significantly alter the underlying direction of economic policy. In South Africa, although there was little space in the transition for radical reshaping of the economy away from the white economic dominance that had long been nurtured and protected by the state, the ANC initially advocated redistribution through the provision of basic needs within a social democratic framework in the RDP. However, in 1996 it too moved towards more fiscally conservative policies in the form of Growth, Employment, and Redistribution Programme (GEAR) that stressed the importance of export-led growth, international competitiveness, and the private sector as the engine of growth.

In the last section of Part IV we therefore examine how two key aspects of this restructuring: market reforms and the restructuring of welfare are gendered. In particular we examine the complex and contradictory effects that these change have had on different groups of women. But women are not simply passive victims of these processes. In contrast to the rather bleak picture offered in some of the literature on women and structural adjustment, it is not clear that levels of gender inequality have unequivocally worsened or that all women's lives have become harsher as a result of economic reform. Instead the specialization (concentration on particular sectors) and polarization noted by Stallings and Peres (2000) as a more general effect of economic reform has also occurred in gender terms. Aggregates say very little about the differential effects of reform on different sectors as well as different genders. Therefore we need greater gender disaggregation. Different women are affected by and have participated in these processes in different ways. Poor women, middle-class professional women, rural women, and urban women did not experience reform in the same ways. Therefore although increased polarization and inequality have accompanied market reforms, these have not been simple or straightforward.

As we have already seen women's roles in the productive sphere varied in non democratic regimes. They had very high participation rates in the paid labour force under state socialism, albeit in gender segregated occupations often in the professions and clerical occupations. At the same time, women undertook a large proportion of the caring activities in the household despite the existence of a comprehensive state welfare system. In contrast, women's participation in formal sector economic activities was much lower in Latin America and South Africa. However, in societies characterized by high levels of inequality and the absence of comprehensive welfare states, participation by women—particularly poor women—in income-generating activities in the informal sector, particularly in the provision of domestic or care services, was high.

There were therefore big differences in state welfare provision at the point of transition. Welfare provision was often minimal under authoritarian regimes but with some variation between regimes. Chile, for example, had one of the most comprehensive welfare systems in Latin America and the third world. But spending was also often skewed towards the elites, for example a very high proportion of education spending was typically directed towards higher education. Very little was spent on poverty alleviation or on measures that would help women's entry into paid labour. Under state socialism, states in East Central Europe had created comprehensive welfare systems that included the provision of health, education, pensions according to need, as well as measures such as maternity provision and family policies that facilitated women's participation in the labour market. The fundamental restructuring of the state-dominated economies and welfare systems has therefore affected men and women differently (Einhorn 1993). An awareness of both general themes and regional differences has to be maintained in any analysis of this kind.

❖ Market Reforms

Market reforms are intended to contribute to the creation of a fully functioning capitalist economy that is integrated into the global economy by freeing the market and rolling back the state. Indeed the need to integrate into the global economy is often cited as a reason for the adoption of these market orientated policies. In East Central Europe this involved more extensive change than in countries that already had some variant of a capitalist economy. Recent market reforms have focused on fiscal discipline through the reduction of public sector deficits primarily through cuts in public spending and the imposition of user fees for education and health services, the privatization of public enterprises, the liberalization of trade and investment regimes, and the deregulation of domestic markets including labour markets. Economic reform programmes that are designed to increase producer incentives particularly in the export sector, liberalize trade and reduce public sector deficits have different impacts on men and women (Gladwin 1999). As we will see, these measures have produced a range of gendered outcomes including major changes in employment patterns. The differential constraints on women's labour combined with differential demands for men and women's labour means that economic reform has not only had very different impact on men and women's employment but on different groups of men and women. We therefore need to examine, not only the overall changes in women's labour, but differences between sectors as well as between different groups of women, looking at both the similarities and differences between the transitions from state socialism and the imposition of market reforms in other contexts.

Women's labour is increasingly important in the restructured capitalist market economies in most of our case studies. Overall women's participation in paid employment has increased. By 1997, 44.5% of women of working age were employed in Brazil (up from 42.5% in 1990) and over the same time period 35.2% of women were employed in Chile (up from 28%) (ECLAC 2000: 149). This increase has occurred at the same time as a sharp decline in the male labour force. In 1986 80.4% of men in Argentina were economically active (a wider definition than the paid labour force) compared to 40.5% of women aged between 15 and 64. By 1995 the percentage of men had declined sharply to 71.1% while the percentage of women who were economically active had increased to 41.3%. In the face of high overall rates of unemployment this has led to an increase in the number of women who are primary earners in the household (ECLAC 2000).

However, a different pattern is seen in East Central Europe where the transition from state socialism has meant a move away from state controlled economies with a commitment to provide employment. As a result, up to 30% of all jobs disappeared and women's employment levels declined (Fodor et al. 2002: 481). By 2001 only 52.4% of women were still employed in Hungary (down from 75.9% in 1990) and 49.7% in Poland (down from 57.0% in 1990) (Fodor 2004*b*: 12). But in the Czech Republic, falls in women's employment were very much smaller. In 2001 67.9% of women were still employed. Men's employment rates declined sharply too. Only 71% of men were employed in the Czech Republic in 2001, 67.8% in Hungary, and 64.3% in Poland (Fodor 2004*b*: 12). Even although large numbers of women left the labour market in Hungary and Poland, women also formed a large proportion of the unemployed (Pollert 2003: 338). In order to understand the role played by economic reform in these changes in employment levels, we need to examine the impact of key areas of market reform: public sector downsizing, and liberalization of trade, finance, and domestic markets on different groups of women, before we can move on to examine their relationship to social sector reform.

Public sector downsizing and privatization has been widespread among countries undergoing market reforms. A number of studies have shown that women are disproportionately affected by public sector retrenchment (van Der Meulen 1999). The public sector typically employs a high proportion of women workers particularly in public administration and social services—often a higher percentage than are employed in the public enterprises (which include male dominated sectors such as power generation, sanitation, heavy industry, or mineral extraction as well as the more female-friendly enterprises such as telecoms and airlines). The dismantling of command economies and the large state sector was a key part of the transition in East Central Europe and the large cuts in public services resulted in extensive female job loss (Pollert 2003: 338). But even after these, 30.2% of women employed in the Czech Republic and 45.2% of those employed in Poland were still to be found in the public sector in 2001 (Fodor 2004*b*: 19). Evidence from Argentina has also shown that female workers also lost their jobs disproportionately in the privatization of public enterprises which took place there between 1990 and 1993. The 28.9% of the total workforce lost their jobs through voluntary redundancy. Of these 23% were women but given that only 12.1% of the total workforce was female, women lost their jobs at a higher rate than men (Geldstein 1997).

In her study of the Argentine telephone and airline companies, Rosa Geldstein (1997) argues that after privatization, worsening working conditions had a disproportionate impact on women. In the telecoms companies, the leave available to look after sick relatives which had been used predominantly by women was cut, the working day was extended, shift patterns were altered to force workers to take the evening shift and salaries were made more dependent on productivity bonuses. As a consequence the workforce became younger and more male-dominated as conditions became more difficult for women with children. But in post–state socialist East Central Europe, there is some evidence that it was men who were exposed to early job and wage cuts when managers of state-owned enterprises were first free to reduce labour costs as men predominated in the labour forces of the industrial state-owned enterprises (Pollert 2003: 341).

Trade liberalization, facilitating the growth of global markets and the global restructuring of production, has also had consequences for women's employment. The production of manufactured goods has increased where production costs are low allowing multinationals to produce cheaply for export. Many goods, such as textiles and other consumer goods, are produced using women's labour. Manufacturing for the domestic market has declined in many of our case study countries as some domestic industries could not face this global competition. Women's employment in light manufacturing fell in East Central Europe after the transition. Only in relatively low wage El Salvador is *maquila* production in labour intensive sectors such as garment production that utilizes female labour for export to the North American market now significant. In the late 1990s women formed 79% of the workers in the Free Trade Zones (FTZs) and tax exempt areas (Hipsher 2001: 159). But there has been an increase in the production of commercial agricultural sector for export in both Chile and South Africa. The production of fruit such as apples and grapes as well as wine is dependent on women's labour, much of it employed on a seasonal temporary basis subject to low wages and poor conditions, often without access to benefits such as sick pay (Kehler 2001). Although most of these forms of production for global export markets employ small numbers of workers, they nonetheless make a significant contribution to the national economy.

The service sector has also increased in these restructured economies. Retailing, telecoms and the hotel, and tourist sectors have all grown in most of our case study countries and provided opportunities for female employment. In the face of an overall decline in the size of the female labour force in East Central Europe, the women who remain are now more concentrated in the service sector (Fodor 2004*b*). At the same time, financial liberalization has led to a growth in banking and financial services with some growth in women's employment in those sectors everywhere. In East Central Europe and Russia, women already dominated in the financial sectors as they were rudimentary and not very prestigious under state socialism (Fodor 2004*b*: 17). However, only a few years after the transitions, men began to move into high positions within these booming sectors resulting not only in a slight decline in the proportion of women employed but also in a much greater increase in the size of the wage gap (Lazreg 1999). In the Czech Republic female workers in banking and financial services formed 70% of the workforce and received 66.9% of the wages of male workers but by 2000 they still made up 61.8% of the workforce but received only 52.1% of the male wages (Fodor 2004*b*). However, it is women in post-socialist East Central Europe who still dominate in the professional and clerical jobs and in the state sector.

Economic reform has therefore had an important impact on the restructuring of employment as jobs have been lost in some sectors and created in others. Male and female employment exhibits different patterns. Male activity rates have fallen in all our case study countries at the same time as female activity rates in paid employment have increased in some of the case study countries (albeit from a relatively low base). Most marked has been the decline in female activity rates in the aftermath of many of the transitions from state socialism. Fodor (2004*b*) argues that although men and women faced a similar decline in employment opportunities, they reacted in different ways. Women were more likely to be discouraged and become homemakers; whereas men were more likely to stay in the labour market and claim unemployment benefits. However, contrary to expectations, the wage gap between men and women in East Central Europe initially declined in the early 1990s but then increased again. There is some speculation that this was because at first large numbers of men were laid off from high paying industrial jobs but subsequently women were less likely to be in the private sector where men appeared to be consolidating their control over the higher paid jobs (Fodor 2004*b*).

But these general trends hide important changes in different women's employment that need to be disaggregated. In post-state-socialist East Central Europe, certain women were more likely to leave the labour market than others. There is evidence that older women often took early retirement; low paid women gave up work, as did some mothers of young children who were faced with reduced access to childcare and increased costs (Fodor 2004*b*). However, many women have not done as badly as had been feared—their high educational levels and their labour market position in the professions stood them in good stead (Fodor 2004*b*). So, although women did not have the same opportunities as men under state socialism, at the point of transition they had a relatively advantageous labour market position compared to many women elsewhere. But most commentators agree that there is little chance of improvement now as their position is still being eroded as men consolidated their grip over new jobs in the private sector.

In our case study, countries in post-authoritarian Latin America the increase in female economic activity was not evenly spread over social strata. Women of the highest socio-economic strata already had significantly higher rates of participation than poorer women and in seven of the twelve countries looked at by ECLAC (2000) it was better-off women who increased their participation rates by more than those in the lowest strata. More highly educated women from the higher income quartiles are able to pay for childcare and tend to command higher

❖ THE STATE AND POLICY OUTCOMES

salaries, which make employment worthwhile while poorer women are less likely to be able to command wages which are high enough to make paid work economic. Heller and Cortes (2000) have found evidence that the female labour market in Argentina became increasingly segmented during the 1990s. The divisions widened between high-skilled women with high levels of education who were taking advantage of the new employment opportunities, particularly in the service sector and professions, at one end; and at the other end women with low educational levels and obsolete qualifications who were often forced into the labour market because of a fall in household income or male unemployment and they often had to accept intermittent low quality employment. The pre-existing gender gap in wages also changed. In a similar pattern to Chile where the gender wage gap at the top end of the employment market was 40% in 1992, but only 10% at the bottom end, in 1992 in Argentina women with incomplete education earned 84.1% of what comparable men earned while women with secondary education and above earned only 65.8% of comparable men's earnings (Montenegro 1999; Heller and Cortes 2000). However, by 1998 the earnings of women with incomplete secondary education had fallen to 76% of comparable males but the earnings of women with secondary education and above had risen to 79.5% of comparable male earnings.

Many advocates of economic reform have been disappointed by the slow growth in employment and the persistently high rates of unemployment that have often been higher for women than men. This reflects both the large numbers of women entering the labour market for the first time, for example in Latin America and the intermittent nature of much of the employment that they undertake. Therefore, while more jobs for women have been created, they vary dramatically in terms of conditions, job security, benefits, and wages with many women forced to take low skill, low productivity jobs in the service sector, particularly in domestic service, micro-enterprises, and self-employment. Only a few 'high quality' jobs have been created in modern sectors such as banking finance and telecoms. As we have seen privatization and deregulation have brought increased flexibility which has some adverse consequences for women workers both in terms of their working conditions and the wage levels commanded by women at the bottom of the occupational hierarchy. But we cannot assess the significance of changes in women's employment without considering how welfare restructuring also impacts on women's lives in both the public and private spheres.

❖ *Welfare Restructuring*

Widespread social sector restructuring was envisaged as an integral part of ensuring the sustainability of market-orientated reforms (Graham 1996). We will examine both the short-term and longer-term changes to welfare provision that have often accompanied transitions to democracy. During first generation reforms, the state provision of social services was cut to reduce both public spending and fiscal deficits. This was combined with an ideology that advocated transferring social service delivery from the state to the market and the private sector. It was believed that this would improve efficiency and accountability as part of the modernization of the state. In the short term, cuts in state welfare provision, such as the introduction of user fees for health and education services and reduction of welfare benefits, predominated, together with the provision of safety nets and poverty alleviation measures directed towards the poor. In the longer term, social security systems have been restructured towards greater market provision primarily through the move from state sponsored to insurance-based systems. All these changes—whether short-term or long-term—have had gendered impacts. As a consequence of men and women's different roles in the productive and reproductive spheres, changes in welfare provision impact on them in very different ways. Despite the evidence of these different patterns, most policies have not been gender aware and there have been few gender-specific policy interventions. When women have been targeted it has often been to take account of their reproductive rather than productive roles (Graham 1996).

At the same time, the imposition of these measures, coincided with increased demand for welfare services because of the impact of economic crisis and the imposition of structural adjustment programmes. Job losses associated with privatization and trade liberalization as well as the effects of price liberalization and falls in real wages led to increased poverty, inequality, and hardship that were often far greater and more enduring than policymakers had envisaged. Economic shocks, policy reform, and old age produce marked gender-specific risks. Women are often over-represented among the poor as are female-headed households. In South Africa 61% of poor households were female-headed and only 31% of poor households were male-headed in 1995 (Chirwa and Khoza 2005: 138). Rates of domestic violence and divorce also increased at times of economic crisis. In Hungary and the Czech Republic the divorce rate had risen to over half of all marriages in 1997 from over one in three in 1989 (Pollert 2003: 337). In some cases, rates of suicide, mortality, and alcoholism have also increased significantly among men. In Russia women now outlive men by 12.5 years compared to a global average of only 4 years (World Bank website www.worldbank.org/gender). In much of East Central Europe and Russia the birth rate fell sharply. Between 1990–9, it declined by 30% in Hungary, 32% in Poland, 38% in Russia, and 40% in the Czech Republic (Gal and Kligman 2000).

The changes in welfare provision have been most pronounced in post–state socialist East Central Europe. Spending on health for example has been reduced substantially. In Hungary healthcare expenditure as a percentage of GDP almost halved, falling from 9.8 to 5.6% (Pollert 2003: 337). In addition, user charges have been widely introduced. Even in South Africa the adoption of the fiscally conservative GEAR in 1996 with its emphasis on cost recovery and public/private partnerships led to the increase in costs for basic services such as water and electricity after the privatization of utilities and justified cuts in social spending (such as social insurance and social assistance funds) (Kehler 2001: 10). As we know, cutbacks in welfare provision impact differentially on women, increasing their caring responsibilities in the household at a time when the pressures on poorer women to generate an income are often increasing.

In post-state-socialist East Central Europe many women's ability to continue to participate in the paid labour force has been affected by these sometimes contradictory pressures: reduced welfare spending resulted in cuts in maternity and childcare allowances at the same time as the resurgence of traditional values and the continuing fall in the birth rate increased the pressure for pronatalist measures. As we have seen, the decline in the birth rate seen under state socialism continued unabated in the majority of East Central Europe. In the Czech lands, the birth rate in 1994 was the lowest ever recorded since the statistics were first collected in 1785 despite a large number of women of childbearing age (Wolchik 2000: 66). Wolchik argues that there are a number of immediate causes: the more widespread use of contraceptives, an increase in the age of first marriage, the availability of new opportunities such as travel, and the impact of social and economic changes such as the increases in unemployment and changes to the welfare system. In the 1990s, for the first time since the Second World War, the birth rate in Russia was lower than the death rate (Marsh 1998: 92). Nationalist discourse in many Soviet successor states that encourages women to have babies for the nation has combined with the more generalized sentiment expressed in 1992 by one of Yeltsin's advisors (and subsequently reinforced by Putin (Chandler 2005) that 'the workplace for a woman is with her children. She is not without work—children are her work' (quoted in Marsh 1998: 95).

As a result of these pressures many countries in post-state-socialist East Central Europe initially extended some maternity benefits. In 1993 in Hungary the Christian nationalist dominated government effectively prolonged maternity leave for any woman with three or more children at home until the youngest child's eighth birthday (in addition to the pre-existing flat rate and earnings related allowances payable after official six-month paid maternity leave had ended and lasting until any child was reached their third birthday) (Goven 2000: 290). After 1989 maternity benefits were not only retained in Czechoslovakia but also extended to women who were at home (Wolchik 2000: 76). Women can have three years maternity leave.

But budgetary constraints often pushed policies in the opposite direction. Significant retrenchment, often part of the wider restructuring of welfare systems, occurred. The level of benefits was frequently low and was often seriously eroded by inflation. Wolchik (2000: 76) argues that the allowance received for caring for children at home in the Czech Republic was below the lowest pension. Across much of post-socialist East Central Europe governments facing severe budgetary constraints frequently abolished other benefits and allowances and many that were retained became means tested. Opposed by the Christian nationalists on pro-natalist grounds, the Hungarian socialist led government, under pressure from the IMF and World Bank, proposed the abolition of the earnings related allowance at the same time as the flat-rated allowance described above would become means-tested (except for women who had three children) (Goven 2000: 294–9; Pollert 2003: 337). In the Czech Republic state subsidized loans to families were abolished in 1991 and after initially increasing them, children's allowances became progressively more targeted in 1993 and 1997 as their value declined as a result of inflation (Wolchik 2000: 76–7).

In Poland, although many of the benefits such as leave to take care of a sick child and childcare leave were maintained, the financial compensation was severely reduced and restricted to families with very low incomes. Heinen and Portet (2002: 153) argue that the leave also 'lost any real significance with the elimination of the right to return to one's job following such leave'. Therefore, although various childcare leave packages continued to exist and in some cases were extended (and sometimes re-titled as parental leave and made available to men), they also became more limited and restrictive with the introduction of means testing and reduced benefits. Perhaps more significantly, some women felt unable to convert their formal rights into actually existing rights in a climate of economic insecurity and fear of unemployment. Between 1990 and 1996, the proportion of eligible women taking maternity leave dropped by two-thirds compared to the 90% of women who had taken all or part of their leave rights in the 1980s (Heinen and Portet 2002). Therefore, in a situation in which many people are fearful of losing their jobs, the risks associated with availing oneself of one's rights are too great.

❖ Poverty Alleviation

Despite the emphasis on reducing state expenditure within reform programmes, short-term mechanisms have also been introduced to ameliorate the poverty that has been caused and exacerbated by economic reform. During the 1990s safety nets and poverty alleviation measures were considered increasingly necessary to bolster coalitions for reform by creating stakeholders as well as protecting the needy. Of the three major mechanisms used to transfer the means of livelihood to the poor— income/cash transfers, in-kind transfers, and public works programmes (later converted to longer-term social investment programmes)—only in-kind transfers initially specifically targeted women and then only in their reproductive roles. For example in-kind transfers in the form of food subsidies, feeding programmes, and other targeted nutrition programmes are frequently directed at young children and pregnant and lactating women. During the height of the recession, the Pinochet regime in Chile established very effective maternal and child health programmes that targeted large numbers of poor women and children using the pre-existing welfare system. Using a different approach, feeding programmes were set up in Peru that utilized unpaid women's labour organized in mothers' clubs and glass of milk committees in Lima. However, these were often established in such a way that they marginalized existing autonomous efforts such as the communal popular kitchens (Barrig 1996).

In contrast, cash transfers such as child allowances have often been made to heads of household regardless of sex. The majority of public works programmes that provide temporary employment have also either not taken gender into account in their design or implicitly have been targeted at men. The programmes have often discriminated against women implicitly and explicitly: both in terms of types of jobs on offer (which have often been 'male jobs' primarily in construction) and in terms of wage levels. As a consequence some funds have employed predominantly male workers (Blum 1997).[11] However, women have also participated in these programmes but often in different and sometimes unexpected ways when compared to men. Men and women often have different criteria for participation. Women will often be less deterred by the very low wages (set so that only the very poorest will participate) but are more affected by timing and location of programmes.

Despite low participation by women in some employment programmes, these factors have also combined to produce what Nina Laurie (1997) has called the 'feminization' of emergency employment. Looking at the Peruvian programmes of the 1980s she argues that the Peruvian government was taken by surprise when jobs that had been designed for men were actually taken up by women. PAIT, the Peruvian temporary employment programme, introduced by APRA in 1985 offered insecure temporary three month contracts with low wages set at the legal minimum wage. However, while 82% of men in the informal sector were earning more than this, only 53% of women were. As a consequence men stayed away from the physically demanding jobs in construction that had initially been intended for them. Large numbers of women joined the programme that offered them employment in their neighbourhood, forming around 80% of the workforce. Once it became clear that the jobs were being done predominantly by women, the rhetoric of the state shifted towards emphasizing welfare element of the programme which ensured its continued feminization as it reinforced the belief that it was 'bad work' for men (Laurie 1997).

However, in general, policymakers have increasingly recognized that within the household, women are likely to pass on a greater proportion of their income and any increase in their income as a contribution to household welfare, and that a greater proportion of income is spent on household welfare in female- than in male-headed households. As a result policy interventions have been increasingly addressed towards women. The National Public Works Programme (NPWP) set up in South Africa to promote infra-structural development and the provision of mainly short-term employment has specifically targeted women. It aimed to

THE STATE AND POLICY OUTCOMES ❖

achieve a workforce comprised of 60% women in part because of this recognition that women will transfer more of their income to help the whole household. Indeed one programme in Kwa Zulu Natal prioritized female-headed households and 95% of its participants were women (McCord 2003).

Explicit or implicit targeting of women has also occurred in the Social Investment Funds (SIFs) that have developed from the transitional short-term programmes to become permanent medium-and/or long-term poverty reduction programmes. They aim to improve the capacity of the poor to escape poverty by not only dealing with the inequalities created by the market reforms that have pushed some into poverty in the short term, but also helping the poor augment their human, physical, and social capital (Inter-American Development Bank 1995). A variety of means such as building social and economic infrastructure (particularly schools, health clinics, and sanitation), the strengthening of community organizations, capacity building, and the organization of productive projects, such as providing credit and developing micro-enterprises, can achieve this. The projects are meant to be demand-driven and determined by local communities. Although they are funded by SIFs, they are implemented by NGOs and local authorities with cost sharing often in the form of free labour provided by the communities themselves. Too many poverty alleviation measures therefore depend on women's unpaid or poorly paid work in order to fulfil their objectives (Molyneux and Razavi 2005).

Initially, few SIFs targeted women directly, but their projects had hugely gendered implications because of women's roles in social reproduction and in their communities. Although not often directly providing jobs for women, projects that build and rehabilitate school and health clinics together with nutrition programmes such as breakfasts for children benefit women as household managers responsible for family welfare. Many of the community organizations and NGOs that should propose and implement projects are composed mainly of women despite being officially described in gender-neutral terms (World Bank 1994).[12] Women's predominance in these organizations is rarely recognized or acknowledged by donors or policymakers. However, participation in SIFs implies important changes for many organizations. First, they are often pressured to become small enterprises rather than being based entirely on volunteer labour. If for example they become businesses with contracts to supply school meals or restaurants or cafes, or if even only some members become paid workers while others remain as volunteers, this implies that they move away from any collective form of organization.[13] Second, there is a new emphasis on professionalization that prioritizes qualifications and experts. As a result some NGOs and local women's organizations are deemed not to have the right training and background to receive funding, which may then go NGOs made up of professional middle-class women. Implicitly recognizing women's participation, some later projects have focused more specifically on them, sometimes requiring project committee members to be women, establishing micro-credit programmes and supporting micro-enterprises for women or targeting them to keep health centres running (Blum 1997; Lewis 1999).

Feminist commentators are divided about the impact of SIFs on poor women. Veronica Schild (1998, 2000) has analysed Chile's social policy since the transition to democracy. The Concertación's emphasis on 'growth with equity' has resulted in policies that are very much in keeping with the philosophy of SIFs. The Solidarity and Social Investment Fund (FOSIS) was established in 1990 with the support of many committed individuals based in NGOs who had resisted the dictatorship. Although underfunded, FOSIS set up programmes such as Entre Todos (Between Us All) that aimed to build organizational and participatory capacities in poor communities facilitated by NGOs and extension workers. Schild (2000: 296) argues that 'without explicitly targeting women, the programme depends on women's community-based and personal skills, not to mention their inordinate capacity to volunteer their efforts' undermining the supposedly gender-free notion of 'human resources' used by FOSIS.

Some of SERNAM's programmes explicitly targeted poor women such as the Programa Jefas de Hogar (female headed households); Programa de Microempresas (micro-enterprise programme) and the Programa de Capacitación Laboral (employment training programme) aimed at enabling women to improve their income generating capacities. Schild (1998) has argued that all these programmes are repositioning the poor and poor women into new narrow forms of citizenship that fit in with a neo-liberal project based on the ethos that it is the individual's responsibility not to be poor through their own efforts in the market. At the same time, women's organizations and state bodies such as SERNAM are compromised in the extent to which they can follow broader agendas around 'women's empowerment'. In contrast, others see positive opportunities for women to become agents of social development through these funds, as long as precautions are taken to diminish the larger workload that they may imply for them (Inter-American Bank 1995).

❖ Social Security Restructuring

Fears about fiscal deficits, inefficiency, and new demands such as ageing populations and increasing health care costs that systems are unable to cope with, has meant that the restructuring of pensions and health systems has been a core component of many economic reform packages. These social security systems provide primarily health and retirement benefits to those workers (and often their dependents) who have made sufficient contributions. Rules regarding contributions, services, and benefits as well as the structure and balance of public and private entities have changed to increase the role of the private sector and competition in the provision of social security benefits. No universal model has been implemented but there has been a move from state sponsored systems that often provide standard levels of benefits (or entitlement on the basis of need), to individual account systems in which beneficiaries receive benefits that are a function of both what they have put in (sometimes termed equivalency) and an assessment of their risk.

The move from standard benefits to individual capitalization with benefits given according to equivalence has strongly gendered implications. While standard benefits systems often contain an implicit male-bread-winner bias in that the right to make claims for social benefits is constructed around a norm of full-time life-long participation in the market-based labour force which many women do not conform to, market-based individualized entitlements contain another form of overt bias which works against gender equality (Elson and Cagatay 2000). In marketized schemes, women are affected differently to men, not only because of their differing ability to contribute but also because of the different ways in which they are treated by them.

In a market-based capitalized system, the actuarial categorization of men and women into differentiated groups—a gender differentiated system—means that women automatically receive lower monthly benefits than men from annuities because of their greater longevity. In contrast, old-style pay-as-you-go pension systems have been seen as relatively more favourable to women who often have a lower retirement age and greater longevity but receive the same benefits as a man of the same salary who has paid in for the same number of years (Arenas de Mesa and Betranou 1997).[14] However, women contribute less because they have lower wages, spend more years outside the paid labour force and frequently have a lower retirement age. This increases the risk that women may not be covered because they do not meet the minimum contribution record (if one exists). Although the gender implications of these changes are now recognized by academics (see below) and are beginning to be acknowledged by some policymakers, as yet no changes to pension and health schemes have been made on this basis despite the implications for poverty among older women in the future.

The best way to analyse how these changes work in practice is to focus primarily on the most radical market-orientated models with the most far-reaching implications for women before looking briefly at some of the less radical versions. The radical Chilean model of social security restructuring was one of the earliest and became a reform paradigm for Latin America and beyond. Pension and health service restructuring was first introduced in the 1980s by the military government as part of its neo-liberal reforms. The Chilean pensions reform allowed those in the state scheme to remain there but workers were given huge incentives to encourage them to move to individual accounts. New entrants to the labour market had no choice but to contribute 10% (plus extra for administration and disability/survivor insurance of around 3%) of their salary into a pension fund (AFP) of their choice. A voluntary scheme for the self-employed was also introduced. A number of problems with this system have been identified. Coverage at around 60% is now lower than the 70% achieved by the state scheme in 1970s, a decline attributed to the larger numbers now in the informal sector. In addition high numbers have joined schemes but are not contributing regularly. The funds are also expensive to administer and yields are uncertain (Barrientos 1996). To receive the minimum pension ($125 per month in 1998) in Chile it is necessary to have contributed to an AFP for twenty years. Many employers in the service sector do not deduct contributions (which is a particular problem for domestic servants who are often excluded) or they under-declare earnings to cut costs paying in only on the basis of the legal minimum wage that is already lower for domestic workers. AFPs' fixed commission charges are also relatively higher for women as their contributions are generally lower (Arenas de Mesa and Montecinos 1999). Finally men and women are also treated differently for the calculation of benefits. For example survivor pensions are only paid out to wives (who receive 60% of the deceased male's pension) and not to surviving husbands unless they are disabled.

The primary implication for benefits is that salary replacement levels (the percentage of their salary the beneficiary ends up with) differ sharply by gender. In Chile women's replacement rates are only between 52 and 57% of their salaries whereas men's rates are between 81 and 86% (Arenas de Mesa and Betranou 1997). According to Cox-Edwards (2000), a woman with an incomplete primary education who retires at sixty (the statutory retirement age for women) will receive only 29% of the pension of the average man with the same level of education who retires at sixty-five (the statutory retirement age for men). Therefore the gender wage gap between men and women increases after retirement. For example women who earn on average 75% men's salaries during their working life will only have 35–45% of men's pensions on retirement. These differences have important implications for the take up of personal pensions. Relatively fewer workers (particularly women) in the informal sector and the low paid are entering the plans as 10% of a low wage not enough to guarantee a pension, and women, particularly married women, are therefore less likely to pay into a scheme (Barrientos 1996). As a result although the coverage of working women increased between 1989 and 1995, it had only reached 50% at the same time as the percentage of regular female contributors to AFPs had declined from 49 to 40% (Arenas de Mesa and Betranou 1997).

Other countries have implemented less radical reforms but these still have some of the same negative consequences for women. Under state socialism, despite their focus on years spent in the paid labour force, women were treated relatively favourably in pensions provision. Women's salary replacement levels were often higher than men's at the same time as caring credits and lower retirement ages also benefited women. Prior to the demise of the USSR, women had the right to retire earlier (particularly if they had brought up 5 children or more) and time out of the labour market to look after children was credited as work time (Chandler

2005). The new systems introduced more 'formal equality' but women's pensions deteriorated significantly as benefits like caring credits were reduced in value at the same time as pensions began to reproduce more closely the inequalities of labour market in terms of wage levels and replacement levels.

A number of countries in East Central Europe, notably Poland and Hungary, opted for a partial privatization of their pensions systems in the mid-1990s, introducing a mixed system in which the public system continues to provide a basic pension and a mandatory individual system provides the rest. Poland revamped its system most radically, also altering its public pension system extensively according to an individualized model. In Poland the maintenance of differential retirement ages between men and women in the new system has also exacerbated women's inferior pensions position (Steinhilber 2004). As a result of reforms in the 1990s Russia also moved towards the social insurance principle although women's right to retire earlier was defended (Chandler 2005). The Czech Republic and Argentina both introduced much more moderate reforms within the existing system during the 1990s—reforming the public scheme at the same time as setting up voluntary private schemes with less deterioration of women's pension position.

The implications for women of the introduction of private health schemes are similar to those of the pension plans. The introduction of health reform has tended to bring in private sector players and encourage competition in the provision of insurance and the administration of compulsory insurance programmes, introducing competition between public, private, and quasi-market forms in the provision of public services. The most radical version introduced in Chile is based on equivalence at an individual level. It takes the form of risk insurance operating with market mechanisms. The benefits vary according to the amount contributed but are also a function of the existing medical risk, which is a function of the age and sex of a contributor and their family group so that two individuals making the same contributions will not have the same levels of coverage and benefits (ECLAC 2000).

Under the Chilean system, employees contribute a minimum of 7% of their salaries to either FONASA (the national health fund) or an ISAPRE (a private healthcare provider). In 1997 32 ISAPRES covered 28% of the population. There is a correlation between those affiliated to pension schemes and ISAPRES as the same better-off people belong to both. As a result of women's lower wages and the higher costs they incur—women of reproductive age have to pay two or even three time as much as men for a health plan—only 32% of ISAPRE members were women in 2001 (Gideon 2005). Benefits are calculated on an individual basis according to risk. Women are assessed as having different risks and therefore if they pay in the same amount as a man earning the same salary they receive different (fewer) benefits primarily because of the costs of maternity. Under this system the cost of having children is therefore paid disproportionately by women.

❖ THE STATE AND POLICY OUTCOMES

The consequences of social sector restructuring clearly vary by gender and class. As a result of the most radical reforms, only certain better-off women in relatively secure well-paid formal sector jobs have comprehensive pension and health insurance coverage. Women earning low wages (often in the informal sector) are unlikely to contribute regularly or be entitled to benefits. Even those women who can contribute, get fewer benefits compared to men earning comparable salaries under the new marketized schemes. And even the more moderate reforms that maintain some elements of the old system also have gendered outcomes that adversely affect many women (Arenas de Mesa and Betranou 1997).

Overall, economic and social restructuring based on market principles and neo-liberal ideas have been implemented to some degree in all of our case study countries whatever their position in the global economy. Although some similar trends can be discerned, there are also differences between the various cases. For example, Fodor (2004b) argues that different gender regimes are emerging in East Central Europe. In Poland the more familial welfare state and the associated changes in family policy encourage women to leave the labour market and assigns them to the home (Fodor et al. 2002; Fodor 2004b). In contrast as a result of somewhat different transitions and welfare reform packages, women are more likely to be economically active in the Czech Republic, but in relatively low positions, and in Hungary middle-class women are doing relatively well whereas poor women have been left behind. Fodor et al. (2002: 489) speculate that in Poland the 'male dominated Solidarity based government combined with the influence of the Catholic Church, contributed to the conservative, family centred nature of the policies'. This was compounded by the rapidity of the structural adjustment that reduced welfare spending and relocated the provision of welfare outside the responsibility of the state.

Differences in outcomes can also be discerned in other cases. In Argentina and Peru, ill-fated attempts to introduce market reforms were implemented by populist presidents with disastrous consequences. In Argentina, debt default and huge increases in poverty and unemployment followed the failure of Menem's economic policies. In contrast both South Africa and Chile managed to maintain economic stability in the post transition period. Overall, social and economic restructuring and greater integration into the global economy have brought increasing polarization and inequality but often in complex and contradictory ways. At the same time as some countries have benefited more than others in economic terms, some women—predominantly the better-off—have benefited while others—often poorer women—have found their access to employment and welfare benefits as well as their conditions of work have worsened.

Despite these variations, it is possible to draw some general conclusions about the impact of social and economic restructuring on women's descriptive and substantive representation, the likelihood of positive gender outcomes, and finally women's ability to exercise their civil and political rights as well as other social and economic rights. The impact of restructuring on overall levels of women's descriptive representation is quite hard to assess. The imposition of legislative quotas for example has few resource implications for the state. However, restructuring can have an impact on who is elected. It becomes harder for poor women to participate in conventional political activity in the context of increasing polarization and inequality, as the demands on their time, both in terms of paid and unpaid labour, have often increased. The tendency for elected women to be relatively affluent can therefore be exacerbated. Improvements in women's substantive representation such as the establishment of effective SWMs have resource implications for the state that can be compromised by market-led reforms that include fiscal restraint. The implementation of certain gender policies can also be circumscribed by limits on state spending. As we have seen the provision of childcare and more progressive domestic violence policies have often been hampered by a lack of state funding. The realization of positive gender outcomes and improvements in substantive representation therefore also requires adequate resources and active state intervention.

Social and economic restructuring have also had an impact on different types of women's organizing. In the absence of state provision, new forms of poverty alleviation strategies often rely on women's unpaid labour within community-based organizations as well as paid professionals from women's NGOs. These strategies can change the relationship between different kinds of women's organizations at the same time as reducing the autonomy of all of them. In East Central Europe, in particular, although women's nominal civil and political rights have increased as a result of transitions to democracy, women's enjoyment of certain social and economic rights has diminished significantly as a consequence of the transition to a more market orientated economy and the reduction of state welfare provision. Overall, the shortcomings in many women's access to social and economic rights reduce their capacity to exercise their newly (re)gained civil and political rights. We are now in a position to sum up all our findings to see whether we can now provide some answers to the question posed at the beginning of the preface to this book: under what circumstances can transitions to democracy result in positive gender outcomes?

❖ NOTES

1 It is estimated that activity rates for Czechoslovakia were similar to Hungary. According to Fodor (2004b: 6), there have been no definitive studies that have explored the differences between the three cases. She speculates that the lower rates in Poland might be due to the conservative Roman Catholic Church influenced culture or because a number of women were classified as 'helping family members' on private family farms.

2 Interview with Gloria Bonder, ex-member of Menem's women's cabinet, Buenos Aires, May 1996.

❖ THE STATE AND POLICY OUTCOMES

3 No representatives from the Consejo were included in the official Argentine delegation to Beijing, which was against abortion under any circumstances.

4 In an interview, Ester Schiavone, Presidenta of the Consejo, was very keen to identify herself as a Menemista, i.e. a keen supporter of President Menem (interview in Buenos Aires, June 1996).

5 Many feminists I interviewed in 1996 argued that two very different Consejos had existed—one before and one after Franganillo's resignation. They were enthusiastic about the first and had no contact with the second.

6 Interview with Mavivi Manzini, July 2003, Johannesburg.

7 Interview with Maria del Carmen Feijoó, feminist academic and member of the 1993 Constituent Assembly, Buenos Aires, May 1996.

8 All the feminists I spoke to in Hungary and the Czech Republic stressed the potential significance of EU accession for enhancing opportunities for improving gender equality.

9 Interpress Service News Agency www.ipsnews.net downloaded 25.4.05.

10 Interview with the Chilean Health Minister, *Women's Hour*, BBC Radio 4 broadcast on 14 June 2006.

11 For example 90–95% of employees in the Nicaraguan public works programmes were men. Women who made up 5–10% of the workforce were doing domestic tasks such as cooking and receiving only half the salary received by the worst paid men.

12 For example, a 'parents organization' in Peru provides school breakfasts (World Bank 1994).

13 Maruja Barrig, interviewed in Lima, August 1996.

14 Some authors have gone so far as to argue that these types of schemes have an implied gender subsidy.

❖ Conclusions

Transitions from non-democratic regimes to polities that are at least nominally democratic have brought some significant changes in citizenship, participation, and policymaking, as well as disillusionment that changes have not been as far-reaching as had been hoped. This book has explored how these changes have been gendered and in particular analysed the circumstances under which gender outcomes can be positive. Through a comparative study of eight primary and two comparator cases, we have examined the extent to which different 'third wave' transitions to democracy have enhanced women's citizenship in terms of women's access not only to civil and political rights but to various social and economic ones as well. In this short concluding section we summarize outcomes in the electoral, bureaucratic, and constitutional/legal arenas as well as policy changes. We can then draw some general conclusions about the main factors that are responsible for them. These conclusions also raise issues that could inform the current debates and future research agendas of feminist political scientists and democratization scholars. We will end by outlining some of these.

Women's civil and political rights have undoubtedly increased as a result of transitions to democracy, but their social and economic rights have not necessarily been enhanced. These discrepancies can, in part, be attributed to the impact of policies of economic and social restructuring and the greater integration into the global economy that has frequently accompanied the political processes of transition. But the extent to which this has happened has varied—it is particularly marked in the transitions from state socialism in East Central Europe—and perhaps least true of South Africa. And as we noted at the end of Part IV, women's ability to access their new civil and political rights is often circumscribed by their socio-economic position and—particularly for poor women—new rights on paper do not necessarily alter women's day-to-day lives. Some women have therefore undoubtedly benefited a great deal more than others, depending for example on their geographical, class and racial position as pre-existing inequalities have often intensified.

But if we focus more narrowly on the opportunities for women to exercise their civil and political rights and participate in political and policymaking arenas, we can identify a range of outcomes. Our analysis of the electoral arena has shown that, with the exception of South Africa, women's descriptive representation was low immediately after the founding election in all our cases. But, mirroring global trends, it did increase to varying degrees. What then explains the variation between Hungary (ranked 103rd in the world) with 9.1% women and Argentina (ranked 7th in the world) with 36.2% women in the lower house in early 2006 (http://www.ipu.org/iss-e/women.htm)? Our explanations can contribute to many of the more general debates that are current within the study of gender and politics.

Clearly the introduction of *effective* electoral quotas, as in Argentina, does 'fast track' increases in women's representation. But this does not happen unless quotas are well designed, appropriate to the electoral system, and properly implemented (which, as we have seen, did not happen in the Brazilian case). However although the design of electoral systems can have an important effect on numbers of women elected, it appears that, particularly in the absence of electoral quotas, parties had a decisive influence in the post transition period. Reinforcing evidence from the first world, it seems that women with a gender agenda can make more headway in parties on the left, including many of the ex-communist parties, than in parties of the right. Indeed in some of our cases the varying fortunes of leftist parties, often operating in relatively uninstitutionalized party systems, can go some way to explain the variations in the levels of women elected over time. But being on the left and relatively open to a gender agenda is not sufficient for a party, the role of women activists advancing that gender agenda within parties—pressing for example for the introduction of quotas and changes in policies—is crucial.

We also assessed the impact of increased numbers of women in post transition legislatures. A number of recent gender and politics debates have focused on the extent to which women representatives will 'act for' women and increase their substantive representation in the electoral sphere. But in keeping with some current scepticism about 'sheer numbers' and 'critical mass', it appears from the case studies that, on their own, larger numbers of women (even a critical mass over 30%) do not necessarily have the impact that some feminists had hoped. An interest in gender issues can, for example, manifest itself in a desire to restrict abortion rights. But, extending the arguments laid out in the previous paragraph, there is evidence of the significant role that can be played by key feminists within legislatures (taking advantage for example of the opportunities for (cross-party) organizing around issues like domestic violence).

Our discussions also considered substantive representation—understood as the representation of women's interest in the policymaking process—and looked at the bureaucratic arena, focusing on state women's machineries (SWMs). SWMs in some form or other were established in all our case study countries in the favourable international context of the 1990s. Echoing studies of SWMs elsewhere, the machineries varied considerably in their effectiveness and the role that they could play. In part this seems to reflect why and how they were set up. Those (such as in Chile, South Africa, and Brazil) that were set up as a direct result of feminist pressure during the transition appear to have achieved the most despite the undeniable problems that they have faced. Others, particularly those established from above and often because of external pressure (for example from the EU accession process) have often done very little. SWMs (such as those in Argentina, Brazil, and Poland) have also been subject to the vagaries of the effects of changes in government and sometimes of presidential whim within less institutionalized post transition polities. Therefore the ability of SWMs to increase women's substantive representation in the post transition context does depend in large part on the role of feminists both within and outside the SWM, its relationship with the government/ruling party and the commitment of the government to the SWM and a 'gender agenda'.

But we also saw that in a number of cases women's rights were enhanced by improvements in the constitutional/legal arena that came out of some transitions. Constitutional/legal change is a significant, and to date, often neglected area for improvement in women's citizenship rights. Constitutions can provide an enabling framework for subsequent gains. But again active women's organizations operating within a favourable context are needed to capitalize on this enabling framework. Two examples stand out here—South Africa and Brazil—where new constitutions were designed as part of the process of transition and feminists were able to have an input into those processes. As a result some progressive gender clauses were included. However, constitutional change did not always result in substantial improvements in gender rights. In Argentina, successful women's organizing around the constitutional process was in part defensive and in our East Central Europe cases constitutional change only began to have a positive effect after the need to incorporate the totality of EU legislation became an imperative. Again the question of what these changes mean in practice becomes important. Will new rights embodied in constitutional reform mean that women can access these rights in their every day lives?

How far has women's enjoyment of certain gender rights been altered by the different policy outcomes that have accompanied many transitions? Our starting point has to be the very different women's rights legacies at the beginning of transitions from state socialism and authoritarianism. In our East Central European case studies, women had access to a wide range of rights, particularly socio-economic ones, on paper. Employment, healthcare, education, pensions as well as divorce, reproductive rights, and a right to equality were all part of this package. At the point of transition from authoritarianism, women in our Latin American case studies had far fewer rights, particularly socio-economic ones, as the state provision of health, welfare, and education was far more limited and societies were characterized by very high levels of inequality. Access to reproductive rights and even divorce was also limited.

Achieving change in this initial gender rights status quo depends on a number of factors. The nature of the particular issue area is crucial. How an issue is framed,

CONCLUSIONS ❖

the openness of the policy environment, the presence of international norms, the cohesiveness of women's movements, and the priority given to that issue all affect the likelihood of achieving change. We examined three gender rights issues ranging from the regulation of marriage—divorce in particular—as a relatively uncontroversial area, domestic violence as a moderately controversial area, to reproductive rights—particularly abortion—as the most contested. We saw that on the whole change is easier to achieve in the least contested areas. Even in Chile divorce is now finally legal. Domestic violence has been legislated against in the aftermath of many transitions from authoritarianism after decades of national, regional, and international women's activism. But as we saw the resources to fully implement the new laws have rarely been forthcoming so their impact has been less than it could have been. But there has been less domestic violence legislation enacted in East Central Europe in spite of the efforts of some of the NGOs active around the issue. Abortion has been a very contentious issue in the aftermath of several transitions, leading to a retrenchment in Poland and El Salvador where the Right and the Catholic Church played a decisive role and liberalization in only in one case: South Africa. For most of our case studies the status quo has been maintained with some access to legal abortion remaining in most post-state-socialist polities and restrictive laws still in place in our Latin American case studies.

We cannot understand this range of outcomes unless we can specify the factors that determine what happens in different contexts. This book has attempted to develop an explanatory framework that can help us make sense of these sometimes seemingly inconsistent outcomes. But, as in the rest of the study of democratization, explanations for different outcomes require us to consider a complex array and interaction of factors.

Overall, this book has found that, while women's organizing seems a necessary condition, it is not sufficient for change in the short term. The nature of that organizing—how far movements are cohesive and interact with the state and the conventional political arena—is important. Influenced by analyses that use the political opportunity structure, historical/institutional frameworks, and studies such as Weldon's cross-national examination (2002) of domestic violence, we saw that organized women are frequently the key to articulating gender issues within transitions. This articulation would not happen without their activities. However, women's organizing on its own is not enough to effect change. More is needed to ensure that these issues then get on the agenda of the transition and are ultimately translated into improvements in women's citizenship.

There are several factors that help to determine whether certain gender issues, once articulated, make it on to the agenda of the transition. Organized women have to make the issue a priority and organize explicitly to achieve this aim. The role of key women, particularly feminists, is often central. These women are present not just within organized women's movements—even though these are often crucial in articulating issues—but also within legislatures, political parties, governments, and bureaucracies in the post-transition period. And these key women often form a range of alliances—both insider and outsider ones with other important actors. But this is not to say that these alliances can be made easily and are always unproblematic. We saw that this happened to varying degrees in Chile, Brazil, and South Africa but did not take place in East Central Europe. Primarily because of the nature and legacy of state socialism, there were no autonomous women's movements in existence or women, organized as women, active at the point of transition.

Furthermore, it appears that gender issues are more likely to get on to the agenda of the transition if they can be framed effectively in ways that resonate in that political climate. In South Africa, feminists were able to insert gender into a broader discourse of rights; in our Latin American cases women's issues were positioned as part of the opposition to dictatorship and state violence and the struggle for democracy. Some issues, such as quotas and domestic violence, were easier to frame in ways that tapped into broad discourses of citizenship and human rights than others such as reproductive rights. There was less opportunity to do this in Eastern Europe whether the opposition was dominated by the Catholic Church or liberal individualism.

The headway that key women can make, whether from within women's movements or within other institutions depends on how open both the transitions and institutions are to them. To be most effective the newly important political arena and the transition itself has to be relatively accessible to women actors. From our case studies it appears that pacted and relatively drawn out transitions with negotiation processes that are relatively open, transparent, and accountable are more likely to be accessible to women actors. Powerful participants in those negotiations, particularly within the opposition, also have to be open to gender concerns and feminists have to be already present or have access to those arenas.

In order to maintain these gender issues on the policy agenda and get positive outcomes in the post-transition period, several other conditions need to be fulfilled. The subsequent policy environment needs to be sufficiently open. It is helpful if some important building blocks are already in place. Gender-friendly constitutions can form one such building block. A government in power that is sympathetic to gender issues with feminists in key positions in the party hierarchy, executive, and legislature as well as an effective SWM is also critical. In South Africa the ex-revolutionary ANC, a party that was relatively open to gender claims, took power. But in contrast the FMLN—relatively more open to gender issues than other El Salvadorean parties—failed to win electoral office and therefore the opportunities for positive gender outcomes were limited.

There is some evidence to show that, in different contexts, activist women will target the arenas that are most accessible to them. At one end of the spectrum, key women were present in all three arenas in South Africa. We can speculate that in Brazil many women, particularly in the immediate post-transition period, eschewed attempting to achieve meaningful change in the fraught electoral arena preferring the bureaucratic and constitutional/legal arenas. In Chile both the electoral and constitutional arenas were relatively closed to women in the immediate post-transition period and a limited presence in the bureaucratic arena was not enough to effect significant change in the restricted Chilean transition. Although we do not have the evidence to allow us to argue that one arena is necessarily more important than another in achieving certain gender outcomes, a presence in only one institutional arena does seem to make effecting significant change rather hard to realize.

But we must be mindful of the danger that our frameworks could become excessively deterministic and push path dependence further than is justified. The question of how far gender issues have to be articulated prior to and during the transition in order for gender outcomes to be positive in the post-transition period is pertinent here. We do not want to over extend that analysis and reach the overly rigid conclusion that it is not possible for gender issues to be articulated and acted upon subsequently if this did not happen earlier. For example in Eastern Europe there are signs that the antipathy to quotas is lessening and that accession to the EU has a potentially important positive impact. It is too early to tell how long-lasting the legacy of state socialism will be.

Having assessed our findings, it is now possible to broaden our horizons. The kind of analysis that has been outlined in this book and the conclusions we have drawn have some general implications for both feminists and political scientists. First this book has reinforced our original contention that the institutional arena and the roles that can be played by key actors within that arena have to be at the centre of any analysis. As women's movements, however cohesive or engaged in the political process, on their own are not enough to achieve positive gender outcomes, other institutional actors must come to the fore. We need to look at the role of insider/outside alliances and in particular what can be achieved by certain strategic alliances of key actors within the institutional arena. Conventional political parties, for example, are key players and women's parties do not appear to be very likely to effect significant change. The state and the institutional arena therefore remain a key part of any study of gender and politics. The analysis in this book can therefore contribute to the emerging debates on feminist institutionalism.

We need also to focus directly on how gender policy outcomes come about. The roles played by organized women or by measures to increase women's descriptive representation such as quotas are part of that process. But more is needed to give us greater insight into how positive outcomes are achieved. For example what kinds of measures can be obtained and what arenas are likely to be more fruitful for feminist actors under different circumstances? How can international norms be used and counter-movements effectively challenged? The significance of issue framing also needs to be incorporated. We have seen that the constitutional arena is not open in all contexts but needs to be exploited if the opportunity is there.

❖ CONCLUSIONS

The electoral arena is often a difficult one for women actors but again under certain circumstances it can yield dividends. If for example parties open to gender concerns are in powerful positions, key feminist actors within them can have some influence. And under the right conditions, SWMs can also contribute to the achievement of certain positive gender outcomes but our case studies confirm that it is unrealistic to expect too much from them as they often have fraught relationships with women's organizations outside the state, are under-resourced, face bureaucratic resistance and a lack of commitment from government.

The findings outlined in this book can also inform the development of future research agendas designed to further our understanding of transitions to democracy. The analysis has highlighted three other important areas that to date have not been given sufficient consideration and therefore warrant further research. First, what are the implications of the gender and transitions literature for the democratization literature? How far do the findings of this book challenge or reinforce some of the assumptions of parts of the democratization literature? What light do they shed on the debates about different modes of transition, of the somewhat unexpected relative ease of transitions from state socialism compared to authoritarianism, of the significance of greater equality and higher levels of education in facilitating consolidation? Do the qualitative gender differences in the Polish transition compared to our other state socialist case studies mirror the differences outlined by mainstream theorists like Linz and Stepan? Do the lower levels of women's mobilization and different framing of gender issues in Poland provide a marked contrast to the transitions from our authoritarian case studies? What are the implications of our gendered analysis of the comparator cases for the understanding of outcomes in the 'grey zone'.

Second, an examination of the socio-economic constraints needs to be integrated more comprehensively into gendered analyses of transitions. Socio-economic changes that might yield positive gender outcomes are hard to achieve as part of transitions to democracy and yet can make an important difference to increasing gender equality. The consequences of economic reform programmes have been negative for many, but not all, women. Some middle-class professional women have benefited from the enhanced opportunities that have resulted from social and economic restructuring. These consequences have also constrained the ability of governments to implement policies that could significantly reduce gender inequality and improve women's access to social and economic rights.

Finally, this book has also shown that a range of international factors is also significant. Women activists have gained much from external factors whether it is the experience of exile, the use of international norms that frame gender debates in domestic campaigns or external funding for women's NGOs. The external context can also have a direct impact on the institutional arena for example the adoption of the *acquis communautaire* has been one of the most significant constitutional/legal changes to occur in East Central Europe with big implications for gender rights. But external factors are not constant and the international climate changed during the period of the 'third wave' and after. It was perhaps most favourable in the early nineties in the lead up to the Beijing Women's conference. Since then we have witnessed a period of retrenchment as the power of religious fundamentalism (of all varieties) and an increasingly conservative American right-wing agenda has grown at the same time as the influence of UN organizations has declined. As a result it has become more difficult to achieve positive gender outcomes in areas such as reproductive rights. However, as quotas have been increasingly accepted as the norm internationally, the improvement of women's descriptive representation has continued. All these concerns also need to be integrated more fully into future analyses.

As an extension of this, we can also utilize the framework developed in this book to explore other types of transition. For example the contentious area of the imposition of democracy from outside, particularly as part of a post-conflict settlement, has become increasingly important over the last decade. More research is needed to assess the extent to which this route to electoral democracy can improve gender outcomes and on the significance of international factors more generally. But in the interim, if we operationalize the analysis put forward in this book to consider cases where democracy is being externally imposed, it would seem unlikely that, in the early stages of the post-conflict period at least, many gender outcomes will be overwhelmingly positive. In few of the post-conflict situations has significant women's organizing existed either prior to or during the period of conflict and transition. At the time of writing, conditions in Iraq and Afghanistan—for example in terms of the security situation—are also unlikely to facilitate an increase in women's organizing. In both Iraq and Afghanistan it seems that few influential politicians or political parties are open to a gender agenda that would enhance women's equality and there a few feminists in key positions in the electoral or bureaucratic arenas. The analysis in this book would also lead us to be sceptical of the significance of the electoral quotas that are often heralded as evidence of the meaningful participation of women in the new polities in Iraq, Afghanistan, and even Rwanda. More significant would be policy outcomes such as the implementation of effective laws against domestic violence and the embodiment of meaningful rights within the new constitutions. The constitutions could then provide an enabling framework and form the basis for future gains that would allow women greater access to civil, political, social, and economic rights. However these concerns do not seem to have been a priority in the final stages of constitutional design in Iraq or Afghanistan.

But we should not be too deterministic. The analysis in this book has shown that outcomes can be contingent and actors can shape events even in the most constraining of circumstances. Transitions to democracy have provided a number of opportunities for the achievement of positive gender outcomes as well as challenges.

❖ CONCLUSIONS

❖ Appendix

Countries	1980	1983	1985	1986	1990	1992	1994	1995	2000	2003
GDP (constant US$ 2,000) in billions										
Argentina	212	198	187	201	182	230	258	250	284	263
Brazil	396	368	418	451	461	465	517	538	602	620
Chile	28	25	29	31	40	49	55	61	76	82
Czech Republic	—	—	—	—	54	48	49	52	56	60
El Salvador	9	7	8	8	8	9	11	11	13	14
Hungary	39	41	42	43	43	37	38	38	47	52
Peru	39	37	40	44	36	37	43	47	53	58
Poland	—	—	—	—	116	111	121	130	167	177
Russian Federation	—	—	—	—	386	313	250	240	260	307
South Africa	95	96	98	99	108	104	109	112	128	139
Birth rate crude (per 1,000 people)										
Argentina	—	—	—	—	21	20	—	19	—	18
Brazil	—	—	—	—	24	22	—	—	—	19
Chile	23	22	22	22	24	22	21	20	17	17
Czech Republic	18	—	14	—	13	—	—	12	9	—
El Salvador	—	—	—	—	30	30	—	—	—	25
Hungary	14	12	12	12	12	12	11	11	10	10
Peru	—	—	—	—	29	28	—	—	—	22
Poland	20	20	18	17	14	14	13	11	10	9
Russian Federation	16	18	17	17	13	11	10	9	9	10
South Africa	—	—	—	—	32	31	—	—	—	25
Population in millions										
Argentina	28	29	30	31	32	33	34	34	36	37
Brazil	122	130	135	138	148	153	157	159	170	177
Czech Republic	10	10	10	10	10	10	10	10	10	10
Chile	11	12	12	12	13	14	14	14	15	16
El Salvador	5	5	5	5	5	5	6	6	6	7
Hungary	11	11	11	11	10	10	10	10	10	10
Peru	17	19	19	20	22	22	23	24	26	27
Poland	36	37	37	37	38	38	39	39	39	38
Russian Federation	139	142	144	145	148	149	148	148	146	143
South Africa	28	30	31	32	35	37	38	39	44	46

Countries	1980	1983	1985	1986	1990	1992	1994	1995	2000	2003
Unemployment as a % of total employment										
Argentina	2	4	5	4	7	7	12	19	15	—
Brazil	3	5	3	2	4	7	—	6	—	—
Chile	10	15	12	9	6	4	6	5	8	—
Czech Republic	—	—	—	—	0.7	3	3	3	10	10
El Salvador	13	—	17	8	10	8	8	8	7	—
Hungary	—	—	—	—	2	10	11	10	6	—
Peru	—	—	—	5	9	9	9	7	7	—
Poland	—	—	—	—	7	13	14	13	16	—
Russian Federation	—	—	—	—	—	5	8	10	10	—
South Africa	—	—	—	—	—	—	4	5	—	—
Male unemployment (% of male labour force)										
Argentina	—	—	—	—	7	6	11	17	14	—
Brazil	3	5	3	2	4	6	—	5	—	—
Chile	11	15	12	8	6	4	5	4	8	—
Czech Republic	—	—	—	—	—	—	—	3	7	—
El Salvador	—	—	12	8	10	8	8	9	9	—
Hungary	—	—	—	—	2	11	12	11	7	—
Peru	—	—	—	3	7	8	7	6	7	—
Poland	—	—	—	—	—	12	13	12	14	—
Russian Federation	—	—	—	—	—	5	8	10	10	—
South Africa	—	—	—	—	—	—	—	—	—	—
Female unemployment (% of female labour force)										
Argentina	—	—	—	—	7	7	14	22	16	—
Brazil	3	5	4	3	3	8	—	7	—	—
Chile	10	15	13	10	6	6	7	5	9	—
Czech Republic	—	—	—	—	0.8	—	5	5	11	—
El Salvador	—	—	24	9	10	7	6	6	4	—
Hungary	—	—	—	—	1	9	9	9	6	—
Peru	—	—	—	8	12	13	12	9	8	—
Poland	—	—	—	—	—	15	16	15	18	—
Russian Federation	—	—	—	—	—	5	8	9	9	—
South Africa	—	—	—	—	—	—	—	—	—	—

Source: World Development Indicators database.

❖ APPENDIX

❖ References

Acker, J. (1990). 'Hierarchies, Jobs, Bodies: A Theory of Gendered Organizations', *Gender and Society*, 4(2): 139–58.

Agosin, M. (1988). *Scraps of Life*. London: Zed Press.

Agüero, F. and Stark, J. (1997). *Faultlines of Democracy*, Miami, FL: North South Center Press.

Albertyn, C. (1992). 'Women and Politics: Choices in Structural Mechanisms to Empower Women in a Democratic Government', Paper at Workshop on Structural Mechanisms to Empower Women in a Democratic Government. University of Natal, South Africa.

——— (1994). 'Women and the Transition to Democracy in South Africa', in F. Kaganas and C. Murray (eds.), *Gender and the New South African Legal Order*. Cape Town: Juta, pp. 39–63.

——— (1995). 'Mainstreaming Gender' National Machinery for Women in South Africa: A Policy Outline', Occasional Paper No. 24, Johannesburg: Centre for Applied Legal Studies.

——— (2003). 'Towards Substantive Representation: Women and Politics in South Africa', in A. Dobrowolsky and V. Hart (eds.), *Women Making Constitutions: New Politics and Comparative Perspectives*. Basingstoke, UK: Palgrave, pp. 99–117.

——— Goldblatt, B., Hassim, S., Mbatha, L., and Meintjes, S. (eds.) (1999). *Engendering the Political Agenda: A South African Case Study*. Johannesburg: Centre for Applied Legal studies.

——— Hassim, S. and Meintjes, S. (2002). 'Making a Difference? Women's Struggle for Participation and Representation', in G. Flick, S. Meintjes, and M. Simons (eds.), *One Woman, One Vote*. Johannesburg: EISA, pp. 24–52.

Alvarez, S. (1990*a*). *Engendering Democracy in Brazil*. Princeton, NJ: Princeton University Press.

——— (1990*b*). 'Women's Participation in the Brazilian People's Church: A Critical Appraisal', *Feminist Studies*, 16(2): 381–408.

——— (1994). 'The (Trans)formation of the Feminism(s) and Gender Politics in Democratising Brazil', in J. Jaquette (ed.), *The Women's Movements in Latin America: Participation and Democracy*, 2nd edn. Boulder, CO: Westview.

——— (1998). 'Latin American Feminisms Go 'Global', in S. Alvarez, E. Dagnino, and A. Escobar, (eds.), *Politics of Culture/Cultures of Politics*, Boulder, CO: Westview, pp. 293–324.

——— (1999). 'Advocating Feminism: The Latin American Feminist NGO "Boom"', *International Feminist Journal of Politics*, 1(2): 181–209.

Alvarez, S. (2000). 'Translating the Global Effects of Transnational Organizing on Local Feminist Discourses and Practices in Latin America', *Meridians*, 1(1): 29–67.

—— Friedman, E., Beckman, E., Blackwell, M., Chinchilla, N. S., Lebon, N., Navarro, M. and Ríos, M. (2002). 'Encountering Latin American and Caribbean Feminisms', *Signs*, 28(2): 537–80.

Angelo, G. (1990). Nuevos Espacios y nuevas practices de mujeres en una situación de crisis: Hacia le surgiemiento y consolidación de una movimiento de mujeres. El caso de Chile, *Cuadernos de la Morada*, Santiago, La Morada.

Arenas de Mesa, A. and Bertranou, F. (1997). 'Learning from Social Security Reforms: Two Different Cases, Chile and Argentina', *World Development*, 25(3): 329–48.

—— and Montecinos, V. (1999). 'The Privatization of Social Security and Women's Welfare: Gender Effects of the Chilean Reform', *Latin American Research Review*, 34(3): 7–38.

Baban, A. (2000). 'Women's Sexuality and Reproductive Behaviour in Post-Ceausescu Romania', in S. Gal and G. Kligman (eds.), *Reproducing Gender: Politics, Publics and Everyday Life after Socialism*, Princeton, NJ: Princeton University Press. pp. 225–56.

Bacchi, C. (1999). *Women, Policy and Politics: The Construction of Policy Problems*. London: Sage.

Bakker, I. (1994). 'Introduction: Engendering Macro-Economic Policy Reform in the Era of Global Restructuring and Adjustment', in I. Baker (ed.), *The Strategic Silence: Gender and Economic Policy*. London: Zed Press, 10–13.

Baldez, L. (2001). 'Coalition Politics and the Limits of State Feminism in Chile', *Women and Politics*, 22(4): 1–28.

—— (2002). *Why Women Protest: Women's Movements in Chile*. Cambridge: Cambridge University Press.

—— (2003). 'Women's Movements and Democratic Transition in Chile, Brazil, East Germany and Poland', *Comparative Politics*. 35(3): 252–72.

—— (2004). 'Elected Bodies: The Adoption of Gender Quota Laws for Legislative Candidates in Mexico', *Legislative Studies Quarterly*, 29(2): 231–58.

—— (2006). 'The Pros and Cons of Gender Quotas Laws: What Happens When You Kick Men Out and Let Women in?', *Politics and Gender*, 2(1): 102–9.

Ballington, J. (1998). 'Women's Parliamentary Representation: The Effects of List PR', *Politikon*, 25(2). 77–93.

—— (2002). 'Political Parties, Gender Equality and Elections in South Africa', in G. Flick, S. Meintjes, and M. Simon, (eds.), *One Woman, One Vote: The Gender Politics of South African Elections*, Johannesburg: Electoral Institute of Southern Africa (EISA), pp. 75–101.

Banaszak, L. A., Beckwith, K., and Rucht, D. (eds.) (2003). *Women's Movements Face the Reconfigured State*. Cambridge: Cambridge University Press.

Barahona De Brito, A. (1997). *Human Rights and Democratization in Latin America: Uruguay and Chile*. Oxford: Oxford University Press.

Barrientos, A. (1996). 'Pension Reform and Pension Coverage in Chile: Lessons for other Countries', *Bulletin of Latin American Research*, 15(3): 309–22.

Barrig, M. (1996). 'Women, Collective Kitchens and the Crisis of the State in Peru', in J. Friedmann et al. (eds.), *Emergences: Women's Struggles for Livelihood in Latin America*, Los Angeles: UCLA Latin America Center.

❖ REFERENCES

Barring, M. (1998). 'Female Leadership, Violence and Citizenship in Peru', in J. Jaquette and S. Wolchik (eds.), *Women and Democracy: Latin America and Central and Eastern Europe*. Baltimore, MD: John Hopkins University Press. pp. 104–24.

Beall, J., Freidman, M., Hassim S., Posel, R., Stiebel, L., and Todes, A. (1987). 'African Women in the Durban Struggle, 1985–1986', *South African Review*, 4: 93–103.

Beckwith, K. (2000). 'Beyond Compare? Women's Movements in Comparative Perspective', *European Journal of Political Research*, 37(4), 431–68.

—— (2004). 'Autonomy and Involvement: Mapping Strategic Engagements of Women's Movements', Paper presented at the Annual Meeting of the International Studies Association, Montreal Canada.

—— and Cowell-Meyers, K. (2003). 'Sheer Numbers', Paper presented to Annual Meeting APSA, Philadelphia.

Blofield, M. (2006). *The Politics of Moral Sin: Abortion and Divorce in Spain, Chile and Argentina*, London: Routledge.

—— and Haas, L. (2005). 'Defining a Democracy: Reforming the Laws on Women's Rights in Chile', *Latin American Politics and Society*, 47(3): 33–66.

Blondet, C. (1995). 'Out of the Kitchen and on to the Streets: Women's Activism in Peru', in Basu, A. (ed.), *The Challenges of Local Feminisms: Women's Movements in Global Perspective*, Boulder, CO: Westview, pp. 251–75.

—— (2002). 'The Devil's Deal': Women's Political Participation and Authoritarianism', in M. Molyneux and S. Razavi (eds.), *Gender Justice, Development and Rights*. Oxford: Oxford University Press, pp. 277–305.

—— and Montero, C. (1995). *Hoy: Menu Popular Comedores En Lima*. Lima: Instituto de Estudios Peruanos/UNICEF.

Blum, V. (1997). 'Social Funds and Gender Social Policy', Working Paper No. 20. Deutsche Gessellschaft fur Technische Zusammenarbeit (GTZ).

Bonder, G. and Nari, M. (1995). 'The 30% Quota Law: A Turning Point for Women's Political Participation in Argentina', in A. Brill (ed.), *A Rising Voice: Women and Politics Worldwide*. New York: The Feminist Press at the City University of New York, pp. 183–93.

Bourque, S. and Grossholtz, J. (1974). 'Politics as an Unnatural Practice: Political Science Looks at Female Participation', *Politics and Society*, 4: 225–66.

Bouvard, M. (1994). *Revolutionalizing Motherhood*. Wilmington, DE: Scholarly Resources.

Bretherton, C. (2001). 'Gender mainstreaming and EU enlargement: Swimming Against the Tide?', *Journal of European Public Policy*, 8(1): 60–81.

Britton, H. (2002). 'The Incomplete Revolution: South Africa's Women's Struggle for Parliamentary Transformation', *International Feminist Journal of Politics*, 4(1): 43–71.

—— (2006). *Women in the South African Parliament: From Resistance to Governance*. Urbana, IL: University of Illinois Press.

Brysk, A. (1994). *The Politics of Human Rights in Argentina: Protest, Change and Democratization*. Stanford, CA: Stanford University Press.

Buckley, M. (1997). 'Adaption of the Soviet Women's Committee: Deputies' Voices From "Women of Russia"', in M Buckley (ed.), *Post Soviet Women: From the Baltic to Central Asia*. Cambridge: Cambridge University Press, pp. 157–85.

Bunce, V. (1994). 'Should Transitologists Be Grounded?', *Slavic Review*, 54(1): 111–27.

—— (1999). *Subversive Institutions*. Cambridge: Cambridge University Press.

Bunce, V. (2000). 'Comparative Democratization: Big and Bounded Generalizations', *Comparative Political Studies*, 33(6/7).

—— (2003). 'Rethinking Recent Democratization: Lessons from the Postcommunist Experience', *World Politics*, 22(1): 167–92.

Bunster-Burotto, X. (1985). 'Surviving Beyond Fear: Women and Torture in Latin America', in J. Nash and H. Safa (eds.), *Women and Change in Latin America*. South Hadley, MA: Bergin and Garvey.

Bunster, X. (1988). 'Watch Out for the Little Naziman That All of Us Have Inside: The Mobilization and Demobilization of Women in Militarized Chile', *Women's Studies International Forum*, 11(5): 485–91.

Bystydzienski, J. (2001). 'The Feminist Movement in Poland: Why so Slow?', *Women's Studies International Forum*, 24(5): 501–11.

Caldeira, T. (1986). 'Electoral Struggles in a Neighbourhood in the Periphery of Sao Paulo', *Politics and Society*, 15(1): 43–66.

Clark, A., Friedman, E., and Hochstetler, K. (1998). 'The Sovereign Limits of Global Civil Society: A Comparison of NGO Participation in UN World Conferences on the Environment, Human Rights and Women', *World Politics*, 51(1): 1–35.

Carothers, T. (2002). 'The End of the Transition Paradigm', *Journal of Democracy*, 13(1): 5–21.

Carroll, S. and Zerilli, L. (1993). 'Feminist Challenges to Political Science', in A. Finifter (ed.), *Political Science: The State of the Discipline II*, Washington: APSA, pp. 55–76.

Caul, M. (1999). 'Women's Representation in Parliament: The Role of Political Parties', *Party Politics*, 5(1): 79–98.

—— (2001). 'Political Parties and Candidate Gender Policies: A Cross National Study', *Journal of Politics*, 64(3): 1214–49.

Kittilson, C. M. (2006). *Challenging Parties, Changing Parliaments: Women and Elected Office in Contemporary Western Europe*. Columbus OH: Ohio State University Press.

Chandler, A. (2005). 'Gender, Political Discourse and Social Welfare in Russia: Three Case Studies', Paper presented at Canadian Political Science Association, June.

Chappell, L. (2002). *Gendering Government: Feminist Engagement with the State in Australia and Canada*. Vancouver: University of British Columbia Press.

Charlton, S., Everett, J., and Staudt, K. (eds.) (1989). *Women, State and Development*. Albany, NY: SUNY Press.

Chimiak, G. (2003). 'Bulgarian and Polish Women in the Public Sphere: A Comparative Analysis,' *International Feminist Journal of Politics*, 5(1): 3–27.

Chirwa, D. M. and Khoza, K., (2005). 'Towards Enhanced Citizenship and Poverty Eradication', in A. Gouws (ed.), *(Un)thinking Citizenship: Feminist Debates in Contemporary South Africa*, Ashgate, Aldershot, Hants.

Chuckryk, P. (1984). 'Protest Politics and Personal Life: The Emergence of Feminism in a Military Dictatorship', Unpublished PhD thesis, University of York, Canada.

—— (1989a). 'Subversive Mothers: Women's Opposition to the Military Regime in Chile', in S. Charlton, J. Everett, and K. Staudt (eds.), *Women, State and Development*. Albany NY: SUNY Press.

—— (1989b). 'Feminist Anti-Authoritarian Politics: The Role of Women's Organizations in the Chilean Transition to Democracy', in J. Jaquette (ed.), *The Women's Movement in Latin America*. Boulder, CO: Westview, pp. 52–78.

❖ REFERENCES

—— (1997). 'Women in South Africa's Transition to Democracy', in J. Scott, C. Kaplan, and D. Keates (eds.), *Transitions, Environments, Translation*. New York: Routledge.

Collier, D. and Levitsky, S. (1997). 'Democracy with Adjectives: Conceptual Innovation in Comparative Research', *World Politics*, 49(4): 403–51.

Collier, P. (1994). 'Gender Aspects of Labor Allocation During Structural Adjustment', in S. Horton, R. Kanbur, and D. Mazumdar (eds.), *Labor Markets in an Era of Adjustment*. Washington, DC.: The World Bank.

Collier, R. and Mahoney, J. (1997). 'Adding Collective Actors to Collective Outcomes: Labor and Recent Democratization in South America and South Europe', *Comparative Politics*, 29(3).

Corcoran-Nantes, Y. (1990). 'Women and Popular Urban Social Movements in Sao Paulo', *Bulletin of Latin American Research*, 9(2): 249–64.

—— (1993). 'Female consciousness or feminist consciousness?: women's consciousness raising in community-based struggles in Brazil', in S. Radcliffe and S. Westwood (eds.), *Viva: Women and Popular Protest in Latin America*. London: Routledge.

Cox-Edwards, A. (2000). 'Pensions Projections for Chilean Men and Women: Estimates from Social Security Contributions', Background Paper for Policy Research Report on Gender and Development, The World Bank.

Craske, N. (1999). *Women and Politics in Latin America*. Cambridge Polity Press.

—— (2000). 'Continuing the Challenge: The Contemporary Latin American Women's Movement(s)', ILAS Working Paper, Liverpool.

Dahlerup, D. (2006). 'Introduction', in D. Dahlerup (ed.), *Women, Quotas and Politics*. New York: Routledge, pp. 3–31.

Diamond, L. (1999). *Developing Democracy: Toward Consolidation*. Baltimore, MD: Johns Hopkins University Press.

—— (2002). 'Thinking About Hybrid Regimes', *Journal of Democracy*, 13(2): 21–35.

—— and Morlino, L. (2004). 'The Quality of Democracy: An Overview', *Journal of Democracy*, 15(4): 20–31.

Dobrowolsky, A. and Hart. V. (eds) (2003). *Women Making Constitutions: New Politics and Comparative Perspectives*. Basingstoke, UK: Palgrave.

Dolling, I. (1991). 'Between Hope and Helplessness: Women in the GDR After the 'Turning Point', *Feminist Review*, 39, Winter.

Drogus, C. (1999). 'No Land of Milk and Honey: Women CEB Activists in Post Transition Brazil', *Journal of Inter-American Studies and World Affairs*, 41(4): 35–51.

—— and Stewart-Gambino, H. (2005). *Activist Faith: Grassroots Women in Democratic Brazil and Chile*. Penn State University Press.

Eberhardt, E. (2005a). Gender Evaluation: Report on the Situation of women in the Czech Republic, Hungary, Poland, Slovakia and Slovenia, Enlargement, Gender and Goverance project, Queens University Belfast.

—— (2005b). 'Equal Opportunities, Mainstreaming and the Reconstruction of Gender in Hungary', Paper presented at the ECPR General Conference, Budapest, Sept.

ECLAC (2000). *Equity, Citizenship and Development*, LC/G.2071(SES.28.3). Santiago, Chile.

Einhorn, B. (1991). 'Where Have All the Women Gone? Women and the Women's Movement in East Central Europe', *Feminist Review*, 39, Winter.

Einhorn, B. (1992). 'Emancipated Women or Hardworking Mums? Women in the Former German Democratic Republic', in C. Corrin (ed.), *Superwoman and the Double Burden*. London: Scarlet Press.

—— (1993). *Cinderella Goes to Market: Gender, Citizenship and the Women's Movement in Eastern Europe*. London: Verso Press.

—— (2006). *Citizenship in an Enlarging Europe: From Dream to Awakening*, Basingstoke, UK: Palgrave.

—— and Sever, C. (2003). 'Gender and Civil Society in Central and Eastern Europe', *International Feminist Journal of Politics*, 7(2): 163–90.

Eisenstein, Z. (1993). 'Eastern European Male Democracies: A Problem of Unequal Equality', in N. Funk and M. Mueller (eds.), *Gender Politics and Post Communism: Reflections from Eastern Europe and the Former Soviet Union*. New York: Routledge, pp. 303–17.

Elshtain, J. (1981). *Public Man, Private Woman: Women in Social and Political Thought*, Princeton, NJ: Princeton University Press.

Elson, D. (1995). 'Male Bias in Macro Economics: The Case of Structural Adjustment', in D. Elson (ed.), *Male Bias in the Development Process*, 2nd edn. Manchester, UK: Manchester University Press.

—— and Cagatay, N. (2000). 'The Social Content of Macro-Economic Policies', *World Development*, 28(7): 1347–64.

Elster, J., Offe, C., and Preuss, U. (1998). *Institutional Design in Post-Communist Societies: Rebuilding the Ship at Sea*. Cambridge: Cambridge University Press.

Feijoó, M. (1998). 'Democratic Participation and Women in Argentina', in J. Jaquette and S. Wolchik (eds.), *Women and Democracy: Latin America and Central and Eastern Europe*, Baltimore, MD: Johns Hopkins University Press, pp. 29–46.

—— and Gogna, M. (1990). 'Women and the Transition to Democracy', in E. Jelin (ed.), *Women and Social Change in Latin America*. London: Zed Press.

—— and Nari, M. (1994). 'Women and Democracy in Argentina', in J. Jaquette (ed.), *The Women's Movement in Latin America: Participation and Democracy*, 2nd edn., Boulder, CO: Westview.

Fine, R. and Rai, S. (1997). *Civil Society: Democratic Perspectives*. London: Frank Cass.

Fisher, J. (1989). *Mothers of the Disappeared*. London: Zed Press.

—— (1993). *Out of the Shadows: Women, Resistance and Politics in South America*. London: Latin American Bureau.

Fodor, E. (1994). 'Political Women?: Women in Politics in Hungary', in M. Rueschemeyer (ed.), *Women in the Politics of Post Communist Eastern Europe*. New York: M. E. Sharpe.

—— (2004*a*). 'Women and Political Engagement in East-Central Europe', Paper prepared for UNRISD.

—— (2004*b*). 'Women at Work: The Status of Women in the Labor Markets of the Czech Republic, Hungary, and Poland', Paper prepared for UNRISD.

—— Glass, C., Kawachi, J., and Popescu, L. (2002). 'Family Policies and Gender in Hungary, Poland and Romania', *Communist and Post Communist Studies*, 35(4): 475–90.

Foley, M. and Edwards, B. (1996). 'The Paradox of Civil Society', *Journal of Democracy*, 7(3): 38–52.

Foweraker, J. (1995). *Theorizing Social Movements*. London: Pluto Press.

❖ REFERENCES

Franceschet, S. (2001). 'Women and Politics in Post-Transitional Democracies: The Chilean Case', *International Feminist Journal of Politics*, 3(2): 207–36.

—— (2003). 'State Feminism and Women's Movements: The Impact of Chile's SERNAM on Women's Activism', *Latin American Research Review*, 38(1): 9–32.

—— (2004). Explaining Social Movement Outcomes: Collective Action Frames and Strategic Choices in First- and Second-Wave Feminism in Chile, *Comparative Political Studies*, 37(June): 499–530.

—— (2005). *Women and Politics in Chile*. Boulder, CO: Lynne Rienner.

—— (2006). 'Continuity or Change? The Significance of Chile's First Female President', Paper presented at the Latin American Studies Association meeting, San Juan Puerto Rico.

Friedman, E. (1998). 'Paradoxes of Gendered Political Opportunity in the Venezuelan Transition to Democracy', *Latin American Research Review*, 33(3): 87–136.

—— (2000a). *Unfinished Transitions: Women and the Gendered Development of Democracy in Venezuela*. University: Penn State University Press.

—— (2000b). 'State-Based Advocacy for Gender Equality in the Developing World: Assessing the Venezuelan National Women's Agency', *Women and Politics*, 21(2): 47–80.

—— (2003). 'Gendering the Agenda: The Impact of the Transnational Women's Rights Movement at the UN Conferences of the 1990s', *Women's Studies International Forum*, 26(4): 313–31.

—— (2006). 'Making Gender Rights Reality: National and Regional Mediation of International Human Rights Norms in Latin America', Paper prepared for Latin American Studies Meeting, San Juan, Puerto Rico.

Friedman, S. (1993a). *The Long Journey: South Africa's Quest for a Negotiated Settlement*. Johannesburg: Ravan Press.

—— (1993b). The Missing 53% in Stephen Friedman. *The Long Journey: South Africa's Quest for a Negotiated Settlement*. Johannesburg: Ravan Press, pp. 129–35.

—— (2003). Paper delivered at Plenary Session, 'What we have learnt from 30 years of transitions from Authoritarian Rule', International Political Science Association Congress, Durban, July.

Frohmann, A. and Valdes, T. (1993). 'Democracy in the Country and in The Home: The Women's Movement in Chile', *Documento de Trabajo*, vol. 55, FLACSO, Santiago.

Funk, N. and Mueller, M. (eds.) (1993). *Gender Politics and Post Communism*. New York: Routledge.

Fuszara, M. (1991). 'Legal Regulation of Abortion in Poland', *Signs*, 17: 117–28.

—— (1993). 'Abortion and the Formation of the Public Sphere in Poland', in N. Funk and M. Mueller, (eds.), *Gender Politics and Post Communism*. New York: Routledge.

—— (2000). 'New Gender Relations in Poland in the 1990s', in S. Gal and G. Kligman (eds.), *Reproducing Gender: Politics, Publics and Everyday Life After Socialism*. Princeton, NJ: Princeton University Press, pp. 259–85.

Gaitskell, D. and Unterhalter, E. (1989). 'Mothers of the Nation: A Comparative Analysis of Nation, Race and Motherhood in Afrikaner Nationalism and the ANC', in F. Anthias and N. Yuval-Davis (eds.), *Women-Nation-State*. Basingstoke, UK: Macmillan.

Gal, S. (1994). 'Gender in the Post Socialist Transition: The Abortion Debate in Hungary', *East European Politics and Societies*, 8(2): 256–87.

Gal, S. (1997). 'Feminism and Civil Society', in J. Scott, C. Kaplan, and D. Keates (eds.), *Transitions, Environments, Translations: Feminisms in International Politics.* New York: Routledge, 30–45.

_____ and Kligman, G. (eds.) (2000). *Reproducing Gender: Politics, Publics, and Everyday Life after Socialism.* Princeton, NJ: Princeton University Press.

Galligan, Y. and Sloat A. (2003). 'Understanding Women's Political Engagement in the New Democracies of Central and Eastern Europe, European Consortium of Political Research Workshops, Edinburgh.

Geddes, B. (1999). 'What Do We Know About Democratisation After Twenty Years?', *Annual Review of Political Science*, 2: 115–44.

Geisler, G. (2000). ' "Parliament is another terrain of struggle": Women, Men and Politics in South Africa', *The Journal of Modern African Studies*, 38(4): 616–19.

_____ (2004). *Women and the Remaking of Politics in Southern Africa: Negotiating Autonomy, Incorporation and Representation.* Uppsala, Sweden: Nordiska Afrikainistutet.

Geldstein, R. (1997). 'Gender Bias and Family Distress: The Privatization Experience in Argentina', *Journal of International Affairs*, 50(2): 545–71.

Githens, M. (1996). 'Reproductive Rights and the Struggle with Change in Eastern Europe', in M. Githens and D. M. Stetson (eds.), *Abortion Politics: Public Policy in Cross Cultural Perspective*, London: Routledge, pp. 55–70.

Gideon, J. (2005). 'Accessing Social and Economic Rights Under NeoLiberalism', Paper given at Conference on Rights Based Development: Feminist Perspectives. IDS, Sussex, September.

Gladwin, C. (ed.) (1999). *Structural Adjustment and African Women Farmers.* Gainesville, FL: University of Florida Press.

Goetz, A. M. (1997). 'Fiddling with Democracy: Translating Women's Participation in Uganda and South Africa into Gender Equity in Development Practice', Paper presented to PERC Workshop on Towards a Gendered Political Economy, University of Sheffield, September.

_____ and Hassim, S. (2002). 'In and Against the Party: Women's Representation and Constituency Building in Uganda and South Africa', in M. Molyneux and S. Razavi (eds.), *Gender, Justice, Development and Rights.* Oxford: Oxford University Press, 306–43.

Goven, J. (2000). 'New Parliament, Old Discourse? The Parental Leave Debate in Hungary', in S. Gal and G. Kligman (eds.), *Reproducing Gender: Politics, Publics and Everyday Life After Socialism.* Princeton, NJ: Princeton University Press, 286–306.

Graham, C. (1994). *Safety Nets, Politics and the Poor: Transitions to Market Economies.* Washington, DC.: The Brookings Institution.

_____ (1995). 'The Politics of Safety Nets', *Journal of Democracy*, 6(2): 142–56.

_____ (1996). 'Gender Issues in Poverty Alleviation: Recent Experience with Demand Based Programs in Latin America, Africa and Eastern Europe', Issues in Development Discussion Paper 11, Geneva: ILO.

Grugel, J. (2002). *Democratization: A Critical Introduction.* Basingstoke, UK: Palgrave.

_____ (2003). 'Democratization Studies, Globalization, Governance and Citizenship', *Government and Opposition*, 38(2): 238–64.

Guzman, V. (2004). Democratic Governance and Gender: Possible Linkages, Serie Mujer y Desarrollo, 48, Santiago: ECLAC.

❖ REFERENCES

Haas, L. (2004). 'Intergovernmental Relations and Feminist Policy Making: A Case Study of Domestic Violence in Chile', Paper presented at APSA, Philadelphia.

Haggard, S. and Webb, S. (eds.), (1994). *Voting For Reform, Democracy, Political Liberalization and Economic Adjustment*. Oxford: Oxford University Press/World Bank.

_____ and Kaufman, R. (1995). *The Political Economy of Democratic Transitions*, Princeton, NJ: Princeton University Press.

_____ _____ (1997). 'The Political Economy of Democratic Transitions', *Comparative Politics*, 29(3): 290–311.

Hardy, C. (1985). Estrategias Organizadas de Subsistencia: Los sectores frente a sus necessidades en Chile, *Documento de Trabajo*, Santiago: PET.

Haskova, H. and Krizkova, A. (eds.) (2003). Women's Civic and Political Participation in the Czech Republic and the Role of European Union Gender Equality and Accession Policies, Sociological Papers no 3, Institute of Sociology, Academy of Sciences of the Czech Republic, Prague.

Hassim, S. (1999). 'Institutionalizing Gender: An examination of State-Led Strategies for Gender Equality', Paper prepared for DAWN.

_____ (2002*a*). Identities, Interests and Constituencies: The Politics of the Women's Movement in South Africa, 1980–1999. Unpublished doctoral dissertation, Toronto.

_____ (2002*b*). ' "A Conspiracy of Women": The Women's Movement in South Africa's Transition to Democracy', *Social Research*, 69: 693–732, Fall.

_____ (2003*a*). 'Representation, participation and democratic effectiveness: Feminist Challenges to Representative Democracy in South Africa', in S. Hassim and Goetz, A. M. (eds.), *No Short Cuts to Power: African Women in Politics and Policy Making*. London: Zed Press.

_____ (2003*b*). 'The Gender Pact and Democratic Consolidation: Institutionalising Gender Equality in the South African State', *Feminist Studies*, 29(3): 505–28.

_____ (2005). *Women's Organizations and Democracy in South Africa: Contesting Authority*. Madison: University of Wisconsin Press.

Hauser, E., Heyns, B., and Mansbridge, J. (1993). 'Feminism in the Interstices of Politics and Culture: Poland in Transition', in N. Funk and M. Mueller (eds.), *Gender Politics and Post Communism*. New York: Routledge, pp. 257–73.

Heinen, J. and Portet, S. (2002). 'Political and Social Citizenship in Eastern Europe: An Examination of the case of Poland', in M. Molyneux and S. Razavi (eds.), *Gender Justice, Development and Rights*. Oxford: Oxford University Press, pp. 140–69.

Heller L. and Cortes, R. (2000). 'El empleo femenino in los 90: nuevos escenarios— "nuevas" ocupaciones?', paper presented at LASA, Miami.

Hipsher, P. (2001). 'Right and Left-Wing Women in Post Revolutionary El Salvador: Feminist Autonomy and Cross Political Alliance Building for Gender Equality', in V. Gonzalez and K. Kampwirth (eds.), *Radical Women of Latin America: Left and Right*. University Park: Pennsylvania State University Press, pp. 133–64.

Howell, J. and Mulligan, D. (2003), 'Editorial to Special Issue on Gender and Civil Society', *International Feminist Journal of Politics*, 7(2): 163–69.

Htun, M. (2000). 'Democratic Transitions and Women's Family Rights in Argentina, Brazil and Chile, Paper presented at Latin American Studies Annual Meeting, Miami, March.

Htun, M. (2001). 'Electoral Rules, Parties and Election of Women in Latin America', Paper presented at 97th APSA, San Francisco.

_____ (2002). 'Puzzle of Women's Rights in Brazil', *Social Research*, 69(3): 733–51.

_____ (2003). *Sex and the State.* Cambridge: Cambridge University Press.

_____ (2005). 'Women, Political Parties and Electoral Systems in Latin America', in *Women in Parliament: Beyond Numbers*, 2nd edn., Stockholm IDEA, pp. 112–21.

_____ and Jones, M. (2002). 'Engendering the Right to Participate in Decision-making: Electoral Quotas and Women's Leadership in Latin America', in N. Craske and M. Molyneux (eds.), *Gender and the Politics of Rights and Democracy in Latin America*, New York: Palgrave, pp. 32–56.

Huber, E. (2003). 'The Role of Cross-Regional Comparison', Comparative Politics Section of the APSA Newsletter, 14(2): 1–6.

Huntington, S. (1991). *The Third Wave: Democratization in the Late Twentieth Century.* Norman: University of Oklahoma Press.

Informe Nacional: Situación de la Mujer en la última década en la República Argentina (1995). Buenos Aires.

Inter-American Development Bank (1995). *Women in the Americas: Bridging the Gender Gap.* Washington, DC.: IDB.

Inter-American Dialogue (2001). *Women's Leadership in Latin America: Trends and Challenges.* Washington, DC.

Jancar, B. (1985). 'Women in the Opposition in Poland and Czechoslovakia', in S. Wolchik and A. Meyer (eds.), *Women, State and Party in Eastern Europe.* Durham, NC: Duke University Press.

Jaquette, J. (1974). 'Introduction', in J. Jaquette (ed.), *Women in Politics.* New York: Wiley.

_____ (ed.) (1989). *The Women's Movement in Latin America: Feminism and the Transition to Democracy.* London: Unwin Hyman.

_____ (ed.) (1994). *The Women's Movement in Latin America: Participation and Democracy*, 2nd edn. Boulder, CO: Westview Press.

_____ (2001). 'Women and Democracy: Regional Differences and Contrasting Views', *Journal of Democracy*, 12(3): 111–23.

_____ and Wolchik, S. (eds.) (1998a). 'Introduction', *Women and Democracy: Latin America and Central and Eastern Europe.* Baltimore, MD: Johns Hopkins University, pp. 1–17.

_____ _____ (eds.) (1998b). *Women and Democracy: Latin America and Central and Eastern Europe*, Baltimore, MD: Johns Hopkins University Press.

_____ and Staudt, K. (2006). 'Women, Gender and Development', in J. Jaquette and G. Summerfield (eds.), *Women and Gender Equity in Development Theory and Practice: Institutions, Resources and Mobilization.* Durham: Duke University Press, pp. 17–52.

Jelin, E. (1996). 'Women, Gender and Human Rights', in E. Jelin and E. Herschberg, (1996). *Constructing Democracy: Human Rights, Citizenship, Democracy and Society in Latin America*, Boulder, CO: Westview Press, pp. 177–96.

_____ and Herschberg, E. (1996). *Constructing Democracy: Human Rights, Citizenship, Democracy and Society in Latin America*, Boulder, CO: Westview Press.

Jezerska, Z. (2002). 'Gender Awareness and National Machineries in the Countries of Central and Eastern Europe', in S. Rai (ed.), *Mainstreaming Gender, Democratizing the State?* Manchester, UK: Manchester University Press, pp. 167–83.

❖ REFERENCES

Jones, M. (1996). 'Increasing Women's Representation via Gender Quotas: The Argentine Ley de Cupos', *Women and Politics* 16(4): 75–98.

_____ (1998). 'Gender Quotas, Electoral Laws and the Election of Women: Lessons from the Argentine Provinces', *Comparative Political Studies*, 31(1): 3–21.

_____ (2005). 'The Desirability of Gender Quotas: Considering Context and Design', *Politics and Gender*, 1(4): 645–52.

Kampwirth, K. (1998). 'Feminism, Antifeminism, and Electoral Politics in Postwar Nicaragua and El Salvador', *Political Studies Quarterly*, 113(2): 259–79).

Karl, T. (2003). Paper delivered at Plenary Session, 'What we have learnt from 30 years of transitions from Authoritarian Rule', International Political Science Association Congress, Durban, July.

_____ (2005). From Democracy to Democratization and Back: Before *Transitions to Authoritarian Rule*, CDDRL Working Paper no 45, Stanford Institute on International Studies.

_____ and Schmitter, P. (1994). 'The Conceptual Travels of Transitologists and Consolidologists: How far to the East should they Attempt to go?', *Slavic Review*, 53(1): 173–85.

Keck, M. (1992). *The Workers Party and Democratization in Brazil*. Yale University Press.

_____ and Sikkink, K. (1998). *Activists Beyond Borders*. Ithaca, NY: Cornell University Press.

Kehler, J. (2001). 'Women and Poverty: The South African Experience', *Journal of International Women's Studies*, 3(1).

Kemp, A., Madlala, N., Moodley, A., and Salo, E. (1995). 'The Dawn of A New Day: Redefining South African Feminism', in A. Basu (ed.), *The Challenge of Local Feminisms*. Boulder, CO: Westview Press, pp. 131–62.

Kimble, J. and Unterhalter, E. (1982). 'We Opened the Road for You, You Must Go Forward', ANC Women's Struggles 1912–1982. *Feminist Review*, 12: 11–35.

Landman, T. (2003). *Issues and Methods in Comparative Politics: An Introduction*. London: Routledge.

Laurie, N. (1997). 'From Work to Welfare: The Response of the Peruvian State to the Feminization of Emergency Work', *Political Geography*, 16(8): 691–714.

Lazreg, M. (ed.) (1999). Making the Transition Work for Women in Europe and Central Asia, World Bank discussion paper no. 411. Washington, DC.: World Bank.

Levitsky, S. and Way, L. (2002). 'The Rise of Competitive Authoritarianism, *Journal of Democracy*, 13(2): 51–65.

_____ and Way, L. (2003). 'International Linkage and Competitive Authoritarian Regime Change in Africa, Latin America and Post Communist Eurasia, Paper delivered at APSA Annual Meeting Philadelphia.

Lewis, P. (2000). *Parties in Post Communist Eastern Europe*. London: Routledge.

_____ (2001). 'The Third Wave of Democratization in Eastern Europe: Comparative Perspectives on Party Roles and Political Development', *Party Politics*, 7(5): 543–65.

Lewis J. T. (1999). Social Funds: Examining Women's Reproductive Health and Women's Empowerment', Poverty Reduction and Economic Management Network, Gender Division, World Bank.

Linz, J. (1975). 'Totalitarian and Authoritarian Regimes', in F. Greenstein and N. Polsby (eds.), *Handbook of Political Science*. 3, Reading, MA: Addison Wesley.

_____ (1990). 'The Perils of Presidentialism', *Journal of Democracy*, 1(4).

Linz, J. and Stepan, A. (1996). *Problems of Democratic Transition and Consolidation: South Europe, South America and Post Communist Europe*, Baltimore, MD: Johns Hopkins University Press.

Lipset, S. (2000). 'The Indispensibility of Political Parties', *Journal of Democracy*, 11(1): 48–63.

Lister, R. (2003). *Citizenship: Feminist Perspectives*, 2nd edn. Basingstoke, UK: Palgrave.

Loveman, B. (1991). 'Mision Cumplida? Civil Military Relations and the Chilean Political Transition', *Journal of Inter-American Studies and World Affairs*, 33(3): 35–74.

Lovenduski, J. (1998). 'Gendering Research in Political Science', *Annual Review of Political Science*, 1: 333–56.

—— (2005). *Feminizing Politics*. Cambridge: Polity Press.

—— (ed.) (2005). *State Feminism and Political Representation*. Cambridge: Cambridge University Press.

—— and Norris, P. (eds.) (1993). *Gender and Party Politics*. London: Sage.

Luciak, I. (1998). 'Gender Equality and Electoral Politics on the Left: A Comparison of El Salvador and Nicaragua', *Journal of Inter-American Studies and World Affairs*, 40(1): 39–66.

—— (1999). 'Women and Electoral Politics on the Left: A Comparison of El Salvador and Nicaragua', *Latin American Perspectives*, 26(2): 43–61.

—— (2001). *After the Revolution: Gender and Democracy in El Salvador, Nicaragua and Guatemala*. Baltimore, MD: Johns Hopkins University Press.

—— (2001). 'Gender Equality, Democratization and the Revolutionary Left in Central America: Guatemala in Comparative Context', in V. Gonzalez and K. Kampwirth (eds.), *Radical Women of Latin America: Left and Right*. University Park: Pennsylvania State University Press, pp. 189–212.

—— (2004). 'Joining Forces for Democratic Governance: Women's Alliance-Building for Post-War Reconstruction in Central America', Paper prepared for UNRISD.

McAdam, D. McCarthy, J., and Zald, M. (eds.) (1996). *Comparative Perspectives on Social Movements*. Cambridge: Cambridge University Press.

Macaulay, F. (1996). Gender Politics in Brazil and Chile: The Role of Parties in National and Local Policymaking, PhD dissertation, University of Oxford.

—— (2000). 'Tackling Violence Against Women in Brazil: Converting International Principles into Effective Local Policy', in S. Jacobs, R. Jacobson, and J. Marchbank (eds.), *States of Conflict: Gender, Violence and Resistance*, London: Zed Press, pp. 144–62.

—— (2003). Sexual Politics, Party Politics: The PT Government's Policies on Gender Equity and Equality, Centre for Brazilian Studies Working Paper no. 46, Oxford: St Antony's College.

—— (2005). 'The Right to Personal Integrity in the Home: Judicialising and (de)criminalizing Domestic Violence in Latin America'. Paper delivered at the Feminist Perspectives on Rights Based Development Conference, IDS, Sussex.

—— (2006). *Gender Politics in Brazil and Chile: the Role of Parties in National and Local Policymaking*, Basingstoke, UK: St Antony's/Palgrave.

McCord, A. (2003). 'The Challenge of Gender and Poverty: The South African Economy Since Democratization', presented at BIG conference in Johannesburg, South Africa.

❖ References

MacDonald, M. (1998). 'Rethinking Labour Adjustment Policy', Paper Presented at IAFFE Conference, Amsterdam.

McFaul, M. (2002). 'The Fourth Wave of Democracy and Dictatorship: Noncooperative Transitions in the Postcommunist World', *World Politics*, 54(2): 212–44.

Mackay, F. (2004). 'Gender and Political Representation in the UK: The State of the Discipline', *British Journal of Politics and International Relations*, 6(1): 99–120.

—— Myers, F., and Brown, A. (2003). 'Towards a New Politics? Women and Constitutional Change in Scotland', in A. Dobrowolsky and V. Hart (eds.), *Women Making Constitutions: New Politics and Comparative Perspectives*. Basingstoke, UK: Palgrave, pp. 84–98.

Mahoney, J. (2000). 'Path Dependence in Historical Sociology', *Theory and Society*, 29(4): 507–48.

Mainwaring, S. (1998). 'Party Systems in the Third Wave', *Journal of Democracy*, 9(3): 67–81.

—— (1999). 'The Surprising Resilience of Elected Governments', *Journal of Democracy*, 10(3): 101–14.

—— and Scully, T. (1995). *Building Democratic Institutions: Party Systems in the Third Wave*. Stanford, CA: Stanford University Press.

—— and Shugart, M. (1997). 'Juan Linz, Presidentialism and Democracy: A Critical Appraisal', *Comparative Politics*, 29(4): 449–71.

Mansbridge, J. (2005). 'Quota Problems: Combating the Problem of Essentialism', *Politics and Gender*, 2(4): 622–37.

Marais, H. (2001). *South Africa, Limits to Change: The Political Economy of Transition*. 2nd edn. Cape Town: University of Cape Town Press.

Marsh, R. (1998). 'Women in Contemporary Russia and the Former Soviet Union', in R. Wilford and R. Miller (eds.), *Women, Ethnicity and Nationalism*. London: Routledge, pp. 87–119.

Matland, R. (1998). 'Women's Representation in National Legislatures: Developed and Developing Countries', *Legislative Studies Quarterly*, 23: 109–25.

—— (2003). 'Women's Representation in Post-Communist Europe', in R. Matland and K. Montgomery (eds.), *Women's Access to Political Power in Post-Communist Europe*. Oxford: Oxford University Press, pp. 321–42.

—— (2006). 'Electoral Quotas: Frequency and Effectiveness', in D. Dahlerup (ed.), *Women, Quotas and Politics*, New York: Routledge, pp. 275–92.

—— and Studlar, D. (1996). 'The Contagion of Women Candidates in Single Member and Multimember District Systems: Canada and Norway', *Journal of Politics*, 58(3): 707–33.

—— and Taylor, M. (1997). 'Electoral System Effects on Women's Representation: Theoretical Arguments and Evidence from Costa Rica', *Comparative Political Studies*, 30(2): 186–210.

—— and Montgomery, K. (eds.) (2003). *Women's Access to Political Power in Post Communist Europe*. Oxford: Oxford University Press.

Matynia, E. (2001). 'Finishing Democracy at the End of the Century: The Polish Roundtable and Others', *East European Politics and Societies*, 15(2): 454–71.

—— (2003). 'Provincializing Global Feminism: The Polish Case', *Social Research*, 70(2): 499–530.

Mazey, S. (2000). 'Introduction: Integrating gender—Intellectual and "real world" mainstreaming', *Journal of European Public Policy*, 7(3): 333–45.

Mazur, A. (2002). *Theorizing Feminist Policy*. Oxford: Oxford University Press.

Meintjes, S. (1990). 'Looking for the Women's League? Leave a Message...', *Work in Progress*, 70/71: 15–16.

—— (1998). 'Gender, Nationalism and Transformation: Difference and Commonality in South Africa Past and Present', in R. Wilford and R. Miller, (eds.), *Women, Ethnicity and Nationalism.* London: Routledge, pp. 62–86.

—— (2003). 'The Politics of Engagement: Women Transforming the Policy Process—Domestic Violence Legislation', in A. M. Goetz and S. Hassim (eds.), 140–59.

Millard, F. (2004). *Elections, Parties and Representation in Post Communist Europe.* Basingstoke, UK: Palgrave.

—— and Popescu, M. (2001). 'The Representation of Women in the Parliaments of Central and Eastern Europe', Paper delivered at ECPR Conference, University of Kent, September.

Molina, N. (1989). 'Propuestas políticas y orientaciones de cambio en la situación de la mujer', in M. A. Garreton (ed.), *Propuestas Políticas y Demandas Sociales*, V. 3, Santiago: FLACSO.

—— and Serrano, C. (1988). 'Las Mujeres frente a la política, *Proposiciones*, 16: 107–26.

Molyneux, M. (1981). 'Socialist Societies Old and New: Progress Towards Women's Emancipation', *Feminist Review*, 8: 1–34.

—— (1985a). 'Mobilization Without Emancipation? Women's Interests, the State and Revolution in Nicaragua, *Feminist Studies*, 11(2): 227–54.

—— (1985b). 'Family Reform in Socialist States: the Hidden Agenda, *Feminist Review*, 21: 47–66.

—— (1991). 'Marxism, Feminism and the Demise of the Soviet Model', in R. Grant and K. Newland (eds.), *Gender and International Relations.* Milton Keynes: Open University Press.

—— and Razavi, R. (2005). 'Beijing Plus Ten: An Ambivalent Record on Gender Justice', *Development and Change*, 36(6): 983–1010.

Montecino, S. and Rossetti, J. (eds.) (1990). *Tramas para un Nuevo destino: propuestas de la Concertacion de Mujeres por la Democracia*, Santiago Chile.

Montenegro, C. (1999). 'Wage Distribution in Chile: Does Gender Matter? A Quantile Regression Approach', World Bank Poverty Management and Economic Management Network. http://www.itam.mx/lames/papers.contres/monteg.pdf

Montgomery, K. and Ilonski, G. (2003). 'Weak Mobilization, Hidden Majoritarianism and Resurgence of the Right: A Recipe for Female Under-Representation in Hungary', in R. Matland and K. Montgomery (eds.), *Women's Access to Political Power in Post Communist Europe.* Oxford: Oxford University Press, pp. 105–29.

Moser, C. (1992). 'Adjustment from Below: Low Income Women, Time and the Triple Role in Guayquil, Ecuador', in H. Afshar and C. Dennis (eds.), *Women and Adjustment Policies.* Basingstoke, UK: Macmillan.

Moser, R. (2003). 'Electoral Systems and Women's Representation: The Strange Case of Russia', R. Matland and K. Montgomery (eds.) (2003). *Women's Access to Political Power in Post Communist Europe*, Oxford: Oxford University Press, pp. 153–72.

Munizaga, G. and Letelier, L. (1988). 'Mujer y regimen militar' in Centro de Estudios de la Mujer (ed.), *Mundo de Mujer: Continuidad y Cambio*, Santiago: CEM.

❖ REFERENCES

Nelson, B. and Chowdhury N. (eds.) (1994). *Women and Politics Worldwide*. New Haven, CT: Yale University Press.

Norris, P. (1991). 'Gender Differences in Political Participation in Britain: Traditional, Radical and Revisionist Models', *Government and Opposition*, 26(1): 56–74.

—— and Inglehart, R. (2001). 'Cultural Obstacles to Equal Representation', *Journal of Democracy*, 12(3): 126–40.

—— and Lovenduski, J. (1995). Political Recruitment: Gender, Race and Class in the British Parliament. Cambridge: Cambridge University Press.

O'Donnell, G. (1994). 'Delegative Democracy, *Journal of Democracy*, 5(1): 5–69.

—— (1996). 'Illusions about Consolidation', *Journal of Democracy*, 7(2): 34–51.

—— (2003). Paper delivered at Plenary Session, 'What we have learnt from 30 years of transitions from Authoritarian Rule', International Political Science Association Congress, Durban, July.

—— Schmitter, P., and Whitehead, L. (eds.) (1986). *Transitions from Authoritarian Rule: Prospects for Democracy*. Baltimore, MD: Johns Hopkins University Press,

—— and Schmitter, P. (1986). *Transitions from Authoritarian Rule: Tentative Conclusions from Uncertain Democracies*. Baltimore, MD: Johns Hopkins University Press.

Palmer, I. (1992). 'Gender Equity and Economic Efficiency in Adjustment Programmes', in H. Afshar and C. Dennis (eds.), *Women and Adjustment Policies in the Third World*. Basingstoke, UK: Macmillan.

Pastor M. and Wise, C. (1999). 'The Politics of Second Generation Reform', *Journal of Democracy*, 10(3): 34–48.

Pateman, C. (1983). 'Feminist Critiques of the public/private dichotomy', in S. Benn and G. Gaus (eds.), *The Public and Private in Social Life*. London: Croom Helm.

—— (1983). 'Feminism and Democracy', in G. Duncan (ed.), *Democratic Theory and Practice*. Cambridge: Cambridge University Press, pp. 204–17.

—— (1989). *The Sexual Contract*. Stanford: Stanford University Press.

Petras, J. and Leiva, F. (1988). 'Chile: The Authoritarian Transition to Electoral Politics', *Latin American Perspectives*, 15(3): 97–114.

Pitanguy, J. (2002). 'Bridging the Local and Global: Feminsim in Brazil and the International Human Rights Agenda', *Social Research*, 69(3): 805–20.

Plattner, M. (2005). 'Introduction: Building Democracy After Conflict', *Journal of Democracy*, 16(1): 5–9.

Phillips, A. (1991). *Engendering Democracy*. Cambridge: Polity Press.

—— (1993). *Democracy and Difference*. Cambridge: Polity Press.

—— (1995). *The Politics of Presence*. Oxford: Clarendon Press.

Pollert, A. (2003). 'Women, Work and Equal Opportunities in Post-Communist Transition', *Work, Employment and Society*, 17(2): 331–57.

Przeworski, A. (1991). *Democracy and the Market: Political and Economic Reforms in Latin America and Eastern Europe*. Cambridge: Cambridge University Press.

—— and Limongi, F. (1996). 'What Makes Democracies Endure?', *Journal of Democracy*, 7(1): 39–54.

Putnam, R. (1993). *Making Democracy Work*. Princeton, NJ: Princeton University Press.

Power, M. (2002). *Right Wing Women in Chile: Feminine Power and the Struggle Against Allende 1964–1973*. University Park, PA: Penn State University Press.

Racioppi, L. and See, K. (2006). 'Engendering Democratic Transition from Conflict: Women's Inclusion in Northern Ireland's Peace Process', *Comparative Politics*, 38(2): 189–208.

Rai, S. (ed.) (2000). *International Perspectives on Gender and Democratization*. Basingstoke, UK: Macmillan.

——— (2002). *Mainstreaming Gender, Democratizing the State?* Manchester, UK: Manchester University Press.

——— and Lievesley, G. (eds.) (1996). *Women and the State: International Perspectives*. London: Taylor and Francis.

Randall, V. (1987). *Women and Politics*, 2nd edn. Basingstoke, UK: Macmillan.

——— (1991). 'Feminism and Political Analysis', *Political Studies*, 39: 513–32.

——— (1998). 'Gender and Power: Women Engage the State', in V. Randall and G. Waylen (eds.), *Gender Politics and the State*. London: Routledge, pp. 185–205.

——— and Svasand, L. (2002a). 'Political Parties and Democratic Consolidation in Africa, *Democratization*, 9(3): 30–52.

——— ——— (2002b). 'Party Institutionalization in New Democracies', *Party Politics*, 8(1): 5–29.

Reading, A. (1992). *Polish Women, Solidarity and Feminism*. Basingstoke, UK: Macmillan.

Ready, K. (2001). 'A Feminist Reconstruction of Parenthood Within Neoliberal Constraints: La Asociación de Madres Demandantes in El Salvador', in V. Gonzalez and K. Kampwirth (eds.), *Radical Women of Latin America: Left and Right*. University Park: Pennsylvania State University Press, pp. 165–88.

Ríos, M. (1994). Socialización, Política y Acción Colectiva: Organizaciones de Pobladoras en Chile 1973–93', Unpublished MA thesis, FLACSO Mexico.

——— (2003). 'Chilean Feminism(s) in the 1990s: Paradoxes of an Unfinished Transition', *International Feminist Journal of Politics*, 5(2): 256–80.

——— (2006). 'Más político que cultural! o cómo llegó en Chile una Mujer a la Presidencia?', *Forum*, XXXVII (2): 31–4.

——— Godoy, L., and Guerrero, E. (2004). *Un Nuevo Silencio Feminista? La Transformación de un Movimiento Social en el Chile Postdictadura*. Santiago: CEM, Editorial Cuarto Propio.

Rule, W. and Zimmerman, J. (eds.) (1994). *Electoral Systems in Comparative Perspective: Their Impact on Men and Women*. Westport, CT: Greenwood Press.

Rustow, D. A. (1970). 'Transitions to Democracy: Towards a Dynamic Model', *Comparative Politics*, 2(3): 337–63.

Safa, H. (1990). 'Women's Social Movements in Latin America, *Gender and Society*, 4(3): 354–69.

Saxonberg, S. (2000). 'Women in Eastern European Parliaments', *Journal of Democracy*, 11(2): 145–58.

——— (2003). 'Czech Political Parties Prefer Male Candidates to Female Votes', in R. Matland and K. Montgomery (eds.), *Women's Access to Political Power in Post Communist Europe*. Oxford: Oxford University Press, pp. 245–66.

Schaeffer-Hegel, J. B. (1992). 'Makers and Victims of Unification: German Women and the Two Germanies', *Women's Studies International Forum*, 15(1).

❖ REFERENCES

Schild, V. (1994). 'Becoming Subjects of Rights': Citizenship, Political Learning and Identity Formation Among Latin American women', Paper for XVIth IPSA Congress, Berlin August.

_____ (1998). 'Market Citizenship and the "New Democracies": The Ambiguous Legacies of Contemporary Chilean Women's Movements', *Social Politics*, 5(2): 232–49.

_____ (2000). 'Neoliberalism's New Gendered Market Citizens: The Civilising Dimension of Social Programmes in Chile', *Citizenship Studies*, 4(3): 275–305.

_____ (2002). 'Engendering the New Social citizenship in Chile: NGOs and Social Provisioning Under Neo Liberalism', in M. Molyneux and S. Razavi (eds.), *Gender Justice, Development and Rights*. Oxford: Oxford University Press. pp. 170–203.

Schirmer, J. (1989). 'Those Who Die for Life Cannot Be Called Dead: Women and Human Rights Protest in Latin America, *Feminist Review*, 32: 3–29.

_____ (1993). 'The Seeking of Truth and the Gendering of Consciousness: The Comadres of El Salvador and the CONVIGUA Widows of Guatemala', in S. Radcliffe and S. Westwood (eds.), *Viva: Women and Popular Protest in Latin America*. London: Routledge, pp. 30–64.

Schmitter, P. (2003). Paper delivered at Plenary Session, 'What we have learnt from 30 years of transitions from Authoritarian Rule', International Political Science Association Congress, Durban, July.

_____ and Karl, T. (1995). 'From an Iron Curtain to a Paper Curtain: Grounding Transitologists or Students of Post Communism', *Slavic Review*, 54(4): 965–78.

Scott, J. (1986). 'Gender: A Useful Category of Historical Analysis?', *American Historical Review*, 91(5): 1053–75.

Seekings, J. (2000). *The UDF: A History of the United Democratic Front in South Africa 1983–1991*. Cape Town: David Philip.

Seidman, G. (1993). 'No Freedom Without the Women': Mobilization and Gender in South Africa, 1970–1992', *Signs*, 18: 291–319, Winter.

_____ (2003). 'Institutional Dilemmas: Representation Versus Mobilization in the South African Gender Commission', *Feminist Studies*, 29(3), 541–61.

Serrano, C. (1990). Chile: entre la autonomia y la integración', in *Transiciones: mujeres in los procesos democraticos*. Santiago: ISIS International.

Shayne, J. (2004). *The "Revolution Question": Feminisms in El Salvador, Chile and Cuba*. New Brunswick, NJ: Rutgers University Press.

Siemienska, R. (1998). 'Consequences of Economic and Political Change for Women in Poland', in J. Jaquette and S. Wolchik (eds.), *Women and Democracy*. Baltimore, MD: Johns Hopkins University Press. pp. 125–52.

_____ (2003). 'Women in the Polish Sejm: Political Culture and Party Politics Versus Electoral Rules', R. Matland and K. Montgomery (eds.), *Women's Access to Political Power in Post Communist Europe*. Oxford: Oxford University Press, pp. 217–44.

Siklova, J. (1993). 'Are Women in Central and Eastern Europe Conservative?', in N. Funk and M. Mueller (eds.), *Gender Politics and Post Communism*. New York: Routledge, pp. 74–83.

Skocpol, T. (1979). *States and Social Revolutions*. Cambridge: Cambridge University Press.

_____ (1992). *Protecting Soldiers and Mothers: The Political Origins of Social Policy in the United States*, Cambridge, MA: Harvard University Press.

Southall, R. (2000). 'The State of Democracy in South Africa', *Journal of Commonwealth and Comparative Politics*, 38: 147–70, Autumn.

Sparr, P. (1994). 'Feminist Critiques of Structural Adjustment', in P. Sparr (ed.), *Mortgaging Women's Lives: Feminist Critiques of Structural Adjustment*. London: Zed Press.

Sperling, V. (1998). 'Gender Politics and the State During Russia's Transition Period', in V. Randall and G. Waylen (eds.), *Gender Politics and the State*. London: Routledge, pp. 143–65.

—— (1999). *Organizing Women in Contemporary Russia: Engendering Transition*. Cambridge: Cambridge University Press.

Squires, J. and Wickham-Jones, M. (2002). 'Mainstreaming in Westminster and Whitehall: From Labour's Ministry for Women to the Women and Equality Unit', Parliamentary Affiars, 55(1): 57–70.

Stallings, B. and Peres, W. (2000). *Growth, Employment and Equity: The Impact of the Economic Reforms in Latin America and the Caribbean*. Washington, DC.: ECLAC/Brookings Institution.

Steinhilber, S. (2004). 'The Gender Impact of Pensions Reforms: Case Studies of the Czech Republic, Hungary and Poland', in OECD, Reforming Public Pensions. Paris: OECD.

Stepan, A. and Skach, C. (1993). 'Constitutional Frameworks and Democratic Consolidation: Parliamentarianism versus Presidentialism', *World Politics*, 46(1): 1–22.

Stephen, L. (1997). *Women and Social Movements in Latin America: Power from Below*. Austin: University of Texas Press.

Sternbach, N., Navarro, M., Chuckyrk, P., and Alvarez, S. (1992). 'Feminisms in Latin America: From Bogota to San Bernardo', *Signs*, 27(2): 393–434.

Stetson, D. (ed.) (2001). *Abortion Politics: Women's Movements and the Democratic State: A Comparative Study*. Oxford: Oxford University Press.

—— and Mazur, A. (eds.) (1995). *Comparative State Feminism*. Thousand Oaks, CA: Sage.

Sundstrom, L. (2005). 'Foreign Assistance, International Norms and NGO Development: Lessons from the Russian Campaign', *International Organization*, 59: 419–49.

Szalai, J. (1998). 'Women and Democratization: Some Notes on Recent Changes in Hungary', in J. Jaquette and S. Wolchik (eds.), *Women and Democracy: Latin America and Central and Eastern Europe*. Baltimore, MD: Johns Hopkins University Press, pp. 185–202.

Tarrow, S. (1998). *Power in Movement: Social Movements and Contentious Politics*, 2nd edn. Cambridge: Cambridge University Press.

Thelen, K. and Steinmo, S. (1992). 'Historical Institutionalism in Comparative Politics', in S. Steinmo, K. Thelen, and F. Longstreth (eds.), *Structuring Politics: Historical Institutionalism in Comparative Analysis*. Cambridge: Cambridge University Press, pp. 1–32.

Threlfall, M. (1998). 'State Feminism or Party Feminism? Feminist Politics and the Spanish Institute of Women', *European Journal of Women's Studies*, 5(1): 69–94.

Tripp, A. M. (1992). 'The Impact of Crisis and Economic Reform on Women in Urban Tanzania', in L. Beneria and S. Feldman (eds.), *Unequal Burden: Economic Crises, Persistent Poverty and Women's Work*. Boulder, CO: Westview.

True, J. and Mintrom, M. (2001). 'Transnational Policy Networks and Policy Diffusion: The Case of Gender Mainstreaming', *International Studies Quarterly*, 45(1): 27–57.

❖ REFERENCES

UNIFEM (2004). Appendix One, in *Not a Minute More. Ending Violence Against Women*. New York: UNIFEM.

Valdes, T. and Weinstein, M. (1993). *Mujeres que Suenan: Los Organizaciones de Pobladoras en Chile: 1973–1989*. Santiago: FLACSO.

Valenzuela, A. (1992). 'Democratic Consolidation in Post Transition Settings', in S. Mainwaring, J. S. Valenzuela, and G. O'Donnell (eds.), *Issues in Democratic Consolidation: the New South American Democracies in Comparative Perspective*, Notre Dame, IN: University of Notre Dame Press.

Valenzuela, M. E. (1990). 'Mujeres y Política: logros y tensiones en el proceso de redemocratición', *Proposiciones*, 18: 210–32.

—— (1991). 'The Evolving Roles of Women under Military Rule', in P. Drake and I. Jaksic (eds.), *The Struggle for Democracy in Chile*. Lincoln: University of Nebraska Press.

—— (1998). 'Women and the Democratization Process in Chile', in J. Jaquette and S. Wolchik (eds.), *Women and Democracy: Latin America and Central and Eastern Europe*, Baltimore, MD: Johns Hopkins University Press, pp. 47–74.

Van der Meulen, Y. (1999). 'Protecting Women and Promoting Equality in the Labor Market: Theory and Evidence', *Policy Research Report on Gender and Development*, Working Paper no. 6. Washington, DC.: World Bank. http://www.worldbank.org/gender/prr/rodgers.pdf

Van Rooy, A. (1998). *Civil Society and the Aid Industry*. London: Earthscan.

Walker, C. (1982). *Women and Resistance in South Africa*. London: Onyx.

Walsh, D. (2006). 'The Liberal Moment: Women and Just Debate in South Africa 1994–1996', *Journal of Southern African Studies*, 32(1): 85–106.

Watson, P. (1996). 'The Rise of Masculinism in Eastern Europe', in M. Threlfall (ed.), *Mapping the Women's Movement*. London: Verso, pp. 216–31.

—— (1997). 'Civil Society and the Politics of Difference in Eastern Europe', in J. Scott, C. Kaplan, and D. Keates (eds.), *Transitions, Environments, Translations: Feminisms in International Politics*. New York: Routledge.

Waylen, G. (1992a). 'Rethinking Women's Political Participation and Protest: Chile 1970–1990', *Political Studies*, 40(2): 299–314.

—— (1992b). 'Women, Authoritarianism and Market Liberalization in Chile 1973–89', in H. Afshar and C. Dennis (eds.), *Women and Adjustment Policies in the Third World*. Basingstoke, UK: Macmillan.

—— (1993). 'Women's Movements and Democratisation in Latin America', *Third World Quarterly*, 14(3): 573–88.

—— (1994). 'Women and Democratization: Conceptualizing Gender Relations in Transition Politics', *World Politics*, 46(3): 327–54.

—— (1996a). *Gender in Third World Politics*. Boulder, CO: Lynn Rienner.

—— (1996b). 'Gender and Democratic Consolidation', Paper delivered at APSA, San Francisco.

—— (1997). 'Women's Movements, the State and Democratisation: The Establishment of SERNAM in Chile', in A. M. Goetz (ed.), *Getting Institutions Right for Women in Development*. London: Zed Press, pp. 90–104.

Waylen, G. (1998). 'Women's Activism, Authoritarianism and Democratisation in Chile', in N. Charles and H. Hintjens (eds.), *Gender, Ethnicity and Political Ideologies*. London: Routledge, pp. 146–67.

—— (1998). 'Gender, Feminism and the State', in V. Randall and G. Waylen (eds.), *Gender, Politics and the State*. London: Routledge, pp. 1–17.

—— (2000). 'Gender and Democratic Politics: A Comparative Analysis of Argentina and Chile', *Journal of Latin American Studies*, 32(3): 765–93.

—— (2003). 'Gender and Transitions: What Do We Know?', *Democratization*, 10(1): 157–78.

—— (2007). 'Women's Mobilization and Gender Outcomes in Transitions to Democracy: The South African Case', *Comparative Political Studies*, May.

Weldon, S. L. (2002). *Protest, Policy and the Problem of Violence Against Women*. Pittsburgh: University of Pittsburgh Press.

Whitehead, L. (1997). 'Bowling in the Bronx: The Uncivil Interstices Between Civil and Political', *Democratisation*, 4(1): 15–30.

—— (2003). Paper delivered at Plenary Session, 'What we have learnt from 30 years of transitions from Authoritarian Rule', International Political Science Association Congress, Durban, July.

WIDE (2003). 'Information Sheet on Gender Equality and EU Accession: the situation in the Czech Republic', Nov. (www.eurosur.org/wide/EU/Enlargement)

Wolchik, S. (1979). 'The Status of Women in a Socialist Order: Czechoslovakia, 1948–1978', *Slavic Review*, 38: 583–602.

—— (1994). 'Women and the Politics of Transition in the Czech and Slovak Republics', in M. Reueschemeyer (ed.), *Women and the Politics of Postcommunist Eastern Europe*. New York: ME Sharpe, pp. 3–28.

—— (1998). 'Gender and the Politics of Transition in the Czech Republic and Slovakia', J. Jaquette and S. Wolchik (eds.), *Women and Democracy: Latin America and Central and Eastern Europe*. Baltimore, MD: Johns Hopkins University Press, pp. 153–84.

—— (2000). 'Reproductive Policies in the Czech and Slovak Republics', S. Gal and G. Kligman (eds.), *Reproducing Gender: Politics, Publics, and Everyday Life After Socialism*. Princeton, NJ: Princeton University Press, pp. 58–91.

Wood, E. (2000). *Forging Democracy From Below: Insurgent Transitions in South Africa and El Salvador*. Cambridge: Cambridge University.

—— (2001). 'An Insurgent Path to Democracy: Popular Mobilization, Economic Interests, and Regime Transition in South Africa and El Salvador'. *Comparative Political Studies*, 34(8): 839–61.

World Bank (1994). Poverty Alleviation and Social Investment Funds: The Latin American Experience, Discussion Paper no. 261.

Yuval-Davis, N. (1997). *Gender and Nation*. London: Sage.

Zielinska, E. (2000). 'Between Ideology Politics and Commonsense: The Discourse of Reproductive Rights in Poland', in S. Gal and G. Kligman (eds.), *Reproducing Gender: Politics, Publics, and Everyday Life After Socialism*. Princeton, NJ: Princeton University Press, pp. 23–57.

Zhotkhina, Z. (2005). 'Challenges for Feminism in Russia Today', Paper presented at workshop on Gender and Citizenship in the Global South and East. London, Canadian Political Science Association, Ontario, Canada, June.

❖ REFERENCES

❖ Index

Items appearing as notes and tables are indexed in bold, e.g. 47**n**

232

Dagnino, E. 51
Dahlerup, D. 10, 11, 128
delegative democracy 24, 27, 91, 158
democracies 1, 2, 8, 26, 33, 35, 36, 44,
    50, 51, 67, 93, 110, 118, 123, 136,
    179
  consolidation 23–24, 50, 95
  definition 16
  imposition from outside 205
  institutional forms 26–27
  quality of 16–17, 24, 33, 37, 44, 50, 119
  regimes 21, 25, 198
  systems 22, 28
democratization 15, 17, 19–20, 22, 24, 25,
    26, 29, 34, 36, 39, 41, 49, 50–53, 93,
    95, 201
descriptive representation 9–11, 15, 38,
    44–45, 79, 88, 91, 93, 97, 132, 134,
    136–137, 139, 140, 195, 198–199, 203,
    205; see also representation;
    substantive representation
developing world 111, 113–114
Diamond, L. 16, 17, 23, 24, 50
dictatorships 19, 23, 24, 25, 67
divorce 45–46, 134, 140, 148, 157, 163, 200;
    see also under individual
    countries
  laws 14, 39, 62, 133, 141, 145, 146,
    164–166, 201
Dobrowolsky, A. 11
Dolling, I. 62, 143
domestic violence 5, 14, 39, 45–46, 59, 63,
    80, 82, 84, 87, 134, 140, 145, 151, 156,
    163, 166–170, 173, 178, 186, 196,
    201, 205
    see also sexual violence; under
    individual countries
Drogus, C. 84

East Central Europe 18, 21, 22, 24, 26, 27,
    29, 31, 44, 51, 64, 68, 81, 82, 95, 96,
    99, 108, 111, 112, 117, 119, 120, 121,
    122, 124, 130, 132, 141–142, 143, 149,
    151, 152, 153, 156, 157, 158, 163, 164,
    167, 171, 179, 181, 182, 183, 184, 186,

    187, 194, 195, 196, 198, 200, 201,
    204, 205
East Europe 26, 42, 115, 117, 118, 123, 148,
    170
East Germany 64, 65
Eberhardt, E. 80, 152, 156
economic crisis 21, 22, 31, 32, 186
economic factors 16, 21, 36
economic reforms 26, 31, 32–33, 45–46,
    181–185, 191, 204
economy 19, 21, 25, 53, 60, 181
  rights 196, 204, 205
education 13–14, 32, 80, 86, 141, 142, 144,
    145, 147, 180, 181, 184, 185, 190, 193,
    200, 204
Edwards, B. 92n
Einhorn, B. 62, 63, 64, 71, 72, 80, 81, 82,
    92n, 98, 130, 132, 142, 181
Eisenstein, Z. 66
El Salvador 18, 22, 42, 43, 44, 55, 59, 130,
    148, 179, 202
  abortion 134, 173, 201
  Catholic Church, position of 57, 173
  domestic violence 167, 169, 170
  elections 30, 73–74
  women 55, 56, 84, 103–104, 183
    organizing as women 60–61, 67, 68,
    72, 73, 89; parliamentary
    representation 94, 108, 118, 121,
    124, 126, 134
elections 16, 24, 28–33, 34, 35, 59,
    100–101, 107, 108, 117, 119, 159, 196
  lists 112–113, 118, 131
  politics 5, 6, 8, 9, 15, 23, 84, 91, 93, 102,
    123, 198, 203
    arenas 15, 45, 91, 93–137, 205
  quotas 7, 10, 11, 14, 35, 37, 39, 88, 97, 98,
    106, 108, 111, 113, 116, 119, 120, 122,
    123, 125, 126, 129t, 130–132, 134,
    136, 162, 196, 199, 202, 203; see also
    gender, quotas
electoral rules 111–113, 118, 123, 136
electoral systems 9–11, 16, 17, 27, 44, 95,
    96, 114–115, 129, 131, 199
elites 17, 20–22, 43, 116–117, 147